Sticks & Wires & Cloth

DATE DUE

APR 2 2 2004			
MAY 1 0 2004			
JUL 0 8 2004			
JUL 1 5 2004			
AUG 1 1 2004			
MAY 1 2 2006			
MAY 2 8			

#47-0108 Peel Off Pressure Sensitive

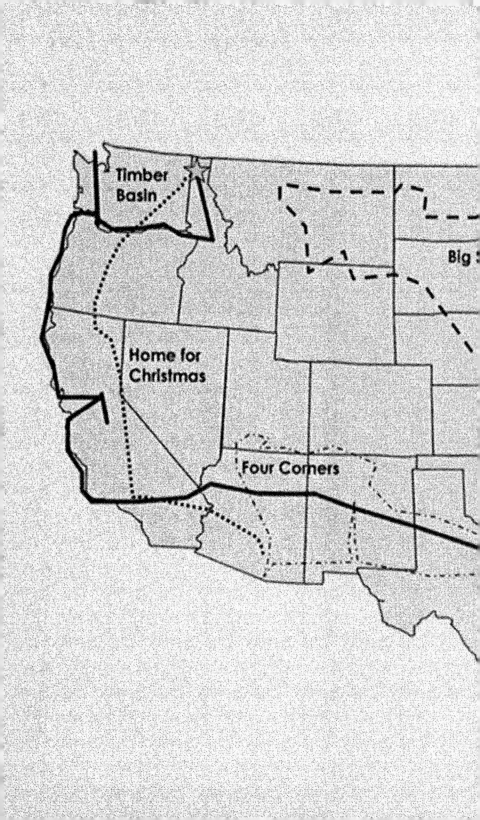

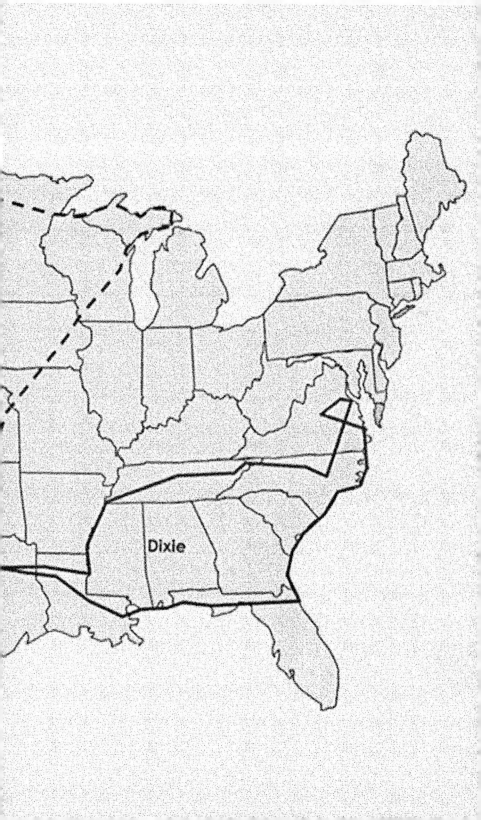

Dixie

Sticks & Wires & Cloth

By

Anne Hopkins

Photographs and map by
Howard A. Richmond II, Duane Binnall, and the author

Published by

Trailing Edge Publishing
P.O. Box 69250
Tucson, Arizona 85737

Published 2003
Printed in the United States of America

Publisher's Cataloging-in-Publication Data

Hopkins, Anne, 1946-
    Sticks & wires & cloth / by Anne Hopkins ;
photographs and map by Howard A. richmond II, Duane
Binnal, and the author.
    p. cm.
    LCCN 2003090816
    ISBN 0-9720015-0-6
    ISBN 0-9720015-1-4 (pbk.)

    1. Hopkins, Anne, 1946---Journeys. 2. United States
--Description and travel. 3. Women air pilots--United
States--Biography. 4. Biplanes--United States.
    I. Title. II. Title: Sticks and wires and cloth

E169.04.H66 2003   917.304'929
                        QBI03-200173

To
Howard

"An airplane is just a bunch of sticks and wires and cloth, a tool for learning about the sky and about what kind of person I am, when I fly. An airplane stands for freedom, for joy, for the power to understand, and to demonstrate that understanding. Those things aren't destructible."

Nothing by Chance, Richard Bach

Contents

Timber Basin

When I climb into Nanna's rear cockpit to begin one of our summer vacations, I strap onto my right leg the blue canvas folder that holds my charts, pen, and notepad. Howard gave it to me years ago. I have used it so often that the yellow "N22TE" embroidery thread in the corner has begun to wear away. I open the cover. The paper is blank. I add column headings "Date… Hobbs… Tach… Comments" and jot down "Off ADS" to note departure from Addison Airport. I always pause to imagine what the final trip leg entry will be, how many flight hours and days hence, on what line or page it will fall, what the lines in between will record—and what they will mean. Last summer the trip ended on page two, line nine, the thirty-eighth line, 66.9^{th} hour, written on the nineteenth day, covering over five thousand miles across seven states, the last one Idaho. The entry: "Timber Basin—hit fence."

Nanna is my Great Lakes biplane, a lightweight open-cockpit fabric aircraft built from a 1929 design. Barnstorming pilots back then considered the Lakes a fine aerobatic airplane. I still do, although it is the waltzing dowager among today's jiving youngsters. Nanna is slow flying, a bit faster than most automobiles, and holds about three hours worth of fuel, enough to match the endurance of a single passenger and a pilot sitting in the open air, fair weather or foul. Nanna is less about transportation than about fun. Just as Dumbo the Elephant is mostly ears, Nanna is mostly wings. Painted on his nose is his formal name, Trailing Edge, which I abandoned soon after the enamel dried on the cowling like the ink on pedigree papers of a family dog.

As in years past, we did not architect this flight. Instead, we built it up from the clay of possibilities that over the weeks we sculpted into "the summer trip" with daily decisions to make a direct line here, dart in there, or pile on large chunks of experience in a single spot. Starting from a metal and concrete hangar of the big-city airport, lifting off, and watching steel and glass skyscrapers of Dallas and Fort Worth disappear, we pulled the prairie sod toward us as though closing a roll-top desk over the clutter of modern life.

The daily baking of the earth's crust was well underway when the sun began warming our shoulders and bare arms. Below my canvas helmet, I could feel rivulets of perspiration washing sunscreen off my neck and dampening my cotton shirt. The air was so laden with moisture already that it would absorb little more from me. Texas was one big steaming pot to escape in summer.

Heading west that afternoon and the following morning, the air cooled as the terrain rose, but relief from the heat came with strong headwinds and turbulence. Pockets of rising air threw my hips and shoulders against the harnesses. The higher I took Nanna the butterfly, the more buffeting he took, held to a record low groundspeed of forty-two miles per hour, less than half our normal rate. To achieve even that, we had to drop down low to hug our highway route. Cars and trucks raced ahead of us. We crept among New Mexico's buttes and mesas as though we were drifting through a river canyon with walls of melted crayons. Farther on lay desert flatlands, ochre and rust paintings on a dusty ground.

At the end of our second day out, we prepared to land at Holbrook, Arizona. The airport lay on a high plateau north of the interstate highway and a modest group of buildings that formed the barren, colorless town. To the south and west loomed taller mountains, but the ground close by rose and fell more subtly. I radioed the airport for landing advisories and heard back, "…winds thirty gusting to fifty-two." Good, the wind was blowing nearly straight down the runway as we had expected. If we hit one of the extreme gusts head on, we would fly above the runway at the speed of a walk, but if the wind shifted to hit us at an angle, it would push us dangerously sideways.

I said to Howard, "I'm going to land long." I was thinking about how difficult it would be to taxi. By touching down closer to the ramp, we could roll out closer to where we would tie down.

"Just land," he said. "Don't worry about where." We had fought tough winds on landing before, and he knew that bad things could happen. In his voice, I could hear how uneasy he felt—he thought we were in for one of those times. These landings were always harder on him than on me. He was the passenger who could only watch, powerless to affect the outcome. Although I could not see his legs from my rear cockpit, I knew that they would be moving and pushing imaginary rudders as we landed, much as a passenger in an automobile leans and slams on imaginary brakes.

The descent to the runway through rushing, dusty air seemed comically slow, as though we were racing toward a carrot forever out of our grasp, suspended from a pole attached to my back. At last, we were floating along above the runway, the dry grass alongside blowing against the earth like flaxen hair plastered back against the scalp. We touched down uneventfully. I inched along, bracing and clinching my teeth as we turned onto the taxiway, exposing our broadside and threatening our wingtips in what was now a direct blustery crosswind. When we pulled into a tie down spot, two men rushed out through the blowing dust.

"We'll be here overnight, fuel up in the morning," I shouted above the wind as I jumped down from the wing.

"Pull it into the hangar," one man yelled back, grabbing a strut to help us pull.

"You can't stay out in this," said the other man, a local FedEx pilot. Neither man wanted to leave the airplane out overnight, blasted by sand and pebbles.

Within minutes, we had pulled Nanna inside and I heard the rumbling doors rolling closed against the howling wind. Bits of sand and rock pelted the metal walls outside, rasping sounds with staccato percussion. Inside everything became peaceful. I wiped my forearms, cutting streaks through dust-caked perspiration. We rolled Nanna into a space on the worn concrete floor among dozens of infant potted trees, as though placing him on display at a show with a shoestring decorative budget, a Charlie Brown sort of event. I wondered how such sprigs would survive out there in the bleak and blowing land.

"What are these for?" I asked the manager.

He smiled and looked at the plants fondly. "We're just a little town out here. We ran a survey find out what people thought would improve our quality of life." He looked down at the pots and chuckled. "'Trees, plant more trees,' they said. So that's what we're about to do."

"Is it always so windy here?"

"Nah. Yesterday it was still as could be. Tomorrow, who knows?"

Holbrook turned out to be like so many towns I happened upon when traveling with Nanna, places that popped up about the time I needed to eat and sleep, places where people lived life plain and simple, and took pride in their communities.

That evening, we drove the airport loaner car for the trip out the main street to the edge of town and back. It did not take long. We stopped to tour the old county courthouse, lovingly preserved, full of the territorial history of this old west outpost, including cramped, unventilated metal-everything jail cells that had to have been hell on earth in the days before air conditioning.

The following morning, we arrived at the airport before anyone else. It had turned into a different place, the air still and clear, no dust anywhere to dull the view or swirl around the ground. Rasping, blowing sounds had ended, replaced by quiet. The scene matched my mood. The dust of my everyday life, too, had settled out, leaving my mind calm.

After two days of headwinds and leisurely progress, the third day brought a tailwind and startling speeds. Everything whizzed by. No car or truck on earth would catch us now. We rocketed along the evergreen forests of Flagstaff, passing south of a fire pushed as relentlessly by those same winds. Before long we crossed the last of Arizona's broad flat valleys and headed for a gap in the last ridge. Craggy pillars rose at our sides as we bolted through to the Colorado River valley, that green ribbon border of California. After days of parched earthen browns and rusts, the startling change of color hit us like a splash of cold water. Across the river, as abruptly as it had appeared, the green vanished. We landed at Needles. When we took off the winds were so strong that we used a taxiway better aligned with the wind instead of the runway.

By mid-afternoon, I was negotiating with the high desert controller at Edwards Air Force base to cut through a corner of his airspace. We crossed our last desert valley with some of the world's longest runways within view but still in the distance. A shuttle could land on those runways after miles of gliding from the edge of space. Yet, if Nanna lost power here, our meager altitude would not even carry us to the edge of the runway. If we could reach it, though, we could easily land on it crosswise.

In the distance across the flats, I saw the mouth of the Tehachapi Valley with hundreds of windmills strewn across the gentle brown hills like white jacks tossed by a giant's hand. Nanna raced over the poles with their tumbling blades like a hand scooping them up to win the game. We rolled over the last hill and, like plopping into a comfortable old chair, we dropped into a sunlit bowl surrounded by familiar soaring ridges, the glider port, and the town. We would visit the glider port tomorrow. This afternoon we landed at the bigger airport to change Nanna's oil.

For the better part of the next day, I revisited the art of soaring. I had soared here many times before when I lived in California. I would rent a Piper Cub, fly up in the morning from Santa Monica, soar until late afternoon, and then scoot back home, feeling smug indeed over freeways choked with traffic.

After my five-year hiatus from soaring, the instructor, a serious young man, needed all morning to whip me back into shape and entrust me with the sailplane. When we started, I could tell that he was not enthusiastic to be working with me, a carefree, older student who showed as little enthusiasm for theory and hypothetical flight as a motorist forced to attend traffic school.

Ground school ended, and we moved into the real world of gliders, tow-plane, and sky. I sat inches from the ground with only a thin shell of fiberglass separating me from the runway. I flew from the front cockpit with my instructor in the rear. As we waited, the sun broiled our Plexiglas canopies and heated the air inside like a greenhouse. The tow pilot swung his Pawnee around as I completed my takeoff checklist, and a line boy attached the towline to our nose. I wagged the rudders. The tow pilot wagged back, and our wheels began rumbling across the rough surface. I used the wings to balance like a tightrope walker uses a long pole. The racket stopped, replaced by the sound of rushing air as our long wings popped us into the air. I was pleased that I remembered how to stay in formation with the tow plane. As we climbed, my instructor had me do various maneuvers behind the tow plane, and then we released to do more.

"You fly better than I thought you would," he said as we began our air work. I suppressed a laugh. By the end of my lesson, he had uttered a bunch of enthusiastic "just rights" and at least one breathless, near religious "perfect." I even got him to smile and chuckle a few times before we were done. I love these guys.

Now I was checked out, but pretty pooped—and it was only lunchtime. After a meal of lemonade and hot dog under big shade trees, ones that I had lounged beneath so many years before, Howard and I took off together in the glider. We flew for just forty-seven minutes. Man that was work. The whole mountainside was pure yucky sinking air. I descended back toward the field, grubbing around over the town for every miserly thermal, fighting for every foot of altitude. The best lift occurred when I no longer needed it, as I turned onto a base leg to land. I did not soar again that day, but knew I would come back again someday. I often wonder why I find hard stuff like this so compelling. What rewards make me return to the struggle? Maybe it is dipping a silent wing into a steep turn to pivot about a stand of trees, then turning my head to gaze up a white wing at a blue sky toward a cloud. Maybe it is the soothing sound of the wind rushing along my cockpit. Perhaps it is the delight of moving freely through the air with just a touch of my fingers, a tap of my toes. More likely, though, it is watching a fellow pilot in a sleek ship break ground behind a tow plane escalating up and up and up as I stand sweating, dehydrated, sunburned, and smiling, and say aloud, "Isn't that pretty?" and to myself, "I can do that."

Leaving the high deserts later that afternoon, we headed west over the coastal mountains into a long, gentle valley. A dry riverbed ran through acres of irrigated fruit orchards and vegetable fields. Sunshine struck the mountain ridge off our left wing, but to the north the ridge was darker and the valley floor was already beginning to shadow. We passed abeam Santa Paula airport where Nanna and I had hitched our fates a half dozen years before. (It was there he had earned his gender-confused nickname by landing in the splay-legged, woofing way that reminded me of Nanna, the nursemaid St. Bernard from Peter Pan.) When we heard "...flight of three biplanes, left downwind..." on the airport frequency, Nanna may have pulled a bit toward the field, but he continued obediently straight ahead. We wanted to beat the coastal low clouds we knew would be forming at Santa Monica.

Soon we popped out of the valley and floated above the coastal plain, feeling the hot, dry air fall behind as cool, moist saltwater mist and smell of the Pacific Ocean rolled in to meet us. Only in an open cockpit can flyers smell and feel a sky's personality. It is like leaning out a farmhouse window to smell fresh mown hay through curtains blowing in the breeze. Flying in a metal and glass cockpit is more like standing trapped behind office windows that never open.

We dove south toward breaking waves along the familiar coast. I asked Oxnard and Pt. Mugu tower controllers to let me pass through their airspace at five hundred feet. As always, they said yes.

"What kind of aircraft is that again?" asked the friendly voice from Pt. Mugu's tower, a U. S. Navy facility.

"Two Tango One Alpha, a gorgeous Great Lakes biplane." I was fishing for an invitation.

"Can you stay in close in so we can have a look?"

"How about a low pass?"

"Low pass approved, advise two miles…"

Once again, Navy folks came through, as they had in previous years at Quantico, Jacksonville, Pensacola, and Corpus Christi. We banked inland in the late afternoon sun over houses and warehouses, crossed the boundary fence, and headed toward the runway. Beyond, I saw the base of a mountain ridge. How fragile I felt as we skimmed a few feet above concrete thick and wide enough to support planes full of tanks and bombs instead of our books and backpacks. Nanna was a hummingbird in an eagle's lair. I have always hoped during these low passes that those watching sensed how much I loved the freedom they defended.

The concrete fell behind as we bid farewell to new and unseen friends and darted back toward the shore. We flew over a flat and sandy stretch along the base of the mountains toward a bulge of earth at the water's edge, Mugu Rock. The coastal highway pinched it off from the mainland like a belt cinched too tight.

Along the coast, we watched the waves breaking on sandy strips and rocky shores, light reflecting from picture windows of beach houses, people sunning on decks, and surfers bobbing in wait for a better wave, all against a backdrop of mountains and foothills dotted with homes. Approaching from the Palisades, breezing alongside the first wisps of clouds aspiring to become the marine layer, I spied the concrete mother ship, Santa Monica Airport, once our home.

Nothing green grew there. Every square inch was paved so we pilots would get off the runway lickity split, no time to loose, nuh-uh. What a kick it was after five years to return, land, and taxi by my old hangar. As we passed, I remembered the day I sat outside, new owner of a biplane without a single scratch or dent, waiting for the wind to drop below five knots, my personal limit at the time. Think of that, only five knots. On this trip we had landed in winds many times that strong. I had learned a lot about wind and so much more since those anxious, early days.

After tying down, I rinsed splattered insects from Nanna's leading edges with water from a collapsible vinyl bucket, covered the cockpits, and secured him for the night. Howard and I disappeared into the gaping maw of civilization.

The next day we confronted the dilemma presented to flyers by the California Coast—be conservative and fly high enough above coastal mountains to glide inland in an emergency or fly low and accept the risk of ditching in the ocean. Wills being in order, we opted for waves, sand, and sea. Nanna must have thought we were silly being concerned about his reliability and his performance, which would be flawless for the entire trip.

We traced the coastline to Santa Barbara in pure golden sunshine. North of the city, I spotted the bluffs and strained to see the sprawling university campus sprinkled with eucalyptus trees. Yes, there were the dormitories and Chancellor's home. As we passed alongside, just offshore, an old memory breached like a whale in the water below. I looked down and remembered how cold it had been the afternoon I jumped off the party boat—right about here—with a couple of other collegiate revelers of similar dubious judgment. I looked along an imaginary path to the beach below the bluffs, where we had straggled ashore, panting, glad the boat had not been farther out. Ah, youth. I wondered if I could do it today. Sure, I could—in a pinch. Still, I sidled closer to shore.

Too soon, we had to leave the ocean and cut inland to avoid the Vandenberg restricted area. I did not call for permission to fly along the coast. (Over the years—long before terrorist attacks taught us all to fear any flying object—I had quit begging the Air Force to do anything not explicitly authorized on page 5.3.1 of the regs. I knew they would not let Nanna pass through, even if all was quiet on the launch pad. The Air Force was to the Navy as the Odd Couple's Felix was to Oscar, no darned fun!)

The inland route did afford different treats, though—pale gold foothills with dollops of green trees casting the long shadows of a waning day. As we passed the sand dunes near Oceano, a marine layer drifted in from the coast like thin lace along our left wing, where it remained for the remains of the day and appeared again the next. The morning of that second coastal day, we swerved inland and climbed to circle the Hearst Castle mountaintop then glided back to waters edge and pushed north. Far ahead, I watched a lone seaside boulder capped with a thin aura of fog. The vapor trailed inland along a spit of sand like a bridal train sweeping down the aisle. Water floating in air—clouds, fog, vapors, and mists—have always seemed more interesting to me than water rolling around the earth in rivers and oceans, but this veil of fog was downright otherworldly.

The coast grew rockier. Breaking waves spewed foam and spray farther aloft toward steeper mountains. At Monterey, traffic controllers denied us transit through their airspace because our transponder had stopped working, so we carved a long seaward arc over choppy, inky waters. We saw that great bay as a sailor high on the mast of a Clipper must have in the old days. The cold dampness swirled in our cockpits making me wish I had worn a lookout's longer pants. We headed back to the north of the bay to land in a stiff wind at Marina Airport and then flew on to Half Moon Bay for the night. There we hiked with our backpacks to the village, ate too well at the local seafood haunt, and slept with windows open to sea breeze and the lowing of foghorns.

From Half Moon Bay to Gold Rush country took only part of a day. We flew below ridges full of trees and, increasingly, homes. From San Francisco airports, airliners bound for the orient and laden with fuel for their Pacific crossing lumbered above us, straining for altitude. They were the whales rising to the top of our shared sky, we the crabs inching along the bottom.

The coastline broke apart, and the great orange span that linked its ends fell into view. We turned right to meander across a sunny bright San Francisco Bay. I had flown this route before, and once again imagined what fun it would be to dive toward the dark and choppy water and fly through the huge space beneath the Golden Gate. I figured out how I would make the approach, how far above the water I would fly, and how fast. Any pilot flying near the bridge must have the same thoughts—even the captains of jets above. These days, few of us would act on such an impulse, though. The bridge fell behind and the fantasy evaporated. Ahead the sun-drenched skyscrapers of the city stood on the hills like ladies, gowned and bejeweled, descending a grand staircase. The Bay Bridge, packed with traffic, headed off across Treasure Island to the lowlands of Oakland.

We swung away toward Tiburon, abuzz with active boats, cars, and people, and Alcatraz, eerily quiet, and then on toward the inland reaches of the bay. Concord and Antioch reminded me of the acreage costs of power generation with all their refineries and assorted infrastructure. Steam and gases billowed straight up. No sea breezes, so strong just minutes before, had followed us to blow them away. Around the next bend, a mothball fleet passed off our port side, gray ghosts tethered line abreast, outermost the battleship Iowa. Mountains and hills had disappeared.

The flatness turned from the bay's silvery water into the tender greens of the agricultural heartland of California. On and on it went. Then, as the sun's warmth crept down the back of my helmet, the ground began to ripple and rise again. I nudged the throttle to ascend with the foothills of the Sierra. Trees grew taller, darker, and denser. The air turned hotter and, with irrigated lands far behind us, crackling dry. Far in the distance lay a rectangular patch of brown on a forested hilltop, likely our destination airport, yes it was, Nevada County. We joined the traffic pattern as an air tanker fighting fires at Lake Tahoe lumbered off the runway. Another tanker fell in line behind us. As we landed, still others reloaded. We were the lark landed among the workers of the sky.

We grabbed a quick cold drink at my sister's home, and headed off on a whim to see the Empire Mines. The following morning, I took my sister for a pony ride—a ride in Nanna, that is. From the air, we located Nevada City's main drag, circled her home, headed to open space for looping and rolling, and then descended low to swoop between hills and along the shores of a nearby reservoir. I dropped her off back at the airport. Nanna, Howard, and I headed off for a day trip to Calaveras County.

My favorite airport logbook entry has long been "The Pond." Flying floats from the pond near Calaveras always makes me smile. It did again that day. The small bit of water was barely long enough for takeoff on a hot day. The pond sat deep inside a ranch. To get there we drove a pickup truck, dodging cattle along the rutted road, hawks everywhere on the hunt in the surrounding hills. A gentle breeze rippled pond grasses that would soon try to choke the water rudder and cut off our path to freedom. The grasses always failed, as they did this year when Terry Campbell and I puttered out in her Super Cub to the far end, turned, and powered up for our takeoff run.

There is a perfect moment in any sport. In float flying, it comes after the labored run across water that pelts the propeller and fuselage with the noise of raging storm and the rush of the torrent below. Like magic, the floats unglue from water and escape into air, held no longer, free. We climbed and hurdled power lines on the way to Melones Reservoir where we landed several times, then hopped over to Don Pedro for more landings and step taxiing, racing along the surface of the water like a speedboat.

Having mastered the basics—again—I decided to spend the rest of my flight time playing. I cut the engine and we floated along like kids on a raft. We tried to sail the plane, but the mild wind generated little force against our open doors. I sat still in the cabin enjoying the quiet with the engine shut down, content to float in the bowl of the surrounding hills like a fly in a tureen of soup. Terry was wearing an ankle brace—she had run over her foot with a float while beaching the plane a few days earlier. Now she removed it to dangle her feet in the cool water. Watching her, I thought that in a former life she must have been Tom Sawyer.

Soon, we headed overland for a new test of skill, a treat, landing in a tight spot on a sliver of water. We neared a straight segment of a narrow river valley that wound through dry brown hills. Dropping into the valley, Terry coached me to aim for a green spot on the hillside, then turn to let down between two ridges, and turn again to plop neatly onto the narrow finger of water. I was overjoyed with my new accomplishment. As I taxied back along the shoreline, a blue heron glided beside us with the ease and grace that both delights and frustrates pilots—now there is a flyer. I reversed course for take-off as the heron landed and looked straight at me, as though to say "Your turn—impress me." I did my unnatural best, lumbering along the sticky water, wrenching free, climbing up with heavy, ungainly floats around the winding course of the waterway. I was thrilled—the heron, I think, yawned.

That day in the Sierra foothills earned a spot in my album of perfect days. I had made four flights: a morning romp with my sister, a trek south along the Sierra foothills to Calaveras to see old and new friends, a frolic in a perky new floatplane on an old familiar pond to oil away creaky skills, and a return to Nevada City to dine and rest with family. Yes, life. Give me more.

The following morning, no sooner had we popped out to the coast on a line from Nevada County to Clear Lake to Mendocino than the wind jousting began. It started as another plain old headwind forcing us to enjoy the rocky outcroppings and aquamarine fringes of water a bit longer, shucky-darn. Then the burbles and buffets near Fort Bragg began, jolting our views. By the time we reached Shelter Cove, (SHELTER Cove?!) we fought for progress, flying above waves no longer pastel and friendly, but inky green, white-capped, and menacing. Finally, along a beach-less, road-less, unpopulated coast where nobody would ever find us, the air careened over the coastal mountains, a genie wind daring us to stay low, gleeful at the prospect of our struggle to climb. He laid one hand on our top wing, pushing down, down, toying with us. He swatted one wingtip, then the other. My heart pounded and my grip on the stick tightened. My legs tensed against the rudders, now in constant motion to keep us upright as I decided what to do. We sidled farther out to sea, watching the shoreline turn into a distant sliver. At last the genie's fingertip grasp weakened and we pulled free of his grip. I cannot say how long it took to climb up three thousand feet, three miles offshore, but it was the same eternity known to age-old pilots.

Breaking a long silence, Howard said, "That was certainly character building."

A day later and on a calmer note, we departed Eureka, stopped at Coos Bay, Oregon, and then continued on to Kelso, Washington for the night. All morning I watched the backdrop of coastal mountains covered with alternating patches of tall trees, medium-height trees, baby trees, and clear-cut areas with no trees at all. Along the shore lay a river mouth, a town, and a lumberyard. Then the pattern repeated with more river mouths, towns, and lumberyards. Wow, do we make a bunch of houses and paper and toothpicks in this country, or what? North of Coos Bay that pattern may have continued. If it did, we could not see it, because we ran into a blanket of whitest clouds. We climbed above it and watched as it floated progressively inland and we flew north toward the mouth of Columbia River. I kept my eye on its inland edge, lest we become stuck on top without a safe way down. The western edge had long been out of sight, miles out into the ocean. Without a break in the cloud layer, I would miss the sight of Lewis & Clark's winter camp area, but I remained hopeful of seeing where their Corps of Discovery first came upon the Pacific. All afternoon nothing but bright, bright white lay below. Mountains and valleys remained in the clear off our right wing. Had someone taken a photo of us from above, it would have shown Nanna nestled in a bed of cotton.

We arrived at the point where the mountain ridges inland promised the river we sought. We had to turn, and still I saw no break in the clouds below. Disappointed, I banked right. Suddenly, the blanket shredded, as though unseen hands had pulled apart the cotton batting, and shafts of evening light fell below us onto the calm blue waters and flat green islands near the wide, wide mouth of the Columbia River. Far in the distance a snow-capped mountain vaulted above the green-ridged horizon. If the Mormon Tabernacle Choir singing "Ode to Joy" had winged by at that moment, I would not have been more surprised. All disappointment of sights missed evaporated. The sameness of our time above the clouds made the variety of color and form more stunning. I was thrilled. Sun at our back, we dropped low to meander among the fish farms, log booms, and barges, all dwarfed by the grand river valley. The mouth narrowed and the hills closed in beside us like velvet drapery. More islands of fields and homes along the center of the river fell below us.

Ahead at another bend lay Kelso. We would rest there for the night and continue north in the morning. There we joined the pattern with a Cessna out for crosswind landing practice. On final, we dipped our own wing down against the wind, landed, tied down, and began looking for water for Nanna's daily sponge bath. The Cessna taxied in behind us and shut down. A man and woman got out and we stopped to visit with them. The student had been working with his instructor, the kind of person who had shared her love of flight with others much of her life— no mystery why she chose to share it here on the shore of the Columbia. Both were interested in our adventure.

"You know you're living every pilot's dream, don't you?" She said it to me more as a reminder than a question.

I nodded. Of course I knew. Not a flight goes by that I do not sit for a moment after engine shutdown and think how fortunate I am to have Nanna and wide-open spaces in my life.

The next morning, our instructor friend had asked a reporter and photographer from the local newspaper to meet us. Reporter Jill got the first pony ride and then scribbled Howard's quotes about our adventure while we launched again, this time with the photographer. In the cramped front cockpit, he strained at his harness for a going-away shot, shooting from the front cockpit toward my face as I pulled Nanna's nose up to frame the river and golf course behind. He had forgotten to fasten the strap of his canvas flying helmet, which the wind caught and billowed up into the slipstream, headset and all. "My gosh, he's going to loose it," I thought, imagining a bludgeoned tail and spiral dive. He slammed his free hand down on his head just in time to keep the helmet from blowing off and like a combat photographer, kept on clicking throughout the averted disaster. Topping that derring-do, he bobbed and weaved, keeping the camera in my face all the way down final and throughout the landing. I reminded myself to spiff up future pre-flight briefings for photographers. We would not see the article until weeks later, but we hoped it would be good publicity for the airport and local aviation.

After our interview, we launched again, slogging northward under clouds as wet and ragged as a cotton mop and through air as damp as a sopping sponge. We headed toward Seattle, keeping the interstate on our wing through rolling hills. The cloud bases rose higher and eventually broke open. "Here there be water, matey," I thought, as we hopped across one finger of water after another through Seattle and on toward Whidby Island. It was there that our unbroken winning streak with the low-pass-no-problem Navy ended—no transponder, no low pass, they said.

My disappointment did not last long, though, because ahead on the northwestern corner of Washington, abeam Victoria, British Columbia, I could see the San Juan Islands. They ranged in crazy shapes and sizes from tiny, maybe a few hundred yards, to small, a few miles. All were full of pines and firs, craggy and rocky with steep edges dropping to the water and only a few beaches, the kind of islands that reminded me of Skull Rock. Even so, enough flat spots existed for about a dozen airports, many public. We picked our destination based upon the same exhaustive research we always do—Howard vaguely remembered that a friend stayed there and liked it. We bypassed all others and headed for East Sound Airport on Orcas Island, the northernmost large island. It was shaped like a pair of saddlebags with the airport running along what would be the horse's spine. We entered a left downwind beside the mountain that distinguished this island from the rest, turned base over the water—no Orcas popped up—and dropped onto final heading back toward the long narrow inlet that divided the island in two.

After landing, a friendly voice on the radio coached us to tie down to the south, so we kept rolling in that direction. Right away I spotted a big and shiny biplane, a bright red one with yellow wings. It was a 1920's Travel Air with "Magic One" and "Rod Magner" painted on nose and cockpit. Rod himself waved us on as we passed. Nanna was home. After our daily button-up and bathing chores, we visited with Rod, biplane-ride entrepreneur, saver of everything he ever touched having to do with flying, and keeper of the hangar that was at once a museum, pilot shop, visitor lounge and office. He helped us find a place to stay and handed us the keys to a loaner car with more idiosyncrasies than features. With practice, Howard was able to get it into gear and we headed off to the Otters Pond Bed and Breakfast, Howard's first-ever stay at a B & B. (How anyone with his zillions of free travel miles could have missed at least one of these establishments I will never know). The pond outside the windows disgorged no otters, but feeders did attract plenty of birds and bunnies. At night bullfrogs emerged onto the lily pads to bellow comic serenades. As I lay awake watching the moon, their croaking reminded me of the hippo chorus I once heard from a floating cabin on an African lake. I drifted off to sleep.

The following day, sunny and mild with a light breeze, we explored. At the airport, we met up with Rod to get a local briefing. He walked me to a map on his hangar wall and pointed to a hole in the center of the paper that would have been his airport had he not pointed at it so vigorously, so often over the years. He offered suggestions about where we could land (or not), picnic, and read. When I lamented that I had not brought along a good book, he led me to a shelf and handed me one of his ancient, musty treasures, *The Airman's World,* a rare book that had been on my must-read list for years. I tucked it in Nanna's lunchbox feeling privileged indeed.

We spent most of that morning aloft tracing island after island, picking out interesting homes, watching the to-ing and fro-ing of ocean vessels, local ferries, and pleasure craft. We found all the mysterious private airstrips tucked away among the trees, including one residential airpark that cut across a fingertip end of Blakely Island. We looked hard for whales, but saw none. All the while, we saw and heard aircraft darting in and out of Friday Harbor. We had considered stopping there for lunch, but as it began to sound like a bustling tourist destination, we decided to pass. Instead, we headed back to East Sound to join up with Rod and Magic to tag along on one of their island tours.

Magic carried two passengers side by side in the front cockpit.

He took off first, Nanna in trail, heading south down the inlet. Rod had told me that he played music and narrated his rides, so I imagined what he was saying and playing as he waltzed about the islands. Suddenly, a yellow balloon escaped in his slipstream and we watched as Magic whipped around and dove after it, like a retriever after a ball, down, down, gaining on it. Nanna, like his romping namesake St. Bernard, banked to join the game of fetch. Magic caught up with the balloon, and I saw it rush between the wings. Then Nanna and I lost sight of the balloon entirely, as puppies learning to fetch often do. (Rod told us later that the trick was to miss the balloon between the wings, but just barely. Once, he caught a balloon on a flying wire and it did not pop, but flapped and thrashed like a living creature in pain, so violently that he and his passengers felt sorry for it. Since then, I think he told passengers that if he hit the balloon, they rode free.) We continued to fly and play, Magic joining up on Nanna's wing until Magic landed. Close behind, Nanna roared by on a low pass for the delight of passengers who had, after all, paid good money so pilots could have fun. The following morning at the Otter Pond breakfast table, the conversation centered on guest sightings of two romping biplanes.

"Magic has never been more than about forty miles away from here. I know that when you take off, we'll want to follow," Rod admitted to me that day.

"Come on along. What a bad parent you to hold Magic back," I said.

"I guess. You know, Little Magic has been farther away from here than Magic ever has, forty miles maybe." Rod turned and looked at the toy biplane, a replica of the original, large enough for a small child. Photos of the toy in far away places hung all over the hangar among the military posters, airplane caricatures, and other memorabilia.

I found it hard to imagine Nanna tethered like Magic, but that is just the opinion of a mother who would soon run her baby into a fence and call it a good day. Nanna and I had spent a thousand hours together and had flown all of the contiguous United States except the Northeast. Magic romped every day, teaching new admirers something they already knew, but needed help remembering. Either way, it worked.

We departed on a Monday to hug the interstate heading south beneath scud and rain again, a near-permanent feature of the corridor that time of year. We met a couple of planes flying in the opposite direction as though the sky, too, were a two-lane highway. When I nudged Nanna across the highway once to keep an eye on an airport runway below, a voice on the radio scolded us for being on his side. Kelso came and went below as we turned upriver toward Portland. Clouds kept dragging lower, and more misty veils fell in front of us until we could no longer see any path to our midday target airport. We probed less ominous tracts of sky, found an airport still in the clear, and landed. It was a big city airport, so Howard was delighted. I called for a weather update and found out that all afternoon we would only see more of the same soggy mess. We would not risk flying the Columbia River Gorge that day.

Next morning, patience rewarded us. The air was calm, clouds few and high, and sunshine plentiful for the trek through the gorge, surely one of the premier biplane routes the world has to offer. We flew a few hundred feet above the ground, overwhelmed by choices of sights: dams, ships, river bends, mountains left and right. I expected to see other planes sightseeing, but saw none. Once I turned my head to discover a waterfall dropping hundreds of feet down a rock face through a green-forested mountain. The view I framed between our wings had been framed, no doubt, in a thousand photos in hundreds of books. I had never seen one, though, so I spied my waterfall fresh, a prize in my box of Cracker Jacks.

The river was wide, even at the narrowest point through the gorge, making the flying easy, giving ample room to pivot about

20

fish ladders, locks, and one barge, which looked like an oversized, open-air, baking pan full of corn. The river was home to massive power generation facilities, including tall power transmission towers marching along pine ridges and frequently down the hillside to cross the river. This danger kept my eyes alert to what the charts predicted and what big orange balls promised. I had once come close to wires, and did not want to repeat that little event. As I flew over the thick metal latticework and heavy cables, I felt like a flying insect bypassing a patio zapper, avoiding certain death.

The pervasive, forested greenness of recent days vanished as the river flowed beyond the nestling mountains to a dry, treeless expanse. It was an abrupt transition. People on the dry side must watch a storm raging toward them from the ocean through the gorge like a vicious beast whose chain yanks it to a halt at mountains edge.

We soon found ourselves beyond The Dalles, buried within a broad tan ravine, seeing nothing but our river pathway, eroded earthen walls, and sky.

"I wonder what's up there." Howard said.

"Want to climb?"

"I think we know what this looks like down here." Ahead was more of the same.

As I pulled the trim cord back and nudged the throttle forward, Nanna's nose tilted up slightly. Slowly, we climbed toward the top edges of the ravine, as though riding a glass elevator up a shaft. Our eyes passed over the flat edge of our destination floor, and we saw a vast barren landscape beyond and farther in the distance a new bunch of mountains. We stuck with the river to Hermiston, then veered right and climbed past Pendleton, Oregon, launching into Idaho's mountains, random shaped like blistered paint. We headed for McCall, Idaho, where Nanna and I would fly for days among backcountry strips scraped from the rugged terrain along Salmon River territory, little changed since the passage of Lewis and Clark.

As soon as Nanna's prop stopped turning on the ground at McCall, Lori and Kathy, two mighty mountain women, bounded out of a screen door along a row of airplanes to welcome us for the mountain flying seminar, the trip's only planned stop. Over our days together, I would learn that Kathy had left San Diego to find a better place to raise six children, all of whom now attended college. Dangling from her neck was a long chain with charms, each related to a child's life. She was the no-nonsense, get-the-job-done kind of woman who motored around town and parked smack dab outside the front door of any establishment where she had business, like a diplomat immune to parking violations. Lori made a career of teaching and commercial flying, a local expert. She flew all sorts of planes doing all sorts of work.

"What's your least-favorite job, Lori?" I asked her one evening.

She thought for a moment. "Maybe flying at night around the mountains—looking for lightning strikes that might start fires."

Yikes.

All the instructors Lori brought in for the seminar were special people, but none more special than Holbrook was. He was the kind of man who could turn a dull gathering of people into a party, yet sought his own joy alone on a motorcycle at sunset or a hike to a mountain hot spring.

"If we take off downriver, we'll climb through the River of No Return," Holbrook said over the radio from Nanna's front cockpit. "How comfortable are you turning tight close to canyon walls? We may have to take off heading that way." He was my flight instructor for the final day, one of three Idaho backcountry-flying veterans who had tutored me over the four days of class. We had been flying for over an hour already that sunny, crisp morning, often just a few wingspans from rocky ledges and treetops. After years of flying these mountains, it was Holbrook's first time here in an open cockpit.

I could see the river heading into a canyon where the walls

grew taller as they converged. To fly in there at river level would be like skiing through a forest down a steep and narrow path. Once in, we would be committed. "I guess I'd be okay." Gulp. All morning, we had been hugging the rocky cliffs and evergreens on the right side of narrow canyons "...keeping the big water under your left armpit" as Lori had drilled us. We had already had a pretty-exciting landing at Cabin Creek, one of dozens of one-way, no go-around, doglegged, dirt-gravel-grass strips in the backcountry. Most strips blended so well into the landscape that aerial photos used thick black arrows to point out where they were.

Now we were about to land at Flying B in a sweeping left arc along Big Creek. To make the approach, we cut low across a ridge—beside a line of amazed horseback riders that I never saw, but Holbrook told me about later—turned to follow the river behind the ridge, contoured the mountainside, and turned abruptly right beyond a bank at just the proper moment to touch down on the grass. This was not flying a traffic pattern. It was running an obstacle course.

Elated to be down and safe, we taxied to a stop so Holbrook could talk to the owner, a wiry man doing chores nearby. To live here was to live isolated. There was no running to the corner store for a forgotten ingredient, no calling in the plumber, no stepping out for the morning paper. The man sounded glad to have company.

As we were about to depart, Holbrook said, "Thanks again for letting us stop by. Can I bring you something next time?"

"Avocados and newspapers," said the owner at once, as though he had been rehearsing his response in case someone ever asked.

Sitting at the end of the grass ready to take off, a dog trotted down the strip, paused, sauntered, sniffed, and kept coming right toward us.

"Surely, he's not going to walk right into the propeller!" I said stepping on one brake and running up the engine to pivot the business end of Nanna away. Even avocados and newspapers would not make up for a butchered pet. Finally, the dog angled away, tail wagging. We powered up, bumped along the rough turf, and lifted off, waving and rocking our wings. Winds of chance headed us away from The River of No Return and left me wondering what might have been.

We flew a total of three hours that glorious, mild morning, the culmination of my wilderness flight training. I watched Holbrook's movements in the front cockpit, his peering out the side watching for horned sheep, raising his face to the sky as though savoring the warm sun, lifting his shoulders with deep-drawn breaths of the cleanest air. As Nanna's pilot, I have flown dozens, maybe hundreds of passengers, striving to give each the perfect pony ride, perfect for each individual. I take pride in my ability to transform neophytes, who are apprehensive that cloth wings can suspend them safely in level flight through perilous skies, into enraptured enthusiasts of rolling and looping flight. I enjoy taking experienced pilots up to plant a seed for The Biplane Dream. This day in the purest air somewhere above the Middle Fork of the Salmon River, Nanna and I hit a new high. We gave Holbrook, a gazillion-hour professional pilot, owner of a dozen-plus planes, a fresh new gift of wings.

Meanwhile, as I caroused around the mountains, Howard pursued the perfect cast in a stream somewhere below, learning the art of fly-fishing in the heart of fly-fishing heaven. That evening he shared with me his new convention for describing The Catch. "I caught nineteen linear feet of fish," he said, leaving the mix of sizes and quantities for me to decide.

The next morning, we struck north toward the fence at Timber Basin.

Before Nanna bounded into my life, I met Tony Blum, a repairer and restorer of aircraft. Tony had designed a stunning paint scheme for a Stearman, hunter green and cream, scalloped wings, and a teddy bear on the nose. It was Tony's sense of the barnstorming spirit of the 1930's that turned into Nanna's distinctive look, the bold blue scallops on creamy wings with a great blue feather arched around his tail. Tony had never seen Nanna except in photos. So, that Saturday morning as we were about to leave McCall to amble above railroad tracks through the northern Rockies, I phoned and arranged to meet him. He was working on a Luscombe at John Burgy's hangar.

"Are you comfortable landing on a grass strip?" Tony asked.

"Oh, sure," I said with confidence. I had just finished landing on some of the toughest mountain strips in America, after all.

Within a few hours, we were circling Timber Basin, a grass strip owned by a community of live-in pilots, and spotted John's hangar, which sat on a hill at the northern, forested end. A pond bounded the south end of the strip with odd poles here and there along the sides. The strip ran up a hill through a narrowing tree-spattered corridor, across a road, and down the other side. We circled the field a couple of times to confirm the wind and details of the strip that Tony and I had discussed over the phone. Everything looked routine enough to me. I felt as confident and unconcerned as I had as a toddler hurling myself off the edge of a pool through the air to a parent who always caught me. Nothing ever went wrong.

We descended into the bowl toward the pond. Our wheels passed over the tall trees. Abruptly the dark green disappeared, replaced by calm blue water. I expected to feel sinking air, but felt no jolt, just a continued gentle descent. The winds were mild, playing no tricks with the changing terrain. The runway cut through the rising meadow like a golf fairway through rougher grass. What I saw descending, though, was only a green meadow. Nanna's nose hid the mowed strip. Any second it was bound to pop into my peripheral field of vision. We skimmed above the water with the edge of the meadow in sight ahead and committed to the landing. I shifted my sight farther downfield to better judge my descent and touchdown. Above the nose, I watched two poles, one on the right with a gently wafting orange windsock and a second farther uphill on the left, a utility pole near the gap in the trees. The touch down and roll out felt routine enough. Then I began performing the series of errors that would keep us out of the air for months to come.

We must have landed well right of strip center. I did not notice any difference between the longer and shorter grass, so as we touched down I did not know anything was amiss. Soon, I felt Nanna pulling abruptly right, like a car with a flat tire. If I pushed the left rudder at all to compensate, I did it with too little force to pull us back to the shorter grass. Whatever it was I tried had not worked. We continued galloping right. Then I did the worst thing a pilot can do in a crisis. I lost my confidence. I ran out of ideas of what to do next. I gave up. It was a brief run— I was now just along for the ride—through long grass and ruts to the fence. I heard Howard yowling as though riding a rollercoaster. CRUNCH, the underside of right wing surfed along a section of wooden fence spikes, SLAM, the right wingtip hit a gatepost and stopped that wing's forward motion, WOOSH, momentum launched the left wing around in an arc to hit the fence as well, and BAM, we stopped!

Mixture full lean, mags off, master off. We had arrived.

"You okay?" I asked Howard.

"Yeah. Are you?"

"Yes."

Nothing human bruised but my ego, we climbed out as the neighborhood gathered. What had been a sleepy, deserted clearing in a forest just moments ago, became a teeming center of human activity.

"Are you all right?" the first man arriving asked. I would soon learn that he was the owner of the fence.

"Anyone hurt?" Another man asked running up from over the hill.

I looked at the weathered, wooden fence and squatted to see

the underside of Nanna's wing. The spikes had been just tall enough to slash the fabric to ribbons like blades of a pasta machine gone mad. Wires still held the thin, splintered, and broken fence slats together in a bent and misshapen line. The metal poles that once held the fence erect now listed in our direction of travel. Nanna nuzzled into a small tree inside the fence, like a bull pausing to smell a blossom before barging into the yard and heading uninvited up the path to the house. Other than the two bludgeoned wingtips, he seemed fine.

The owner of the fence moved closer to me. He was an old-timer, a wiry, graying man. He had been the original developer of the private residential airpark, so he had seen so much happen here over the years, and he had struggled through all challenges and hardships that came with such an undertaking. "I saw you set up to land," he said, his voice calm and friendly. "Looked good to me. I started walking back up to the house, so I didn't see. What happened?"

"I don't know. It happened pretty fast. I kept pulling right."

"Hmmm." He looked back toward the runway, puzzled.

"Sorry about the fence. Just let me know what I owe you."

He laughed. "Don't worry about it. It's not worth much." I glanced at the fence again. He was probably right about that. He continued, "Don't get down on yourself. Stuff happens."

"I suppose." I sighed. I was just recovering from an adrenaline rush. As I stood, trying to calm down, I remembered another biplane from another time damaged in another grass field. I began murmuring what its pilot had later written. "An airplane is just a bunch of sticks and wires and cloth, a tool for learning about the sky and about what kind of person I am, when I fly. An airplane stands for freedom, for joy, for the power to understand, and to demonstrate that understanding. Those things aren't destructible."

"Anne!" Tony's head appeared first as he jogged over the crest of the hill. He had an open, pale-bearded, rosy face topped with soft curly hair that rolled over his shirt collar, the kind of face that another thirty years might turn into a Santa Claus. His body was compact and strained the buttons of his shirt. Tony's expression looked puzzled and worried at first and then relieved when he saw that no one was hurt. He had been waiting for us at the far end of the field, away from the scene, out of sight. "What happened?"

I told him my best guess of a puzzling sequence of events.

"Can you start okay?"

"Sure. I shut down normally." I glanced at Nanna's aluminum spinner poking over the fence and chuckled. To describe shutting down a swirling propeller just inches from tree branches as normal was a stretch.

We rolled Nanna back from the fence and foliage and then swung his tail around. I climbed back in, started up, and taxied slowly down the hill to the far end of the field with Tony walking my wing. We turned up a dirt track toward the hangar where Tony had been working when we first passed overhead, and I called him on the radio.

There I met John Burgy as he stood in the summer breeze that blew into the hangar through the wide open door. Inside rested two airplanes surrounded by parts and tools. He and Tony rearranged everything to make room for the biplane that had dropped in unexpectedly.

John was a big, white-haired, blustery crust of a man with a liquid-center soul. "Don't beat yourself up about it," he said, as he poked and prodded at Nanna like an emergency room physician. "No big deal. We'll get you going again."

"Doesn't look so bad, does it, John?" Tony asked, picking off shreds of fabric dangling from the lower wing like the tattered hem of a street urchin's rags. "A temporary repair should do it." He turned to look at me, smiling. "We'll have you on your way in two, maybe three days." I tried to smile back.

Within twenty minutes, still more people who knew and loved airplanes dropped their Saturday projects to commiserate and console, remove fabric, diagnose damage, cut new sheet metal, and formulate the repair plan that would get us back on our way. I listened to Howard and Tony debate the best approach to removing an aileron, and I marveled at Tony's patience. I watched John working at a section of wing as he sat on the soles of his feet, a big, meaty man as limber and graceful as a Geisha performing a tea ceremony. A young student pilot arrived to fly John's Zlin, taking off and landing several times—perfectly centered—right in front of John's hangar. Tony's sons shouted and romped on the grass outside, adding their voices and the sounds of caught balls to the neighborhood chorus. Deer began to appear along the edges of the forest. I felt as though I was watching life distilled. All was right in the world—at least it was at Timber Basin.

"Look at this," Tony said. "Spar's cracked."

"Oh no," I said, my hopes for the quick fix dashed. Nanna was not going anywhere anytime soon. Dents and torn fabric were like scraped knees and elbows. Slap on a bandage and away you go. A cracked spar, though, was like a fractured arm—hard to fly with a broken wing.

Despite the setback, work continued. John and Tony offered to take on the repair job. Tony would bring his family up from their Spokane home on weekends. Everyone involved rearranged life to help me.

Amid the flurry of activity, Pam Burgy appeared and walked me up to her and John's home farther up the hill. "Let's get you away from this for awhile," she said and led me along the winding dirt driveway up the hillside to the yellow house that she and John had labored for years building. It had a large picture window that looked down the hillside and out over the meadow and airstrip. "Stay here as long as you need to," she said, her voice as soothing as a trainer calming a skittish filly. She sat me down at her kitchen table with a glass of water and listened patiently as I lectured myself for making errors that I would never fully understand.

"If only I'd pulled the mixture right away…how could I have wound up so far right…maybe my tailwheel hit a rut." I replayed the events in my mind and talked about what might have been if only I had done this or that differently. She nodded with empathy. Pam was the kind of woman who made everything comfortable for her family and friends, even strangers, no matter the cost or inconvenience to her. She reminded me of the pioneer women who first settled in these remote places.

We stayed with John and Pam that night. They were our most gracious hosts of the trip, strangers who opened their home and their hearts to us.

I learned a lot of stuff on that June day, including that if you need to smash your biplane, be sure to do it at Timber Basin, Idaho.

Imagine

The Timber Basin Trip—it might have earned a grander title, perhaps the Big Mountain Trip, had we completed the loop of the Rockies—was the most recent in the meandering summer series Nanna and I have flown since we linked up over seven years ago. We had already flown trips nicknamed Dixie, Rio Grande, Big Sky, and Four Corners, any of which qualified as a once-in-a-lifetime adventure. Altogether the trips covered thirty-two states, over 250 hours in the air, and over twenty thousand miles across the ground.

How different my life became when I ignored inner voices that nagged about impracticality, frustration, and danger, to heed instead the one that whispered, "Imagine."

I was not one of those kids who dreamed of flight or looked up whenever an airplane engine droned overhead. The possibility that I might fly an airplane did not cross my mind, nor did any of the many pilots I encountered growing up suggest that I could fly. I did not earn my way into the air by dogged determination and soulful looks toward pilots willing to take me for a ride in exchange for an airplane wash. I came to flying late in life, alone, curious, and on a whim.

It began on a bright Saturday morning nearly twenty years ago, when I padded out to my patio, clay tiles warming my bare feet, coffee cup in hand. I looked up at the lone, tiny cloud against the blue, blue Arizona sky and said, "Today would be a good day to learn to fly." So I did, motoring out, sunroof open, "I Heard it Through the Grapevine" throbbing its primal rhythm from the speakers, to Deer Valley Airport north of Phoenix. There a fresh-faced young instructor waltzed me through the introductory lesson, which exploded into several months of training and my pilot license. Several additional pilot ratings and another dozen years would pass before I became an aircraft owner.

During those years, I never considered buying a real airplane. I did buy a gift for myself, though, a small model biplane, an origami sculpture constructed from business cards, caught in a bottle, flightless, trapped. I would sit at my desk, staring at it, as I thought through problems. The paper model still rests on my desk beside a feather I found upon my front porch one perfect California day. Together these two images must have been conspiring in my subconscious to bring themselves to life. Today, a third item sits beside them, a scale model of Nanna, blue and cream colored like the business cards and with a large feather painted on his tail—imagine that.

As my flying progressed, it occurred to me that I did not have to keep renting airplanes. I could own one. But what kind? I considered what I might do with an airplane, and it became clear that a single plane would not do. Finances and hassle aside, ideally, five were necessary: one for pure fun, another to move from point A to point B, a third for soaring, a fourth seaplane, and finally a blistering fast point A to point B plane to cover long distances. I had noticed that flyers who sought too many attributes in one aircraft wound up dissatisfied with the compromise machine. Reasoning that I could rent all other types but the fun-only airplane, I began jotting down ideas about that one.

Meanwhile, an acquaintance from Hong Kong visited the United States on a flying vacation and invited a group of pilots to join him at a nearby airport for a day flying open-cockpit Stearman biplanes. The day of the rendezvous, I rounded the corner of a hangar and saw two huge, sturdy silver ships with crimson accents. One guzzled oil from a five-gallon can like a baby elephant feeding from an oversized bottle, then drooled a lot of it through its radial engine back onto the ground. I was smitten. Later, Hartley Folstad, owner of the air show fleet, took me up for my first-ever biplane ride, including a dogfight and mild aerobatics. This was a category one fun airplane—in the air. On the ground, it was big and heavy and would be as hard to push around by myself as a stubborn mule. The idea of a biplane did appeal to me, though, with all that beautiful wing.

The next month I was wandering around Santa Paula Airport checking out the variety of antique aircraft housed there and the possibilities of aircraft ownership. As I stepped out from a row of hangars, I saw the most beautiful biplane I had ever seen. Sunlight glinted off the tan fabric with bold red, white, and blue stripes. The top wings swept back in a jaunty way. Painted on its graceful round tail was the logo for the Great Lakes Aircraft Company. As I walked around admiring the biplane, a fellow strolled over.

"Beautiful plane," I said. "Yours?"

He nodded. We introduced ourselves and shook hands. His name was Jim.

"Would you buy another one?"

"In a minute."

He answered questions about the plane and whether it might be right for me. When I sensed he was ready to move along, I thanked him for his time.

"I'm going for a little acro practice. Care to come along?" He said it as nonchalantly as offering a lift to the corner gas station, but his words stuck me like an offer to fly to the moon, it was so unexpected.

I accepted—never mind that I knew nothing about the man, his skills, or his judgment. To have declined such an invitation on that warm California day would have sentenced me to a lifetime of wondering "What would have happened if…" We grabbed another parachute out of his hangar, saddled up, and took off for a half hour of bounding around the skies. Months later, my friend Jim spun that same Great Lakes into an orchard near where we had flown—and spun—that day.

Right away, I began taildragger lessons in a J3 Cub and aerobatic training in a Super Decathlon. Meanwhile, I continued pestering other pilots, comparing biplanes: Great Lakes, Pitts, Starduster,

Waco, and Tiger Moth. I already knew I would buy a Lakes, but I needed to help my head catch up with my heart's decision.

The clincher came late in the afternoon on a mild November Sunday at Santa Paula, when another Great Lakes slipped from downwind to final in a sweeping left arc. It tilted toward those of us on the ground as though hung from a string attached to its right wing, its whole orange and blue-striped topside presented to us. Right over the numbers, it collided with a small Grumman flying straight in to the runway. I heard the collision and saw both planes collapsed on the runway. Everyone ran toward the accident. Both pilots walk away unharmed. The Lakes caught fire. It was quickly extinguished, the biplane was dragged off the runway, and everything settled down. I thought, "What are the odds that I would witness two Great Lakes crashes in one lifetime?" I had just witnessed one, so odds were good that I would never witness another involving this scarce model. Therefore, for my own airplane, I should get the safe choice, a Great Lakes 2T-1A-2.

This is the sort of logic that caps the decision to purchase a fun airplane.

Reincarnation

The hunt for the right Great Lakes biplane took several months, despite the small universe of those still flying – well under two hundred, I had been told. I wanted one with a solid engine and airframe. If the fabric were shabby, that would be okay. I wanted to replace it anyway. While the search progressed, I began noodling on a 1930's look to replace the bold disco-era stripes typically painted on at the factory. I began by jotting down notes about a plane's personality to complement my own, the colors I had in mind, and a few graphic elements that had been swimming about in my thoughts.

An acquaintance suggested I look at the design work of Tony Blum. I phoned him and we met at Cable Airport. When I walked out of the bright sunshine into the dark hangar, I must have gasped as my eyes adjusted, stunned by developing image of that most statuesque of biplanes, a Stearman. The hunter green scallops gleamed along the big cream wings. I was accustomed to seeing yellow or gray military livery, so this Stearman was unusual, a refreshing change, and resonated with what I had in mind for my plane. Little touches made it special: the nose detailed with a Teddy Bear image, beige leather seats embossed with "Stearman," and floorboards that gleamed like fine antique furniture. Then there were the modifications and upgrades Ken McCullough, the owner, had made to engine and avionics. I had not even considered adding instrumentation to fly in clouds. Right away, I asked Tony to design a similar look for my airplane.

Sketches and notes passed in the mail. Within a couple of months, we had the conceptual design locked. The plane would be dark blue and cream with lighter blue accents, scalloped wings like the Stearman, a large Great Lakes logo on both sides, the plane's name "Trailing Edge" on the nose, and a huge feather to accentuate the tail.

I needed an artist to design the graphics and quickly settled on a new commercial artist, my daughter's roommate. Julia listened to my idea that the wind should blow the name along the sides and a feather should focus attention on the tail. We discussed the challenges of shaping straight feathers onto a round form and we poured over photographs and drawings of feathers. I watched her sketch ideas of windblown letters, intrigued by the seemingly effortless way she worked, tilting her head, tucking a fallen strand of hair behind her ear, wrinkling her brow when dissatisfied, and nodding when something worked. Then I left her alone to do that magic thing that artists do with nebulous ideas from weird clients.

Her first drawing a few weeks later approached perfection. She had bent the feather in a natural way that hugged the rounded edge of the tail section. Most of the feather fell on the first section of the tail. The rest flowed onto the rudder behind, so that when I pushed the rudder pedals back and forth the feather would wag. She had created splits and points along the quill that made it look like a real working feather. After one small adjustment to taper the quill's base, the feather was perfect. I produced transparencies of the name, logo, and feather, which I would later project onto the fuselage and tail to determine sizes for the production of painting masks.

I had the design, but still no airplane to put it on.

When an airplane changes hands from one pilot to another, it is reborn. Whatever it had been changes—its lifestyle, its personality, its capabilities, frequently its appearance, and even its gender. It was like that for my new airplane.

He was not new and he smelled. When I first climbed in, I wondered what the half-life of manure odor was. For years, his original cotton fabric had marinated in air at a home near the feedlots and pastures of Chino, California. He was white with the bold red and blue stripes given him at the factory in Wichita,

Kansas, in the spring of 1976. He bore serial number 728 in the series of over a thousand built in the 1970's and 80's from the original 1929 design modified with newer engines and avionics. He had flown on average seventy hours a year. The FAA knew him as N824GB. If he (or she) had a nickname, I did not know it, much as I would not have known the name of a stray dog that appeared on my back porch. Most of this would change.

First, we would learn about each other as we were that first day together, the mild and sunny Friday I drove to Santa Paula, sunroof open, tunes blaring. It was one of those days that darned near guaranteed that nothing could go wrong. Once at the field, I worked so hard. Everything seemed foreign. I did not know where to look or reach for this gauge, that lever. Given the scarcity of such items in an old biplane, this should not have been so difficult, but strange is always difficult for me. When I was learning aerobatics in the Decathlon, my instructor, Rob, kept having to remind me, "Relax!" and told me how strained my voice sounded calling my position in the pattern. He was patient with me those first five hours in the air doing pattern work and landings, air work, stalls, emergency procedures. I felt awkward. After the first day, I felt a little discouraged.

I had read all the literature, watched all the films, and attended the gatherings of pilots that laud the natural flyer. That is the novice who climbs into an airplane and in the first few minutes gets the flick, moves the controls in an intuitive way, needs little or no instruction on coordinating stick and rudder, and seems to have eyes and feelers on the plane's belly showing exactly when to flare for landing. I am the other sort, the pilot that has to work very hard at flying. If I do not practice regularly, if for some reason I cannot fly for a few weeks, I amaze myself with how unskillful and forgetful I have become. As frustrating as this is to me, on those rare days when I do everything smoothly and perfectly, my sense of satisfaction is all the higher, knowing I have overcome something gargantuan to achieve my little corner of nirvana.

It is difficult now to remember how awkward I felt on land and aloft those first hours. On the ground, even climbing and settling into the cockpit, which today is as routine and familiar as tugging on a T-shirt or lacing my feet into a pair of tennies, was fraught with challenges. I learned not to step here, sit there, kick the windscreen, carry in pebbles from my shoes that might chafe the fabric, or, sin of sins, drop anything. Coins, pens, clips, flashlights, and most any other solid object could migrate to and jam exposed controls causing serious aerial mishaps, so I had to retrieve everything no matter how painful the contortions to twist, see, find, and grasp. I learned to take inventory of everything I took into the cockpit and to check that I took it out with me.

I became familiar with taxiing using S-turns to see ahead of the high nose that stuck up between my path and me. I had been flying a Piper Cub and found the biplane handled similarly on the ground, except that I could not see as much of the ground nearby due to the extra lower wing.

At some point, everything clicked. The stick became an extension of my arm, then of my mind. Think left turn, stick moves left. Think right, it moves right. My feet pushed on the rudders automatically whenever I felt heavy on one side. I got used to how the airplane behaved with different power and trim settings and noticed my fingers pushing and pulling at levers and cord without orders from central command. No longer did I have to think about everything all the time. The sight picture and peripheral vision on landing telegraphed when to round out and flare. I began to sense when the wheels would touch and knew to expect a gleeful chirp or dreaded bounce.

Then I noticed the behavior that made this machine come to life for me and become my new friend. His landing gear hung straight down in the air. When he landed, though, his gear would splay outward and mush down as his weight sank into the lubricated rope coils packed inside the landing struts. He touched down with a "Whooommmmpppphhhhh, whoommpphh, whomph" sound and feeling, a plopping down, bouncy-ball action, reminiscent of a lumbering St. Bernard during play, dropping his head between outspread legs. I got so when we touched down, I punctuated the event by saying "Whoommppphh" to myself. I think I described it to Rob that day by holding out my arms, doing a little jump, and bobbing my knees a few times as I said "whomph, whuuf, whuuf." Soon, my brain was making associations of that behavior and an animal playing, until one firing synapse shot into the story of Peter Pan, smack in the middle Wendy & Michael's nursery. There in the corner sat the nursemaid and playmate St. Bernard—Nanna. Over time, that became the enduring personality and name of my biplane. Never mind that he already had a perfectly good, formal name, Trailing Edge, destined to be painted on his cowling and formal enough for registration with the American Kennel Club. Never mind that my airplane had always been a boy and Nanna was surely a girl's name. Never mind that I recognized the contradictions and avoided calling him that out loud for some time. One day during those first few months we were together, I stopped fighting it, and the nickname stuck—Nanna. The world and I would have to learn to ignore the contradictions.

Then came time for the solo, in many ways more memorable than my first as a beginning student pilot. We were landing to the west that day, coming in low over the metal hangars, and past rows of airplanes tied down on the left of a runway not much wider than a road. A number of the locals coming in at the end of a day of flying had gathered to watch the show. Nanna and I were the evening entertainment. Rob waved me off on my own and then stood beside the runway in his familiar stance, arms crossed and hands tucked under his arm pits, legs set wide, body tilted slightly back. He smiled and spoke with the other bystanders, comfortable and unworried. I tried to sound relaxed and confident calling over the radio. The long weekend of learning was ending.

I do not recall if we flew one circuit or two, but on the last one, rounding the corner from left downwind to base, the low sun warming my sunburned face, shadows lengthening, peace came over me. All thoughts of technique, procedures, worries, fell away. "If I never fly this airplane again, I'll be happy for this one perfect moment."

After we landed and taxied to a stop, the small bunch of observers dispersed. I saw Rob walking toward me, beaming. As I climbed out, he repeated a local pilot's compliment. I felt as satisfied and happy as a kid balancing on a two-wheeler for the first time.

In my logbook that Sunday night, I wrote seven lines for the weekend's flights, the last "Happiness is a horizon between two wings, and the wind, the wind."

In the days that followed, mechanics and restorers unbolted and tore that functional, good-looking biplane into a skeleton stripped of all fabric and paint. The hunt for imperfection was on. A wingbow, repaired years before, needed rework now. The tailwheel needed replacing. Plastic tubing, brittle with age, had to go. On one visit to the carcass, I stood in a dark and cluttered hangar before pieces and parts of wood and metal strewn about the stained concrete floor. What could I have been thinking to pay such a substantial sum for this pile of rubble? Just weeks ago when I landed the biplane for the last time before the restoration, every cent felt well spent. What was special and valuable about the biplane would never be visible on this concrete floor any more than my own value would be apparent from my components, a few dollars-worth of chemicals and a couple buckets of water. Assembly required—and batteries to set us in motion.

A summer and fall passed before the repairs and restoration were nearly completed. The only items left were the finishing accents—logo, feather, and name. I lugged my adjustable-height ironing board, overhead projector, and three transparencies to the hangar. I shined each piece of artwork onto the new, doped fabric and freshly painted cowling, experimenting with image sizes and angles. When satisfied with each, I jotted down dimensions. A few locals strolled by the open hangar, curious about my odd technique. The next day, I mailed my graphics files and dimensions off to a mask maker who returned to me a complete set of stencils. On an early morning weeks later, a local artist arrived and by dark, using the masks, little paper cups, brushes, paint, and a talented, steady hand, popped those elements onto the fuselage and tail. When he finished, I stood with him outside the open hangar door. Warm light spilled toward us as in a Vermeer painting, having already illuminated the central subject of "The Biplane."

California Meanderings

Winter was half-over when we finally rolled Trailing Edge out of the hangar into the bright sun, cosmetically perfect and mechanically sound, ready to fly again. Within a couple of days, instructor Rob had helped me scrape the rust off my landing skills.

Time came to cut the cord with Santa Paula and make our way home. Before the restoration, I had taken comfort knowing that if I goofed flying, landing, or taxiing and I damaged something, I could repair it as part of the project. Now that the biplane was perfect, I felt the dread every new vehicle owner feels awaiting the arrival of the first scratch or dent. Please, please, don't let it be today. We launched into a partly cloudy sky. Instead of heading toward the Pacific, we took the higher, inland route to Santa Monica so we could slip down through the forecast scattered cloud layer from the drier east side, then scoot into the airport under whatever layer had formed.

The temperature dropped as the biplane and I climbed, and a cool, moist air swirled around my arms. The sound of the engine rumbled through my headset and vibrated through my feet. I had been anticipating this time for months, eager to get on with our life together. Yet, as we climbed through the scattered clouds, I grew uneasy. Something felt wrong up here in the open air. Had I not practiced enough? Was I not ready? Unease turned to discomfort. The higher we climbed, the more anxious I became. We did not belong up here, this high. I was afraid. In enclosed cabins, my comfort level had always risen with the safety of altitude. In the biplane, it did not. The higher we flew, the more I felt we were out of our element. The biplane wanted to be earthbound, riding on the blanket of air above the ground with the birds and bugs and smells. To fly higher was to waltz with a partner not in our arms, but across the room, remote and disengaged. Whether it was this detached feeling or anxiety that the clouds or poor visibility would prevent my landing, this overwhelming sense that something was wrong turned us back to Santa Paula. To this day, I feel strange when we fly more than a thousand feet above ground.

A couple of days later, I returned to fly him home. In clear skies and sunshine, we flew comfortably low and slow to the Pacific Ocean. Coastal mountains swept along above our left wing, and diners at Malibu's popular seaside restaurants waved as we passed. It was our premiere. I felt like we were parading along a red carpet through an adoring crowd. But, I was not the center of attention, only the anonymous escort on the arm of the hunk. I realized then that whenever we were out together in the future, my best tactic for getting what I needed would be to say, "I'm with him."

At the Palisades, we turned inland and introduced ourselves to the modern world of air traffic controllers and big city airports.

"Santa Monica Tower, Great Lakes biplane November-two-two-tango-echo," I said, reading the number on the tag on the biplane's panel. The call sign was still new and unfamiliar to me. "Palisades inbound with Zulu."

"Say again type aircraft," the controller replied.

"Great Lakes biplane, a two-tango-one-alpha." I would have this conversation again with all new controllers we radioed. They never knew which four-character designator to type into their system for this unusual aircraft.

We received our instructions and continued toward Santa Monica Airport. Landing there was like parking a car in a big, empty lot. Its runway was several times larger and far less tricky than Santa Paula's, where planes were tied down within a few wingspans and the traffic pattern ran alongside a mountain. Landing at Santa Paula had been more like driving into a crowded garage, down steep ramps, and through narrow aisles to squeeze into a narrow space. I was glad that we had practiced there. It made this airport seem easy.

In the following weeks, I sat home or at the hangar with the biplane and waited for perfect conditions more than we actually flew. If the wind was too strong or at too great an angle to the runway, we did not fly. This was the first airplane I had ever owned, and the experience was not unlike the anxiety following the birth of a first child, when every little gurgle and movement conjures disaster—something is wrong and you are on the verge of making one horrible mistake after another. Screw up and you will kill your child. Do not risk a crosswind landing or let that nick on the cowling go unattended by professionals. Luckily, with airplanes as with children, newborn anxiety fades.

Years later, I noticed how much I had changed. One day, after practicing gusty crosswind landings, I was working in the hangar, dabbing extra dope that did not quite match onto a spot on the tail. The old dope had rubbed off in some mystery event a couple of years earlier. I had reminded myself to repair it often enough but never seemed to get around to it. As I worked, I noticed that where the fabric stretched over bolts and tubes, the blue paint of the feather had worn away in the wind the way river stones wear smooth in rushing water. There were plenty of other nicks and scars, like all kids get. Some came from my mistakes, like shoe-born pebbles that fell out, lodged between fabric and wood, and cracked the finish. Others came from exploring the great wide world, like chipped paint from propeller-tossed rocks. Looking back, like all mothers I laughed at myself thinking about those early fretful days.

The hangar at Santa Monica where I sat and waited for perfect conditions was in a building shaped like clover. Each hangar compartment had a rounded sliding door. It sat at a busy taxiway intersection. As I waited to fly, I sat in a lawn chair to watch airplanes landing and taxiing and to listen to their growls and whines. I washed the biplane's windscreens when they were barely dusty. I took pictures to mail to friends and family or add to the

49

growing scrapbook. I learned which camera angles showed the biplane to best advantage. Many people who had taken an interest in the restoration now came to visit and admire. Sometimes they flew with me, sometimes not, depending on wind, weather, and mechanical status or how adventuresome—or not—they felt.

Still, I managed to log over thirty flight hours the first two months, flying day trips at first back to Santa Paula, inland to Cable Airport to show off the biplane to our Teddy Bear Stearman friends, and then extending our reach for an overnight camping trip to Oceano, a small strip near Pismo Beach. During those early flights, I discovered all the little mechanical things that new airplane owners always find. And, I learned about the black art of rigging biplane wings, this prompted by a persistently weary right thigh muscle from having to push the rudder peddle too hard, too often, meaning almost always. When one local expert opined that major surgery on a warped rudder was the only solution, I decided to live with the problem, much as someone with a bad knee will live with it rather than undergo surgery. I was to find a masterful rigger two years later, who put it all right in a couple of hours using only a practiced eye and proper tools. Soon after that, my overdeveloped right thigh returned to normal.

During these early days, weeks and months, the mistakes I made led to practices and procedures that are with me still, refined and improved over time. To avoid dead batteries—or worse, people dead from an accidental prop start—I do not allow my feet off the brakes and rudders until I have turned off the ignition and master switch. I fold all charts before engine start to avoid refolding airborne, where an edge caught in the wind will yank the chart away. To avoid difficulty of removing hard-cooked insects, I wash the leading edges, all thirty-one of them, at the end of every flying day. I add an extra "G" for "goggles" to the pre-landing checklist to be sure an extra lens over my glasses does not distort my vision: "GGUMP" for "Goggles, Gas, Undercarriage, Mixture, and Prop." I put the cockpit cover on before nightfall to be sure no person drops anything in that might jam the controls and no critter crawls in to sleep—I can tell they try from muddy paw prints on the fuselage. In the hangar, I move the front wheel chocks, but leave the back ones positioned on floor marks to guide the biplane into position. It would take more years and significant damage to inspire the latest practices: I stop taxiing when trying to solve a problem, and I make a low pass before landing at any strip with peculiar features or squirrelly winds.

Who knows how long the biplane and I might have progressed this way, trips growing longer, forays of more and more miles. Instead, I needed to work in the San Jose area for a couple of months and then move to Dallas, Texas. So, one Sunday afternoon in late March, instead of wheeling my suitcase onto an airliner, I heaved it into Nanna's front cockpit—I had given up calling the biplane anything but Nanna by then—and buckled it into parachute and harnesses like a rigid, uncomplaining passenger. We launched for the valleys of Central California and on to San Jose. We landed at Harris Ranch, more restaurant than airport, and taxied back to the fuel pump for the first time ever on an unpaved surface, little more than a dirt tractor path, weeds brushing the underside of the wings as they bobbled up and down as the wheels bounced along. Afterwards, I noticed that everybody else taxied back on the runway. Departing with the sun perilously low in the sky, we turned west toward the calm, blue San Luis Reservoir, followed the winding road west over the pass. From there we breezed north along deep green ridges into approaching twilight where automobile lights flowed like pale red and white currents toward the two parallel runways at our destination airport.

For the next two months, Nanna and I led a temporary existence, playing together in the lengthening evenings after work among California hills gone greenest green from winter rains. On weekends, we explored the San Francisco Bay and points south to Santa Cruz, east to the Sierra foothills, and north toward the wine country.

It was trying to reach Mendocino, thwarted by weather going bad, clouds dropping lower and lower as hills rose higher and higher, that I first bathed dust from Nanna using nature's handy washrag, a gentle fall of rain. We had just turned around and were flying beside a wide-spaced procession of clouds marching up the slopes, each cloud dragging behind it a veil of gray water. I picked out one slender, transparent shaft and we turned toward it. At first, tiny beads of moisture tapped the windscreen. The force of the wind, much like the blower in a car wash, pushed the beads up and away, back out into the surrounding air. Right away, the beads grew into large splats pelting the metal and fabric like a drum roll. The water raced along the windscreen and disappeared behind. I stayed dry. I watched the wing surfaces as sheets of water formed on the leading edges then flowed back, taking with it months of accumulated dust, and disappeared behind us like water spewing from a waterfall. The thundering noise stopped. As quickly as the drops had grown, they shrank once more into the tiniest pinpricks of moisture, then nothing but clear air, drying all the surfaces at once. We turned back on course. I was delighted and a little surprised that I had stayed dry in the back cockpit. Howard was not so fortunate in front. From the edges of his windscreen, Nanna drooled.

Finding Texas

Finding Texas should be easy. From the Bay Area, fly down California's valleys and coast until you see smog, work your way along the foothills of the Los Angeles basin, find the windy pass with a big interstate highway heading east, and follow it until you run out of mountains. Bingo, Texas. I knew little about the state that was to become my home and less about my target city, Dallas, only that it was flat and far from an ocean. Like the dozens of other places I had ever lived, it would reveal its charms if I would be open to them and not pine for places in the rear view mirror.

It was early May, the sun casting the faintest glow to backlight the hills behind Reid Hillview Airport in San Jose. I stood before a fuel pump. The pump being a self-service, all hours sort of affair, I had put off filling the tank. If I had not, rising temperatures in the morning would have made the avgas expand, vent, dribble, and ultimately slobber onto the fabric wing. That Friday morning, the fuel supply was gone. A precious hour passed before I managed to drum up a fuel truck, fill up, and launch into a clear sky, just Nanna and me.

Thus began my follow-the-road navigation, the first road being Highway 101, and the beginning of my confidence that the method was foolproof. When I could also see definite mountain ridges, large valleys, and the Pacific coastline, it was. I had no plans to rely on my compass, nor had I paid any attention to it in these first few months, as it bobbled about at the top of the panel. Everything I needed to know about where we were came from looking outside the cockpit for features that matched my memory or my charts: coastline, mountains, roads, and landmark buildings, mostly.

After more than sixty hours together in the air, Nanna and I had become a decent team. He accepted my shortcomings: flaring a bit high now and then to land with a thud rather than a whisper or letting him fly through the air a bit skewed as I forgot about the rudder and pondered some mystery of life. I accepted his, holding that darned right rudder and left aileron all the time. By then, I had developed a technique for cruising where I rested the heel of my tennis shoe atop the rudder peddle, letting the dead weight of my foot hold the rudder without straining my thigh muscle. If it got bumpy, I had to give up relaxation and put my heels back on the floorboard so the balls of my feet could push one side then the other to keep the nose straight. Unfortunately, I had no solution for the aileron, and eventually got used to a weary arm. Yes, we were ready for our longest trip. At the end, a new home and hangar awaited.

Aside from my confidence in flying with Nanna, other elements promised a fine trip. I was at the end of one chunk of my working life and about to begin another, a boundary where old stresses and challenges no longer mattered and new ones had yet to ensnare me. I felt like I did at the end of a run or a bike ride, breathless, blood pumping, and worn out, yet satisfied to have met my goal. In time I would feel fit and eager to do it again. I relished this period of relative peace, knowing that I had the days ahead to look forward to the newness of "a whole 'nuther country" that was Texas. And, my younger daughter Amy would fly with me from Los Angeles to San Antonio for a brief visit with her grandparents. Just how brief it would turn out to be would have surprised me that morning.

With this sense of well-being, I rode with Nanna into fair skies and gentle winds. Leaving Silicon Valley behind, passing above the wafting garlic aroma of Gilroy, and angling across fields and hills toward Salinas, I glanced at my watch and thought of Amy. She would be preparing to drive to the airport to meet me. I wondered if her idea of packing "...just the few things you really need" would map in any remote way to the space available in the small storage compartment I called the lunchbox—probably not.

The highway pulled Nanna and me toward Salinas, but we let go of it to cut the corner between the town and hills, which surely had names, but no one had marked them on my chart. All around us lay fields of green and tender produce. This was Steinbeck country, lettuce fields enough for Cal, the shimmering waters of Monterey Bay in the distance, and unseen canneries I knew to be along the docks. In 1932, maybe '33, some other Great Lakes, a new-fangled one flown out from the Cleveland factory, must have barnstormed around this valley in this sky at the time those stories fermented in Steinbeck's mind and flowed from his pen into the American psyche. Think of it, this very same sky.

Every valley has a stream or river or at least a dry drainage channel running through it. Like any elementary school child, I had learned about tributaries, rivers, and oceans. Although I had flown over countless valleys before, miles above them in airliners, thousands of feet in small, metal private planes, this time was different. We flew low. We flew slowly enough, could see far enough, and had so few flying tasks that I could pay attention. This particular valley, the Salinas, was darned long, but narrow enough that I could take in the big picture, how all the pieces worked together. I noticed how foliage colors matched the waters' flow, why towns had grown up where they did, and how the roads connected them along natural paths. Years later, I would read Isak Dinesen's description of this awareness: "Every time that I have gone up in an aeroplane and looking down have realized that I was free of the ground, I have had the consciousness of a great new discovery. 'I see:' I have thought, 'This was the idea. And now I understand everything.'"

I have since had the same thought when flying Nanna over the grandest of scenery: Bryce Canyon, Monument Valley, Zion, the Mississippi River, the Big Bend of the Rio Grande, the Chesapeake Bay, the badlands of North Dakota, the San Juan Islands, to be sure. But it happens, as well, flying above less dramatic places: the little gum drop hills of south Texas; a river that still winds through a man-made reservoir during a drought; rows of crops, contoured by farmers to fit the land; forests of Minnesota and Canada stretching past a hundred horizons and beyond; the Texas panhandle, where the continuous plain stops after hundreds of miles and splits off abruptly into the ravines, buttes, and mesas of New Mexico; the gradual changes of the earth that make Texas so special and subtle for all its human bravado, from Gulf Coast wetlands, ancient receded seas, piney forests, high plains, and in the end, mountains. That day in the Salinas Valley, peering down at checkerboard fields along the valley floor and the river itself growing narrower and narrower, and then across at mountains that grew taller and closer together, I began to know Earth.

We followed the highway across the valley's last ridge heading for the coast and stopped south of Pismo Beach long enough to refuel. For the next leg, all was clear through the valley and along the mountain ridge that cut the Santa Barbara coastal plain. There, as we hurdled over to the coast, a tabletop of clouds had formed over the city, south as far as the eye could see, and out to sea for a few miles. I knew the terrain, so we continued above the clouds, mountain peaks to my left. North of Oxnard, the clouds thinned as the sun boiled them away. A hole appeared, and we spiraled down to fly low along the shoreline. The Pt. Mugu tower controller reminded me that the rifle range was hot and that I had best not drop any lower approaching Mugu Rock. I felt sad, knowing that Nanna and I would not romp along this sparkling coast again for a long, long time.

At Santa Monica, we landed and shut down in the area reserved for transient aircraft close to a sunning Amy. She had been waiting for a couple of hours. While I called to check the weather, Amy set out on a mission to find us a bite to eat. We sat on ground with our picnic of soft-shelled crab and spring rolls, joking that such fare might be difficult to find down the road.

After refueling, I stood, holding open the flap to the lunchbox, looking at the meager space remaining, and comparing it to the mass of Amy's belongings stacked on the ground below. Her bag of cosmetics took about as much space as the wheel chocks, which I considered chucking in the final minutes. After packing and repacking, we admitted defeat and agreed that one sizeable plastic bagful of clothing would fly under Amy's left leg and I would sit on her jacket.

Haze, mist, and smog stayed with us for our departure from the Los Angeles Basin. It seemed fitting to me that I should leave it looking and smelling the way it usually did. We hugged the bowl of mountains and stayed low to avoid the maze of airspace restrictions. I picked out golf courses and ball fields among the buildings for my imaginary hopscotch game. As we flew by one emergency landing spot, I looked for another within gliding distance. Interstate-10, the world's longest emergency runway and navigation aid, fell under our wing for the first time as we banked left into Banning pass. There we encountered none of the strong winds against which other biplanes have struggled.

Clear of the great city and its hazards, I relaxed a bit. I reached forward around Amy's seat and tapped her with a book of road maps. I had ordered them from the auto club especially for her. "Here, you can follow along."

She took them. Within a couple of minutes, I felt something tapping against my foot and saw Amy's hand and the map book re-appear. "Not now. Maybe later." Then she squirmed. "This parachute pack sure is firm."

"Would you like to learn to fly?" I was about to run off the edge of my chart and needed to refold it. My plan was to teach Amy to hold Nanna straight and level while I changed and refolded charts along the way.

"Not right now. Maybe later." As she spoke, she adjusted her music earphones beneath the radio headset.

My hopes dashed, I began manipulating a five-foot wide chart within a two-foot wide cockpit. Air rushed by outside, ready to seize and yank out anything poking up the way a sneezing person would snatch a tissue from a Kleenex box. The departed chart would then float to earth, unless it happened to catch on the tail, where it would hang like a slipcover for all to see until the engine blast stopped and it slipped pitifully earthward. With care to avoid such embarrassment, I held the stick between my legs as I unfolded the chart.

"Mom, what's going on?"

"I'm folding a chart," I said, looking up to see the wings at a sharp angle to the horizon and the nose well below it. I pulled Nanna out of the diving left turn. So it went for the whole trip, periodic excursions of altitude and heading when I ran out of visible chart area and began refolding. Amy would wake and ask, "Are you folding charts?" to confirm that I was awake.

At the northwest end of the Salton Sea, Thermal Airport sits about a hundred feet below sea level. It was wickedly hot and dry when we landed. Amy had by now lost one earring post (in flight, never to be found) while rearranging her headset atop earplugs of her compact disc player. On the ground, she leaned over and one lens of her sunglasses fell onto the cement and broke. I, still wearing a cotton turtleneck under my dark blue flight suit, sweltering, offered what sympathy I could muster. We escaped into an air-conditioned building to replenish body water and cool down. I peeled off a layer of clothing. At the snack machine, I pointed at the selections. "Hmmm. No soft-shelled crab."

By the time we took off toward Phoenix, the extra plastic bag had found its way into my cockpit and Amy had taken back her coat for extra cushioning. Lifting off the searing runway, we labored for altitude and turned north. We crossed the highway, saw eighteen-wheelers heading east, and settled in to tag along. About fifteen minutes into the leg, I wondered why the Salton Sea was not dropping away. I looked carefully at the chart, checking mountain ridges, roads, and towers. Turns out, eighteen-wheelers drive on any old road, not just I-10. We were following the wrong road. As we circled back, Amy perked up as the hazy, late-day sun streamed through her single dark lens. We agreed that we should backtrack to Thermal rather than strike out across a desolate, mountainous shortcut. Sure enough, we found the highway fork I had failed to notice and picked up the real I-10, leaving the imposter road to fork off to wherever it darned well pleased.

The day was wearing away too fast. My plan to be well into Arizona by days end had long fallen along the wayside. I began frequent calculations of time and distance, worried that we might not even make it to the next airport by sundown. It would be tight. I had never landed Nanna in the dark and did not want to try it for the first time with any passenger—let alone my baby. Bright lights appeared in the distance and looked like a city, but turned out to be a prison. I was disappointed as we flew by and worried that we would not reach the airport in time. By the time we touched down, the sun had set, and I needed the runway lights to judge where the runway was. Phoenix lay far down the road. We were behind plan, but we were down and safe. It had been a good day.

Within minutes, the desert night fell like the blackest curtain. We organized our belongings and made our way toward the phone booth, aided by one strange, bright light from inside the only hangar on the field. Amy pointed a flashlight at the local yellow pages, as I searched for a taxi company, always an iffy business in the middle of nowhere. An agricultural pilot landed, bounded our way like a puppy heading home, and offered us a ride in exchange for use of the phone. He dialed his girlfriend's number. After fifteen minutes of busy signals, he handed back the receiver, defeated. I called the only cab company in town. In another fifteen minutes, our cab arrived and our bewildered pilot, still unanswered, piled in with us. At his house, visible through the window, the girlfriend stood talking on the phone. As he walked in the door and we pulled away, she was still at it. I always wondered how long he was home before she hung up.

Early Saturday morning, after a quick stop for coffee, rolls, and a supply of beef jerky, we refueled and launched out of air that had already warmed twenty degrees since sunup. The dry air a bit higher up would swirl around the cockpits and keep us comfortable. Immediately, Amy made good on a prediction she had made to me months before when I took her for her first flight in Nanna, "I could sleep in him." Most of that day, she slept, recalling later that evening, "I'd be sleeping, then half-wake thinking I was in a dream. I'd look around at another view and remember, 'no, this is real, I'm flying with my mom.'"

The calm morning air would not heat up into rumbling thermals until midday. As Amy slept, I flew on, sorry that she was missing the long flat valleys and mountain ridges. Still, I was happy that she felt comfortable enough to sleep. I could watch her slumbering head while I enjoyed solitude in a mystic land, flying by layers of orange and rust with patches of sage and brown. By midmorning, saguaro cactus began popping up with increasing frequency. We were entering lush desert, a description introduced to me years before by a Tucson realtor. We skirted around the southwest edge of Phoenix, passing beside the Estrella Mountains, where I had soared in the past. Soon, the magical leg ended. Amy awoke as I made a radio call to Avra Valley, the airport where I had landed on my first solo cross-country flight twelve years before. We landed hungry.

"What's the best way to get through Tucson airspace," I asked another pilot at the airport restaurant. "Will the controllers let me follow I-10?"

"Yeah, they're pretty agreeable," said one fellow.

"If you like to talk to those guys," added the second. "Me, I prefer running around the back side of the mountains here and pop out south. Same thing at El Paso, heck they don't care if you stray into Mexico a little there—you can always glide back into the state, needs be."

After lunch, sun overhead, away we flew, around the southwest Tucson ridges, and picked up the highway. The air was choppy, the compass bobbing and, as usual, I ignored it. Who needs the compass when you have the road? After flying for awhile, enjoying the green river valley tucked between hills, I wondered why the town below was larger than any I expected to overly. Soon, we flew over an airport that was not where I expected it to be and with runways running in the wrong direction. I turned on the GPS and discovered that the nearest-airport function came up with Nogales. In denial, I did not believe it and continued flying along the highway, although now it looked more like just a road. The sun was not straight overhead any longer, but beginning to warm the right side of my head. I was in Mexico.

As we banked and reversed course, Amy awoke. "Wrong road again, huh. I guess we're going to lose more time on this one than the last." She did not sleep again until we landed at Cochise, where she lay under Nanna's wing and napped, shaded from the heat of the day, while I folded and studied charts inside the cooler pilot's lounge. Soon, we were again on our way.

Having failed to follow the right road twice so far, once at the Salton Sea and just that morning into Mexico, and confused now by the mismatch of the terrain I saw, the chart, and the GPS, I began to doubt the identity of the highway below. I needed to be sure. Amy happened to be awake and highway traffic was light. We dove toward the highway. I pulled back the power to glide down low, transforming cars from scale models to full size with alarming speed.

"There. That green sign. Does it say I-10 East?" I called over the intercom, dipping a wing so both Amy and I could glimpse the text whizzing by.

"I can't...." Amy began, her canvas helmet snapping sharply to the right in front of me as she tried to read, "...see it."

I saw it. "Yep, we're on the right road. It said I-10." On we flew.

We made short work of the rest of Arizona and New Mexico, wide flats punctuated by mountains and, sadly, smoke from distant forest fires. The mountain ridge at El Paso loomed ahead by late afternoon. I had abandoned any thoughts of scooting around the mountain into Mexico and cast my lot instead with the El Paso air traffic controllers, asking for a transit of the city low along I-10. "Transition approved. I can't see you yet because of the mountains. Report passing a smokestack." That was easy to find. It sat right by the highway that I was not letting out of my sight for a second. The controller could not have been nicer, giving me constant signposts and vectors to an airport at the edge of the city. Once there, I decided instead to push on another few miles to Fabens, Texas. It was already Saturday evening, and we still had a huge chunk of Texas to cover tomorrow morning.

The sun lay low in the sky as we circled above a runway half-covered with shifting sand, like a scene from the Sahara Desert. Everything looked white except the few buildings close by. We had long since left lush desert behind. The wind favored a westerly landing. On final approach, blinded by the glare of the sun, unable to see straight ahead, we descended to about fifteen feet off what appeared might be the runway, but I decided to go around.

"Let's just land the other way," Amy said over the engine's roar as though reading my mind as we bounded away. We pulled up and maneuvered for the other end of the runway. The tailwind was negligible, the landing uneventful. Taxiing was another story—we saw no signs of life until we reached the far end of the airport where a group of folks chatting in a hangar caught our attention. We made a quick pit stop and hopped back into Nanna to squeeze in a last one-hour leg before sunset.

Ca-chunk, ca-chunk, the propeller turned twice, then we heard nothing but the sound of silence as only West Texas can do silence. The prop would not turn over and catch. We needed a new plan.

I found a rope buried beneath shifting sand and tied down Nanna's tailwheel, wondering how deep the sand would be by the time we left.

A mechanic, Pina was his name, strolled out of the hangar and greeted us. Quitting time had come and gone. "Sounds like a dead battery. I know what it's like to be flying away from home and have trouble. We'll get you going again first thing in the morning." Bless their hearts. We pulled out the battery and he carried it into the hangar and hooked it up to the charger.

Before we left the hangar, Amy and I stood with our overnight parcels in hand, talking with mechanics and pilots who had lingered after work. It was a scene familiar at any small airport, a bunch of local flyers interested in the folks passing through. I gestured too broadly, and my plastic bag fell open, spilling its contents onto the grey hangar floor. One fellow leaned down to help pick them up, but stopped short when I scooped together underwear and T-shirt and said, "dirty clothes."

As night fell, Lucy, the airport matron, gave us our first West Texas ride in a red pickup truck, faded and dusty. She dropped us at a motel. Amy and I took turns trying to unlock the flimsy door that opened into a room with shag rug and orange walls from an ancient psychedelic age. The bathroom window opened onto flat land with tall dry grasses and coyotes calling in the distance. The truck stop across the road did not offer soft-shelled crab, but the corn dogs were not bad, and who could ruin chocolate milk? Homogenized Motel 6 travel had not found its way to this place. This was my first night in the wilds with Nanna, and I was glad to find when we returned from dinner that not even hard rock candy had magically appeared on my pillow.

Morning broke. Lucy fetched us at the motel. When we rumbled up to the airport gate, tires crunching against the gravel, guard dogs barked and growled to keep us outside the fence. One of the canine pack limped and staggered from a life of hard knocks, but did let Amy pet him as we waited. I was beginning to worry about the time. We had a long way to go. Finally, Pina pulled up.

Battery replaced, fuel topped off, strapped in, I turned the Nanna's key. I expected to see the propeller swing four or five times, and then catch with a loud bleating roar. Ca-chunk, ca-chunk, and then silence were all I heard. The battery was just plain dead and would not hold a charge. Pina cannibalized one from another airplane he was working on and within a few minutes sent us on our way. I wondered if we would have been so fortunate at the big international airport.

East of El Paso, things got flat fast. Amy agreed to stay awake to help me find another major highway. The fork leading in one direction to Dallas and the other to San Antonio should be obvious, but I could not take a chance of missing it. It was now Sunday morning, the day of Amy's return flight. We had become pretty good at this road-following business by now, although missing fuel supplies and excursions to the Salton Sea and Mexico had put us far behind schedule. We hit the fork, headed southeast, and Amy went back to sleep until her head wobbled into the slipstream. At Fort Stockton, we called my parents to warn them of our tightening schedule, and launched for the final push to San Antonio.

This leg surprised me most. The desolate country, pale and hilly, looked as though someone had melted a huge sheet of earth into liquid, dropped a boulder into it to make waves, and then cooled the rippled sheet solid again. The turbulence was the worst we encountered on the trip, and we hugged the highway, knowing that an emergency landing elsewhere would have been perilous. When trees and houses began to appear again, I was debating with myself pushing on to our final destination, Twin Oaks, or stopping sooner for fuel. Amy awoke feeling queasy and asked that we get out of the turbulence, up or down, she did not care. We landed at Kerrville, winds blowing twenty knots straight down the runway, thank goodness, as a direct crosswind of fifteen was Nanna's limit, and ten would probably be more than I could handle with any confidence.

At Kerrville, Nanna experienced his first red carpet arrival—there would only ever be a few. We taxied slowly to the ramp and pulled up beside a twin-engine airplane with a large cabin. Its door was open with steps folded down. On the ground lay a red carpet. As soon as we shut down our engine, a young man in a natty uniform of Bermuda shorts and shirt ran up to our side and placed a similar carpet beneath Nanna's wingwalk. Amy looked back at me and we laughed. Boy, were we at the wrong airport. Soon, Amy's stomach settled and we piled back in Nanna, taxiing a long, long way to one runway—the wrong one—then all the way back to another, got ourselves headed into the wind, and popped back into the sky for a short, but thrilling leg.

To say that Twin Oaks is nestled in a residential neighborhood does not do justice to the word nestled. We could not see the airport until the GPS showed that we were almost on top of it and the San Antonio International Airport traffic controller kept requesting that we, "Report airport in sight." That big, commercial airport was only a few miles away and its runways were already clearly visible. Directly over the tiny field, I told him I had the field in sight. According to the wind direction, we needed to land over tall trees and downhill. As we came in over the treetops, I saw houses falling into view just yards off my left wing. People stood by fences watching.

"This can't be the airport. It's just an alley," I thought, watching the blur of people and fence whiz by. Reacting more than thinking, I pushed the throttle full forward, and we bolted back into the sky. As we pulled up and turned crosswind, I looked back to see that, yes, windsock, hangars, and airplanes sat alongside an honest-to-gosh runway—wow, what a place. I forced the surrounding obstacles out of my mind, looked only at the runway, dropped down over the trees again, ignored the peripheral flashes of color so close to our wingtips, and landed. We rolled uneventfully downhill.

We taxied back and stopped in front of a small building next to an open hangar. The tall oaks that had looked so menacing as they snatched at our wheels when we landed now seemed to welcome us with friendly, rustling sounds. Bill Fowler, owner of Twin Oaks, met us as we shut down and climbed out.

"You came in the hard way," he said, smiling. He was tanned and gray, a big man with a friendly open face.

"Oh?"

"Unless the wind's over ten knots, we usually land uphill."

"Next time, I'll remember that. Seemed like about that strong to me."

We introduced ourselves, and he led me to a telephone in a cluttered office furnished with unmatched furniture. I called my folks and checked the weather for my solo leg to Dallas. As we waited for my parents to arrive, Amy made friends with a miniature horse, and I chatted with Bill.

Decades ago, after retiring from the airlines, he had bought this country strip for his personal use. Friends asked to use it. He agreed. They suggested that Bill pave it so they could come and go in the messiest weather. Bill did. Lights, fuel? Sure, why not. Like Topsy, the bare strip grew into a little airport, and the city grew around it. Someday, no doubt, the city would choke it to death.

My parents soon pulled up to the airport gate. Amy and I trotted out to help them open it and exchanged customary hugs and kisses. My plan to leave Amy and fly Nanna on to Dallas that afternoon had already fallen apart with news of bad weather in the hill country to the north. Such weather never stops the airlines, though, and Amy's flight home would soon depart. She had spent two days flying with me and would have only two hours to visit with her grandparents. We rushed home so she could have a quick shower—she could not bear to travel bedraggled— and dropped her at the airport for a two-hour commercial flight back to Los Angeles. Time was so short at curbside that neither of us could go soft and sloppy about our parting. Gone were the days when she would drop in to do her laundry and share a meal or ride bikes with me to Marina Del Rey for Sunday brunch. Like all those forks in the roads we had just flown, she was winging off in one direction, I in another.

Two days later, the weather cleared, Nanna and I bounded out of Twin Oaks alone under low ceilings with a non-stop tailwind. All was quiet along the rural route we would come to know so well as a series of hops between reservoirs no more complicated than a stroll across a familiar park. I could not stand to complicate such a peaceful flight by barging across the busy Dallas airspace. Instead, we skirted around to the east and slid into the pattern at Addison Airport.

"Two-tango-echo, can you make a short approach?" the tower controller asked. The voice was professional, yet friendly, boding well for the thousands of interactions we would have as Nanna and I came and went over the coming years.

"Affirm." I chopped the power and dropped onto Nanna's left wing slipping in over a line of planes ready to depart. For the first time ever, their pilots watched the wonderful machine with the blue tail feather. Chirp. Home.

Two things stick in my mind about this trip with Nanna. First, nothing is harder about a long trip than a short one except laundry management. When mechanical troubles arise, someone will magically appear, knowledgeable and eager to help. All journeys are just a series of legs lasting no more than a few hours each. Others have flown every leg before, and any pilot will share the tricks and pitfalls of flying it. Nanna and I could fly almost anywhere in the world by piecing together legs, the way a child can chain strips of colored paper together to coil around the largest Christmas tree.

My second memory is Amy's singular achievement—open-cockpit sleeping. By her own estimate, she dozed seventy percent of our flying time. I am not surprised. I had discovered her extraordinary ability to sleep when she was a baby. I would find her in the driveway, napping, rump in air. Once, she used a big Tonka dump truck as a pillow and awoke with its shape impressed on her cheek. When Amy tired, she lay down and slept, period.

Recalling our flight together to Texas, I can still feel the light turbulence and see the back of Amy's head in the front cockpit bobbing gently up and down, back and forth, as she sleeps. A feisty air pocket hits us and she wakes briefly. Minutes later, her head is bobbing again. After awhile, it drops sideways into a ninety mile an hour slipstream that whacks her awake briefly. As I keep pushing her aerial pram onward, the pattern repeats.

To the best of my recollection, I did not sleep.

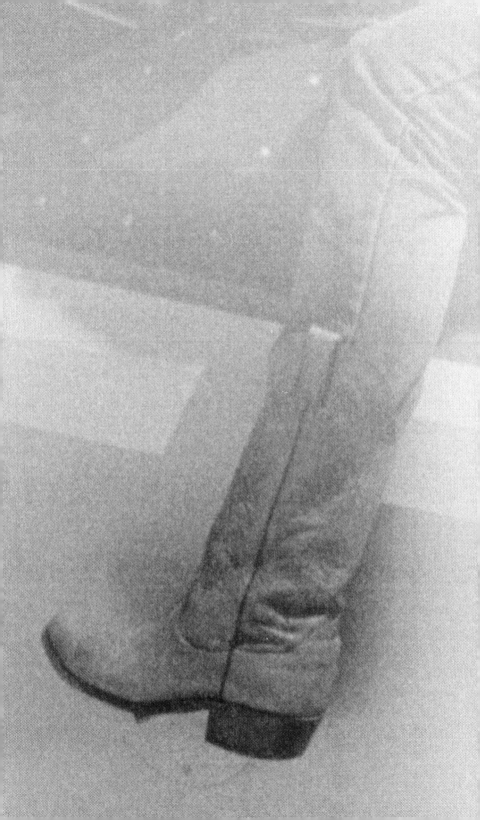

A Whole 'Nuther Country

What I had expected to be a couple or three years living in Texas stretched beyond five. I lived in only one home during that time, but Nanna moved through four hangars. His first was satisfactory, except for a leak in the metal roof that dripped rain onto his top wing, which then dribbled onto his cockpit cover. The second hangar, situated as it was about midfield, had no leaks and turned out to be quite satisfactory, but the airport soon condemned it to make way for a tunnel beneath the runway. Evicted, I moved him to the far south end of the field to a third hangar, an ancient metal structure with a small concrete pad on a dirt floor. Critters—rabbits, cats, and mice—slipped in from an open field overgrown with weeds at the airport perimeter to escape the heat, cold, and rain. I often saw them scurrying away in the early morning, or noticed their droppings or tracks in the soft dirt. Once in awhile, the top of Nanna's dark blue fuselage showed a line of paw prints. Still, we might have been content to share our space and satisfied to remain if prevailing winds had not forced us to taxi over a mile for take-off. The final move came when Nanna popped to the top of a waiting list for a midfield hangar. This last home was the best of all. Not only was it conveniently located, waterproof, and free of wildlife, but on our way out to fly we taxied by the local flight museum and could watch vintage airplanes, some on display and others preparing to fly.

During these years, I reshaped my lifestyle and leisure time around Nanna. I honed the skills of loading people and baggage and making simple fabric repairs. I discovered what to wear flying in fair weather, rain, or snow in temperatures ranging from well above one hundred degrees to below freezing. I made all of the stupid mistakes a biplane pilot could make, one each. I survived bent propellers and airframe dents and the associated long repair periods banished from the skies. I discovered the magic of grass strips and tasted formation flight. I grew to appreciate my fellow aerial creatures. I recorded a mental library full of flights to play again in my mind in years ahead. I discovered my country and the strength and goodness of its people.

Nanna and I, frequently with Howard along, scooted out from under the massive airspace around Dallas-Fort Worth, where we had to speak to and get permission from air traffic controllers. Once free of that territory, we explored the countryside, unencumbered. Rarely did we use the radio.

On our first local flight, I despaired at the sameness of it all. How would I keep from getting lost among rectangular look-alike fields, featureless roads, where mountains and coastlines did not exist for hundreds of miles? How would flying here stay interesting? By the second flight, I had noticed that reservoirs had distinctive shapes, that highways angled off relative to the section lines of the farmland, and it was darned easy to spot multiple Dallas skylines from a long, long way away across open prairie. Navigation aids and natural beauty were subtle, not a word I would associate with much else in Texas. I learned that comparing flying in Texas to flying in California was as pointless as comparing the art of Monet to that of Mondrian.

Most flights stayed within striking distance of Dallas. Local friends and out-of-town guests gave me a favorite excuse to fly, flights I called pony rides. I enjoyed seeing flying through the new set of eyes in the front cockpit. Other times the cockpit was empty, and I would play alone with Nanna, practicing aerobatics or flying along familiar routes. Just as I never tired of walking or running along a familiar footpath and observing changes—the crocus popping out, a new puppy racing out to greet me, fresh white paint on an old picket fence—I never tired of this local flying. I spent hours in the air watching crops and foliage change, flocks of water fowl migrating in and out, new homes spilling north onto farms and ranches that stretched beyond the horizon, and boating populations growing and shrinking with changes of season and water levels of the reservoirs.

On weekends, we explored dozens of small airports nearby or flew the few miles to our favorite grass strip to picnic, read, nap, and watch other airplanes practice landing. Occasionally, we ventured farther out across our new home state, even as far as the Gulf coast and Big Bend, distances which anywhere else would cross whole states, regions, even countries. The main event, every year, became the summer flying trip. We made four of these trips in Nanna exploring the United States, for short: Dixie, Big Sky, Four Corners, and Timber Basin. It was on these trips, as concerns of daily life blew away in the slipstream, that I ceased seeing earth as packages of discrete features—here a sea, there a forest, beyond, prairies and mountains—but as a continuous flow from one form into another, "…a piece of the continent, a part of the main," as Donne wrote. I saw the great blanket below, less as a patchwork quilt than as an afghan knit from a single yarn that changed color and texture, sometime gradually, other times more abruptly. I developed a fondness for everyday people I would have met no other way and empathy for people long dead I would imagine at historic sites above which we flew.

Along the way, life got better.

Room Enough for Memories

In 1929, the first owner of a Great Lakes biplane climbed into the cockpit. It was cramped. Stashing baggage and living out of that cockpit for weeks at a time have challenged pilots of the breed ever since. Whatever lessons in coping we have learned since that first day are like folklore of a preliterate society—nobody writes this stuff down. Each new owner learns by trial and error, occasionally commiserating with a fellow owner who offers up a useful suggestion.

"There is only one way to get into this airplane easily," I coach my passenger, "Watch. Right hand, right foot. Don't step on anything that isn't black," I thump on the pale fabric skin beside the wing walk and demonstrate the starting hand and foot positions to a waiting passenger. "Left hand to the blue bar, pull up, right hand to the center handhold, left foot on the step, both hands to the center, step on the seat. Now, in slow motion pull in your left foot. Try not to kick the windscreen. Use all that upper body strength to walk yourself down. Don't sit on the top." I thump on the metal between the two cockpits. "Keep the stick between your legs. I'm going to reach behind you now to hold up the parachute so that it doesn't slide down." Most get it right and wind up sitting properly in the cockpit. The rest suffer for their originality.

The seat is not adjustable, but one-size-fits-most, bolted to the frame. Who does not fit, does not fly. I have already guessed if the passenger needs one or two extra cushions on top of the parachute pack. If they are long in the body, I take the parachute out and replace it with a cushion. If one thin cushion is still too much, the passenger sits on the bare metal of the seat pan. The leftover cushions or chutes stuff into one of two large black nylon zippered parachute bags on a shelf in the hangar. The largest person ever to ride was six foot five, long legged, but short-bodied, and weighed 250 pounds. Once in, he suffered from extra wind blowing against his forehead and could squirm only a couple of inches left or right.

Installing the lone passenger in the front cockpit takes five to ten minutes, depending on ability to follow instructions. Some start grabbing and attaching various combinations of thirteen separate latches and buckles, a futile endeavor for the uninformed. When someone jumps the gun this way, I stop instructing and wait. Having failed, he (rarely she) looks up with a sheepish grin and I continue, "Now, look for the thick black and red belt on the floor to your left. That's right. Thread the left shoulder strap onto the post…" Once lashed into the three separate systems: the parachute harness, a five-point harness, and an extra General Motors type seat belt, I teach Parachutes 101 and give the fear-of-God briefing about not pushing the three engine-control levers on the left and not stepping on the two black knobs on the floor, the brakes. Finally, I help my passenger retrieve the flying helmet from the stick and put it on.

Although I have never done so, one biplane pilot advised me to remove the control stick from the front cockpit, explaining, "Heck, it'll be exciting enough when one of them tries to use the throttle as a door handle." No door to the cockpit exists in Nanna, but still I am wary of a rider, when we are momentarily upside down, realizing that nothing lies between head and ground but air. A primal survival instinct might then rampage out of the brain stem demanding a handhold. When Howard flies with me and begins thrashing about doing his personal cockpit preflight procedures (adjust baggage, position water bottle, cock head to read and set GPS), I rest my hand on the throttle lever, lest we roar off inadvertently when he hits it.

I enter the cockpit using the same procedure as my passenger. It is second nature to me now, like slipping my hand into a glove. The space is cozy for me, a medium size human. Once in, I see my passenger's head through a Plexiglas windscreen and Nanna's nose and propeller beyond, hiding anyone or anything else straight ahead. The rim of the cockpit is rolled in black leatherette, laced on like a steering wheel cover in a sports car. The instrument panel is a rough-textured black metal and sits about ten inches in front of my face. To read the few instruments mounted there requires small head movements or an occasional duck to see dials blocked by the cockpit rim or to shade them from the glare of the sun. These instruments tell me: how hard the engine is running, whether it is getting a lean or rich mixture of air and fuel, if oil is properly circulating, how fast the propeller is turning, how high we are above sea level, how fast we are moving through the air, roughly which direction we are heading, and how many times the force of earth's gravity we are pushed in our seats or pulled against our harnesses. When other flyers stand alongside peering in at the panel, they sometimes ask, "No artificial horizon? Fuel gauge?" I point to the wings and say, "Just those. Keep them parallel to the horizon," and to a test-tube-like device hanging down from the top center wing, "Fuel gauge. When the float touches the red line, it's about time to land. If it sits on the bottom long, you will land."

In the cockpit, I stick to set procedures that I have refined over time to avoid repeating all the mistakes I have made. First, I turn sideways, a maneuver possible only in warm weather when clothing is no bulkier than T-shirts and shorts. (In winter, I am confined to a forward-facing position and make do, frequently winding up with a stitch in my side.) To don the parachute, which is designed like a jacket with the chute itself doubling as the seat cushion, I gather the two black and red shoulder harness straps that I will need later, stack them right-above-left on the blue parachute shoulder. Then I slip my left arm under that bundle while turning forward, shrugging and bouncing to align all the pieces. I continue pivoting right, ducking as I lift the right shoulder harness over my head. I lay it on my right shoulder and slip my right arm into the remaining parachute armhole. A few more shrugs and everything settles into place. I snap the chest strap first taking care that the harness straps lie on the outside (one of life's little disappointments would be finding upon an emergency departure from an airplane, one's parachute caught on the harness). If I am wearing shorts, I tug them down my legs to keep any bare skin from depositing onto the chute any body sweat, oil, or salt that might cause deterioration. Then I pull straps around each leg and snap them closed.

The first woman ever killed while flying bounced out of an open cockpit in turbulence. I wear two restraints. The ends of the five-point harness are heavy, so I grasp the left metal post and begin threading onto it the loops for the left shoulder, crotch strap, and right shoulder. I lug up the right hip belt with the ratchet hardware, taking care not to poke the inside of the cockpit fabric and latch all the pieces together. Then I ratchet the belt so tight that I cannot move my hips at all, knowing that the flesh that seems immobile now will, once inverted, flow away from the seat like yeast dough rolling from a bowl onto a breadboard. The final bit of security, a red seat belt like those in automobiles, snaps in place without fanfare. Chute on, belts on, I tuck in straps so they cannot dangle in my face later. I remove and tuck my baseball cap beneath all the nylon straps woven across on my chest or turn it around to wear under my helmet so the bill can protect my neck from the sun. Finally, I remove the flying helmet from its customary perch on the control stick, slip it on, adjust the goggles on my forehead, and move the mike to my lips. I tuck the headset cord under my right leg and turn my head left and right to be sure the cord is loose enough to move without leaving slack to float around. Thus ensnared, I think of Nanna as an airplane put on and worn flying, rather than one entered and flown.

At this point, I pause and think if I forgot to check the fuel and oil, remove the wheel chocks, or latch the lunchbox door. If I did, I undo, get out, correct the oversight, and re-enter. This does not happen much anymore. Back in place, I adjust my sunglasses to fit comfortably beneath the headset ear seals, a maneuver which sometimes results in enough distortion of the frame to pop out a lens. Rarely, the lens will fall on my lap. More often, it lands on the wooden floorboard, where I cannot see it. I freeze. Then slowly, I remove gloves if necessary, and gently stretch one hand at a time to grope slowly along the floor. I used to move too quickly and sank a great percentage of putts through the hole that led to a final resting spot on the belly fabric. Thump.

What falls is not always a lens. Sometimes it is a pen or the little foam muff that covers the mike to keep wind noise down. A whole pair of sunglasses is a popular item for a passenger to drop. Howard's favorite is his portable GPS, an easy save because I see it drop and push it with my foot back into the hand frantically groping around the base of the front seat.

The items most difficult to retrieve are those propelled toward the back, not straight down. All except the wimpy muff, which I can safely ignore, require one of the following techniques. The out-of-cockpit excursion involves lying on the ground, always dusty or dirty, usually oily as well, sliding on my back to thump the fabric, listening for the lost item to bounce like a penny on a drum. Once located, there is the difficulty of retrieval. The item may be close by an inspection hole. If so, I slide off the cover plate and reach in to nab the renegade item. Items falling behind the pilot's seat involve: squeezing down onto the cockpit floor on one side of the stick; plastering my head against the side of the cockpit to get one eye positioned to sight down one side of the belly; shining the flashlight and seeing something; zipping the flashlight back into my pocket before I drop it, too; putting my head on the seat as I stretch my arm back for the blind, groping capture. Magnets and yardsticks come in handy, but are rarely around.

Fortunately, I have learned to stabilize frames and lenses while adjusting sunglasses. I carry an extra mike muff. I clutch my pen—never the kind with a separate cap—as my great grandmother clutched a paper of pins, as though it is the last one on earth. As to fumbling passengers, I can only sigh.

An object not found that is sturdy and solid worries me. It might wedge in and stop the movement of the control stick or rudders. Some benign items have never turned up and must have departed the cockpit over the top of a loop or more purposefully during cockpit cleaning. (The cleaning procedure is to force wind to swirl around the cockpits by flying askew, and then turn upside down to dump whatever did not already blow out.)

Any trip lasting longer than a day and which does not end back at the hangar requires carting more than just pilot and passenger. The compartment for luggage measures 5" X 18" X 22" of rigid metal, a bit more than one cubic foot, enough space for, say, a case of soda pop OR beer (cans, not long necks) OR one stereo component OR four shoe boxes. I began calling it the lunchbox back in the dawn of my biplane life. On a trip, most of the lunchbox space is consumed by Nanna's carry-ons: tie down ropes and stakes, extra oil, cockpit and pitot tube covers, wheel chocks, extra charts, collapsible bucket and washrag. A bag of dirty laundry, a baseball cap, a couple of apples and string cheese, a small bubble-wrap pillow, two boomerangs, and a book or two will fit as well. Once, we went camping and stuffed in a tent and a tiny stove for coffee. There is always room for one more thing, so long as we do not put too much stress on the three butterfly catches that hold everything in.

Sleeping bags, ground cloths, and backpacks full of clothing do not stand a chance to get space in the lunchbox, so they go in the cockpits, lodged behind pilot and passenger legs. This makes the cockpits crowded and hotter, because little room is left for air circulation. It also calls for an additional pre-landing checklist item, "Baggage secure?" I would hate to abort because underwear stood between me and a full back stick. I also tie my blue picnic cloth roll to the back of the front seat, so that it dangles above my knees, back behind the instrument panel, ready for any unplanned picnic. I suppose a bush pilot might tie oars, canoes, and such to the outside, maybe around the landing gear or along the fuselage, but I have never been so daring, although I once flew a flag from Nanna's belly.

That accounts for all available space, except for the map case, a gray metal box mounted on the back of the front cockpit seat, within my reach from the back seat. The lid is spring loaded to stay closed when inverted. Attached to the front of the case is a clear plastic sleeve that holds the airworthiness certificate, aircraft registration, and a few other documents that someone from the government from time to time will ask to see. The plastic is yellowed and cracked in several places, so I have patched on bits of clear tape to hold it together. I began these repairs one day after we had flown on knife edge—the airplane looks like a cross flying sideways through the air—and noticed the important papers seeping out the side, one actually taking flight around my ankles, trying hard, but failing to escape into the open air. That adventurous document now sports a tennis-shoe print.

Add together what fits in the lunchbox, in the cockpit, and in the map case and we are talking perhaps a half dozen cubic feet for all inanimate objects traveling. There is no room for unnecessary stuff.

Yet, on every single flight, I cart along unnecessary items. They do not take up much space resting at the bottom of the map case under utilitarian items like airplane manual, chart, and flying gloves, but I still have to pack them down just so to be sure the lid always springs shut. An unspectacular plastic bag holds all but one of my useless, priceless, items. I rarely take out the bag. It is enough to know it is there and to think about the contents from time to time.

The rock is a little over an inch long. It is dark gray, narrow with a smooth but irregular surface. My first flight instructor—I called him Coach—picked it up from the side of the runway as he watched me line up to land on the wrong runway. He signed his name and printed the date of my first solo flight on that rock.

Another friend, Paul, gave me bits of two airplanes known to all biplane pilots who read literature. One is a scrap of fabric with pinked edges, doped yellow with decades of ground-in dirt. A note on the back declares it to be "…genuine aileron fabric from the biplane itself—N499H…" The other is the plate from Paul's plane: "Luscombe Airplane Corp, Dallas, Texas, U.S.A., Model 8E OPT, Serial 4448, Date 12-21-46." Whenever we cross the Mississippi River, I imagine the biplane and Luscombe in the distance in search of whatever little something or nothing that chance might bring.

The next item is a dog tag to identify the wearer as "668770 USN." Howard had worn it while rescuing downed pilots and, later, during an unusual Navy assignment commanding an onshore outpost in Viet Nam. Military service had prepared him for the heat and excitement of riding in Nanna's front cockpit.

My only memento that did not come from a pilot lies protected within a tiny aqua Tiffany & Co flannel pocket. When Mother died, I added her wedding ring to my package.

Years before that, Daddy had sent me a package and written a letter describing items he thought I might like to include:

-- A pair of gold wings given to me by the Commander of the Cadet Regiment as the "Outstanding Naval Officer" of the class

-- A copy of the letter presenting the "Cutler Wings"

-- The original page from my log book starting my new log as my original log lies in 26,000 ft. in the Southwest Pacific presumably within the sunken Hornet

-- First page covering flights after return to the States following the Hornet sinking

-- The last two pages of my log book covering my last flights as a Naval Aviator in 1964

-- And—flight clothing record showing the date of receipt of a "Jacket, Leather, Intermediate" on 8-16-43. That is the jacket you now have!

I rolled these papers together and secured them with paper clips at each end. To uncurl and read them is to struggle with ancient scrolls.

Not in the bag of memories, but above the altimeter, glued and wired to the instrument panel, sits a small brass placard with the inscription: "Farmboy   Midway 6B12   Admiral." Below those words, tarnished by the oils of my fingertips, are Daddy's wings.

High Couture

"Sigourney Weaver didn't look good bald, and you won't either," Amy warned. She stood on the tiles in my front hallway, dressed for our weekly bicycle ride, bin of laundry in her arms as she studied my haircut, the most recent iteration of what I called my barnstorming hairdo. She wore the facial expression that all mothers recognize as the "Oh, Mother" look of disapproval.

A quarter-century before, Amy the baby had tugged at the long curls that cascaded down my chest from elastic bands below my ears. My flower-child look had given way to a series of shorter hairdos, most recently the cap of tight curls that stopped mid-neck like the actor's signature style. It had been years since I snipped off my Sigourney curls. For the last few months, I had been cutting my hair progressively shorter in hopes of finding the length that could be finger-combed into tidiness when I removed my flying helmet. After flying, strands of hair more than a couple of inches long twisted and bent into abrupt angles like barbed wire gone awry. What did not twist or erupt skyward flattened under the helmet like grass mashed under Nanna's tires. I looked like the cat that lost the fight.

On this last haircut, I had finally arrived at a length where just a little dab of moisture—tap water preferably, but sweat or spit more likely—would smooth out any spikes. My skull was not overlarge, so even when the hair was freshly washed, plumped up and fluffy, my head looked a bit small atop substantial shoulders on a medium-tall frame. Still, I was disappointed at my daughter's unfavorable reaction, because I had hoped I could declare victory in this one aspect of biplane life and move on to the next problem on the long list.

"Okay, I'll ease up next time."

"Good idea, Mom." She shook her head in disbelief as she bounded up the steps toward the washing machine with her own long dark ponytail bobbing from side to side. I had not asked her or my other daughter Allison for advice on my biplane wardrobe. A mother can take only so much.

Dressing for flights in a biplane like Nanna was not easy at first. It has taken me years to get it right. The item that started the biplane wardrobe was a pair of flying shoes. Their most important feature was a sole smooth enough to keep pebbles and grit out of the cockpit, yet rigid enough to push against rudders. The shoes were white canvas painted with big yellow arrows on the top pointing toward the toes. By the arrows, I had painted "Push Right Rudder" and "Push Left Rudder." I called them my taildragger tennies. This particular pair was the first in the series I had created after my first biplane flight in a big Stearman. I had smudged the spanking-new tennis shoes by wedging my toes underneath the oily rudder pedals so I could adjust for my leg length. That night I had scrubbed the toes, but oil stains persisted, so I applied the paint to divert attention from them. Rarely have I flown Nanna without these shoes. As I have produced three additional pairs as replacements, there must be superstitious tendencies rattling about in the back of my mind.

When I began exploring the countryside in Nanna, I discovered that dressing for the outing was not as simple as donning blue jeans and sweatshirt for a drive. A car held all the incidentals a driver might need: box of tissues, screwdriver, map, coins for the toll roads, lip balm, and other items. I could toss a hat and purse on the seat or floor. In a car, I had all these items within reach without making any special arrangements regarding clothing.

Nanna's cockpit contained no areas for stashing anything. The cockpit was as Spartan as a bleacher seat. The map case was hard to reach and had room for little more than legal necessities. Neither side pockets, nor a glove compartment, nor any other enclosed storage space existed. No seat lay at the ready for hat or purse, and even if it had, anything there would likely have blown away after bumps or maneuvers invited whirlwinds into the cockpit.

Whatever I needed for the flight, I had to attach to my person. Pockets, especially ones with closures—a necessity for inverted flight—became the center of my paraphernalia strategy. My first idea was to take a page from military professionals and go for the flight suit littered with pockets. These one-piece, zip-up-the-front marvels had pockets for pens and knives, maps and money, extra underwear, and whatever else a well-equipped sky warrior might carry. I bought my first, a navy blue, lightweight cotton one, at a surplus store. The arms were too long, so I rolled them up, the waist too full, so I tied the belts together in a knot instead of sticking the Velcro ends in place. Into the two breast pockets, I loaded fuel tester, Swiss Army knife, pens, ignition keys, extra mike muffs, allen wrench, tailwheel air-stem adapter, eye drops, Chap Stick, and a tube of sunscreen. The large leg pockets I loaded with different things depending on my flight, but often gloves, neck warmer, charts, portable GPS or radio, and a rag for wiping oil off my hands. I sent off to have my name embossed on the brown leather patch that attached just below the left shoulder. The blanks for these patches all came with a military wings insignia, none of which looked like civilian biplane wings, so I picked the plainest looking one. Later, I had to chuck my patch when my dad turned up his nose at wings that designated an Air Force pilot. I bought one with the Navy wings, still wrong, but not nearly so offensive.

The flight suit worked well, so long as I flew within about a forty-degree temperature range, easily done in California, but impossible in Texas. At the warm end of the range, I wore only underwear with the flight suit. At the cold end, I added turtlenecks, long underwear, and sweaters underneath and sometimes a windbreaker or leather jacket on top. My Texas and Oklahoma flying in the dead of winter reached temperatures as cold as twenty degrees, so I added neck warmer and face mask, and substituted fur lined gloves for my everyday Nomex ones. Once on, this stuff was no more removable than a suit of armor until we landed, so I matched my wardrobe carefully to each flight leg. I once took off a neck warmer in flight, but even that was a battle with headset wires and engine noise. I nearly lost it all in the slipstream.

After several years with the ill-fitting flight suit, I knew enough about my flying needs to have one custom made. The new one was also navy blue, but heavier-weight cotton. I added baby blue stripes and embroidered name, and had pockets added. I have never run out of pockets, but have never felt I had too many, either. Instead of looking like an urchin in hand-me-downs, I now look darned official, too much so, I sometimes think. People might expect too much from me, all duded up.

Dressing for cold weather was simpler than for hot. The need for pockets stayed constant, yet the desire for less fabric touching the body rose with every degree of temperature and percent of humidity. My first solution to this problem was to invent a device I called my biplane buddy. I could wear it over any comfortable summer shorts and shirts. I sewed two large, subdivided pockets that zipped shut. Then I lashed the pockets together with strapping and rings. The top pocket was a bib front with straps over the shoulders, across the back, and around my waist. The second pocket was larger and hooked onto the waistband like a small apron. The bottom pocket could be attached or not depending on the mission. This getup lasted one summer. The large bottom pocket, filled and heavy, kept slipping lower down its adjustable straps. I found myself continually hiking it back into position along the waistband. I also got tired of looking at pictures of the goofy pilot who looked like a sagging kangaroo.

My second Texas summer, I latched onto bib overall shorts and have stayed with them ever since. The front chest pocket and two hip pockets came with Velcro-closed flaps. When I purchased the first pair, I wondered about having enough space for everything I needed to carry, but everything fit. I had no leg pockets for extras, but found I could manage by stuffing charts and portable GPS between the bib front and T-shirt. Parachute straps held it all in.

The greatest challenge was keeping the shorts fabric from riding up. If I did not, sweat from the back of my legs would soak into the parachute and eventually rot the canopy and risers. I worked out a procedure. Before I slid down onto the parachute pack, I loosened the shoulder straps for the shorts so they sagged like a toddler's droopy drawers. I usually remembered to tighten the straps again when I stood up to get out. If not, within my first few steps away from the plane, I usually noticed how uncomfortable the sagging shorts felt.

I now own three pairs of bib overall shorts, two blues and one beige, colors that match Nanna, a minor nod to fashion. Next to them in my closet hang the two flight suits, one slightly heavier than the other. In a bureau drawer in my bedroom lie my foul weather add-ons, waiting for winter. I am ready for any biplane outing.

For luck I wear a gold or silver biplane necklace. Every morning, whether I am flying that day or not, I clasp the chain around my neck so that the biplane always flies toward my right arm—that seems like west to me. I have owned several of these miniature biplanes. I wear one, keep two spares, I have lost one, and I have worn one out. That one I gave to my friend. It had been with me even longer than Nanna had, and had protected me during our first flying years together. The fragile propeller and one of the wing struts had been crushed by repeated snagging, banging, and smashing of parachute and harness buckles. Though broken and worn, it had a patina of fun and adventure as it sat on Paul's windowsill in the months that his life slipped away.

Recently, I looked in the mirror at my latest fresh haircut and remembered that other day years before. "Sigourney Weaver didn't look good bald, and you won't either." I was not bald, but no strand of hair exceeded one and a half inches, a length that had inspired the original comment. Both daughters live far away

91

and we are all sufficiently busy to see one another infrequently and then only with considerable preplanning. I will have time enough to grow it out before they arrive.

Pony Rides

"Pony Rides: Nancy, Lloyd, Ray, Jim, John, Henry." In my logbook are scores of entries like this one, although most bear the name of only a single rider. This particular entry of cousins and uncles' names noted flights made a Sunday afternoon in June after a family reunion, the first I had attended since childhood. I flew one rider at a time from the Carolina grass field, which from the moment I saw it I called "Grantham International," even though aviation charts designate "Cox-Grantham" as an unpaved, private airport, and it is a fraction of the length required for any sort of modern transport suitable for international commerce. Shoulder-high summer corn bounded the runway on three sides and trees poked up smack dab at the arrival end where they had stood since perhaps the Civil War. Nearby sat the clubhouse with a porch running along the front where folks could sit and watch the takeoffs and landings of the few small planes that lived there and any vagabonds like Nanna that dropped in. A member pilot had given us a key to the door as he left. "Just turn off the A/C and lock up when y'all are through."

On the ground, Howard briefed my riders, then helped them up the windy wing walk into the front cockpit and hovered over them to fasten buckles. I waited in the back cockpit with the engine idling. As soon as Howard finished, off we went. For twenty minutes in the air, each of my kinfolk looked down upon the family farm as they had never seen it before. There stood the ancient pecan trees where Uncle Joe's hound dogs ate after supper, while the rest of us split watermelons brought up cold from a nearby spring and ate with juice dripping and forming little mud balls in the dust. Beyond, ran the dirt road to the back pastures and the pens that used to hold huge sows, testy and grunting at squealing piglets. The barn where Grandmamma Stevens had cured and graded tobacco used to be there, we decided. We circled where the old farmhouse had stood. It had been sold and moved to another county where another family's memories now seeped into its sturdy timbers. Each flight ended with a steep descent, wheels whisking over the trees, a gentle plop onto the grass, and a rush of corn higher than our heads blurring by on both sides until we rolled to a creep and swiveled around to trundle back to the clubhouse.

I do not recall when I adopted the phrase "pony ride" to describe such passenger flights, but I do know why. My sisters and I had grown up as suburban kids. Every summer, though, our two-tone, green and cream, family Chevy rolled up and down country roads through moist summer heat to farms of grandparents and cousins. Some owned horses. I looked forward to trotting and galloping along the dirt roads, and for free, not even spending my allowance. So it was that when I invited friends or family or colleagues for a flight in Nanna, I watched them approach their flights much as I had my pony rides, with high expectations and sometimes a bit of fear.

I think Nanna and I pleased them all. I have my favorites.

Twenty-something, fresh-faced Emily arrived late, rushing to meet me after work. We planned a sunset tour of California hills, green as Ireland from the heavy spring rains. Bubbling and gushing as always, Emily stopped chattering, paying close attention as we buckled her into the parachute and I pointed out the metal ring. "If I tell you to, or if the intercom isn't working and you look around and I'm signaling like this," I gestured frantically UP, "or, heaven forbid, I'm not there, get out any way you can. Open the harnesses like this—one, two." I flipped my finger above the two latches. "Leave the blue buckles alone. You're wearing the parachute like a jacket, so it will stay with you. Once clear of the airplane, look down at the chute and see orange, then pull the ripcord, here. It's important that you look down for the color behind the cord so you don't grab the wrong piece of metal and then panic when it doesn't work. Got it, Em?" I watched her nod. "Then, steer with the back risers. Try to miss power lines and keep your feet together if you can't. Okay, now that you understand, we aren't going to do that. Never have." The briefing was necessary should the unthinkable occur. Besides, her mother, my sister, would never forgive me if I killed her this time. Soon, we were racing in Nanna down the runway, then up into the air southbound over houses, offices, and stores of Silicon Valley until cities faded away and gentle hills rose to meet us.

Emily had never flown in a small plane of any type before. I turned Nanna gently left and right, sweeping alongside a reservoir.

"How you doing?"

"Fine. This is fun." Her nervous giggles had stopped.

We flew in silence for a few minutes, making steeper turns to look at the occasional home or to follow the bend in a road. I watched the back of her head as she turned to one side, then the other, and then up, drinking in the unfiltered sights. I had not flown many non-pilots before, so I was apprehensive about doing anything too rambunctious with Emily. Also, I remembered the day that I had been chatting with her mother when toddler Emily snuck by us and fell out my second story window, plunging through a marble tabletop and landing on concrete. She had suffered only a mild concussion and minor cuts. She has remained a charmed, special cherub to me ever since.

"Can we do tricks!" Emily's voice came across the intercom full of mischief and joy for life.

Gulp. What? No first time flyer would want to do more that just fly right side up, I had thought. I was unprepared for the request.

"Gosh, are you sure 'Em?"

"Yeeeeeeessssss."

"Okay. It'll take me a minute to put some stuff away." I tucked my chart and other loose paraphernalia into my flight suit and zipped it up tight. "First I'm going to turn to be sure nobody is around us. Check again to be sure your seatbelts are on and tight." I made two half circles, scanning for traffic. Nobody around. "Now, I'm going to dive a little for speed and we'll do a loop. That's like a backward flip. Okay, here we go." I pulled Nanna's nose firmly skyward. The upward thrust pressed us against our seat backs, until we could see no ground at all. Emily began giggling. "Now, look out to the left and you can see the horizon." The giggles got louder and louder as we floated upside down over the top of our circle. "Tilt your head back now and look for the ground." Guffaws, snorts, and yelps came across the intercom as the G-forces mashed us against our seats.

"That was sooooooo great. Let's do it again!" And we did. And spins, and rolls. Later, at dinner, she ate heartily, showing no signs of an upset stomach caused by the wild slinging about of the liquid in her ears.

What surprises me most about pony rides is that only a few non-pilots have ever declined aerobatics, or the offer to fly the plane themselves. Holly, a high school student, skimmed over fields, rode through loops and rolls, and took the controls to fly herself. Back on the ground, her younger brother Jerrod looked down at her beaming face for reassurance. Every bit of his lanky frame looked hesitant and nervous, just as it had when Holly and I took off. I half expected him to say he had decided not to take his turn. Holly grabbed his arm and said, "Go. Do whatever she says you can!" I flew Jerrod that day, including loops and rolls. He flew the plane himself and seemed to enjoy being in control. He traveled farther and faster along the journey from fear to joy as I have seen.

I do not brief pony riders on use of the sick sack any more. I used to. For years I kept one tucked into the parachute within easy reach of my passenger. Only one rider ever became queasy, and that due more to mid-summer Texas heat than the motion of flight. I took him for a second ride on a cool day, and he felt fine.

A big part of a pony ride is the route. Over time, I perfected my Dallas route and sequence of maneuvers, from gentle to extreme. Mary took the last of these rides in Dallas, perhaps, the best one. It was May. A storm had passed through, leaving the air fresh and clear. Bundles of whitest white clouds, widely spaced, skated across the countryside, dragging their shadows diagonally across fields lined up like a north-south, east-west plaid of vibrant greens and rich-soil browns. We had left the bustling city airport behind. I turned off the radio.

"We don't need to talk to them anymore. How are you doing?"

"Just fine. Oh, Anne, isn't it pretty?"

"Yes, ma'am. There's Lake Lewisville." Ahead lay the marina protected from the shimmering reservoir by a thin strip of land, scrubby with trees on both ends of a narrow inlet. Beyond the trees lay farmland and the golf course that I had watched emerge from the wilderness years before. "I'm going to drop down low so you can see what it was like to fly back in the old barnstorming days."

The noise of the engine grew quieter, as I pulled back the throttle and descended in a left turn. We headed for the end of the dam that marked the beginning of my low pass. To our right, a sailboat approached the inlet, heading for the reservoir and a day's sailing. The coast was clear. We turned right and dropped down over the trees until we passed twenty feet above them. We flew a gentle slalom course between two sandy shores. As we crossed the inlet, the sailor looked ahead toward us and waved as we streaked across his path. Soon the rush of trees fell behind. We dropped in over the utility lines to run across a field, row after row of lush, dark green plants, close enough to the ground that we could have landed in a few seconds. We crossed a hedge to another field plowed and ready for planting and then over a fence to a pasture where cattle stood off a ways in a shaded corner. At the far end of our run, over a narrow finger of the reservoir, I added power and we climbed toward the main channel, and then along the shore to the northwest. Jet skiers charged in toward us from another branch of the waterway like Spectre agents out to get James Bond, but they could not catch us. The winds were light, water calm, so we continued low above the surface, level with the houses along steeper banks.

We left the reservoir heading northwest toward tall buildings of Denton. I played a game with Mary that I played with most of my riders—Find the Airport. About two miles from the grass strip, I said, "We're going to land at a little airport in the middle of a ranch. Tell me when you think you see it." I watched Mary's head turn left and right.

"I don't see anything."

"We're about a mile away." Soon I angled toward and turned parallel to the field. "Got it yet?"

"No, where?" Her head still turned in all directions as she searched.

The sound of the engine changed as I changed the angle of the propeller and reduced power in preparation for landing. We turned left, descending.

"See it?"

"No!"

We turned onto final, heading directly toward the field, about a half mile away.

"Is that it?" Mary pointed to two hangars.

At the moment she spoke, I cut Nanna's engine and plopped down on the grass. "Yep." We rambled along in a wide circle so Mary could take in all the sights: wildflowers growing in and alongside the runway, brightly painted grain silos, the cottage on the hill, the dilapidated old fuel pump, hangars, windsock, hawks soaring above, hay barn in the distance, grasshoppers jumping on our wing. Through Mary's eyes I saw it all again, an airfield from another time. It was 1930 again. We lingered for a few moments, Nanna's engine purring.

We took off to the south, and then turned north, spiraling up through large gaps between the clouds. Higher and higher we went, the air growing cooler as we worked our way farther north to another reservoir. Mary's head kept turning this way and that as one cloud or another came closer. We began circling about them, one at a time, feeling the denser moisture on our bare skin the nearer we drew.

"Do you know what a cloud feels like?" We maneuvered closer and closer to one that had captured Mary's attention. It was perfect. One side of it jutted out like a cotton boulder. It grew larger and larger as we approached. Finally, I watched Mary sneak her left hand up to the edge of the windscreen, testing the force of the wind with her fingers. Suddenly, she stuck her hand way out, just as Nanna's left struts sliced through the edge of the cloud.

A week later, Mary called. "I had to let it set for awhile. But, I just had to call and tell you—it was so special." She said it in that lilting Texas drawl that I always hear when I think of my friend. "Just think of it, Anne. I touched a cloud."

I had taken Lorie on a different route. The sun was below the horizon, only a pale glow, the gray-tinted promise of sunrise. A smattering of clouds moved high above. The January air was cool and crisp, but we had dressed warmly and the heater pumped enough engine-warm air back to us so that we were not cold. We headed east toward two reservoirs separated by a narrow band of land traversed by a railroad track. On the far side of the north reservoir, smoke from stacks floated skyward. No winds or boats yet disturbed the smooth surface of the water as we raced across and I began planning my gift for Lorie.

Just a minute or two before the colors of morning would erupt, we turned back west toward a duller, grayer sky. We dropped lower and lower toward the water in sweeping turns. Every few seconds I turned my head to gauge the progress of the sky's canvas behind us. At last, a stroke of nature's brush completed the work. It was ready to be presented. I banked Nanna slowly so that his wings became more than just tools for maneuvering in the sky. I made them frames for the masterpiece "Sunrise."

Lorie gasped. The sky before her had changed in that half circle from a murky paint pot of gray sameness and faint outlines. Now it blazed pink with cloud and brightening lavender sky, with a streak of electric yellow where sunlight grazed the horizon. As the wings continued to roll, they pulled into the frame a mirror of water reflecting tall stacks, belching not smoke, but a tower of pink cotton candy. For a few minutes, I framed and reframed our picture as pieces of the sky's larger canvas exploded in new color and form. If one bright cloud lost its tint and below it, another caught the light, I tilted Nanna's wings downward to make a new picture. When the sun rose over the horizon, too bright to view head on, we turned to moved it off to one side. Finally, "Sunrise" between our wings disappeared, washed away by the cleansing rays of light. We turned away, back toward the west where we found another gallery favorite, "Bright Morning," being crafted with distant clouds and shiny copper and diamond buildings.

Lorie and Mary were my dreamers, my romantics, my riders of unicorns. For them the beauty of flight was the big payoff, their greatest joy. For me, these rides levy a creative tax, but pay the biggest satisfaction dividends. To bring someone to flight for the first time is like guiding a child for a first step, a first word, a great ah-hah moment.

It was different with the pros like Dan and Kevin. Professional pilots are at once my favorite and least favorite pony riders. Of course, they are not really riders at all—more like Kentucky Derby jockeys—because they will fly the whole darned flight without any help from me. On these occasions, I am simply along for insurance purposes. Pilots are favorites, because words are unnecessary. Flying lives in the same corner of their souls as it does in mine. We think the same thoughts. I can sit happily, feet on the floorboard, hands resting in my lap, and enjoy watching them play, or I can ignore them and drink in the countryside passing below me. Often I learn something from them. Occasionally, they deign to ask me some small technical question, perhaps to make me feel needed. They are my least favorite riders, too, because when they fly Nanna, it makes me sad to know I cannot fly him as well as they can.

Dan, a young flight instructor who had once checked me out to rent a Piper Cub, was the kind of man who you want to have a million of if you ever have to go to war: rock solid dependable, strong, pragmatic, capable, and a loving father to boot. We had finished about half our flight when he set up for a landing at the grass strip. "Show me how it's done," he said, jolting me out of my passenger status.

"Okay, I've got the airplane," I said moving my feet back to the rudder peddles, then grabbing and shaking the stick to acknowledge that I was now flying. I overshot final and never stabilized the approach. To top it off I hit tailwheel first, and not in the full stall of textbook technique, but planting us hard and with a bounce. Thanks goodness, only one bounce. "I decided to show you how it's not done," I said as we rose again into the pattern. "You've got the airplane. It lands pretty much like the Cub." I slumped back into my seat. Dan shook the stick, flew the pattern perfectly, touched down with a whisper, tearing not a blade of grass. Doggonit.

Kevin and I had shared the skies dozens of times in separate airplanes, me in Nanna, he in either the local air museum's Stearman biplane or the heftier AT-6 low-wing military trainer. The day Kevin and I took Nanna out together, Kevin ran the whole show. The air traffic controllers at Addison knew both of us and the unusual airplanes we flew. As we completed the preflight check, Kevin called on the radio. "Addison Tower, Great Lakes biplane November-two-two-tango-echo, ready to go, northwest."

"Oh, no you don't. You're in the wrong airplane!" the controller blurted.

"It's okay," I said. "I'm here."

"Well, okay. November 2-2-Tango-Echo, Cleared for takeoff."

Kevin flew as though he had been born in that cockpit. He used just the right amount of rudder, flew a perfect loop first time around, and did it all with the ease and grace that surround all natural pilots. Doggonit, again. Why is it so much harder for me?

I spend time with riders who made me laugh, as well. Wally worked a good five minutes adjusting his parachute, tightening the leg straps, easing out the chest strap, inspecting the ripcord, fitting the length. I stood by on the wing walk in a cold December breeze, waiting.

"Criminey, Wally, we're not going to use these things."

"Maybe so, but it's gotta be right," said our family's Special Forces member. If I had encouraged him, I have no doubt he would have bailed out just for the fun of it.

Aaron, our family's rock guitarist, was so long in the body that he had to sit on the bare metal seat pan, no parachute or cushion, to keep the top of his head protected from the wind above the screen. Over the reservoir, I noticed his head bobbing and weaving, and I knew that somewhere in his head, Paul or George or Mick or Rod, were rocking out. I did not interrupt.

Lewis had learned to fly in a biplane, the Navy's "Yellow Peril" Stearman trainer. Before climbing onto Nanna's wing, he glanced into the back cockpit and noticed the Navy wings mounted on the instrument panel. "How about that!" he said, smiling. Lewis was another long-in-the-body rider, which made the flight uncomfortable for him, as I had not yet discovered the trick of removing all the seat cushions. After about twenty minutes, we landed, not the perfect landing I had tried so hard to make, but okay. He was a good sport about the wind beating his forehead. That evening, I invited him to sign my logbook. He did: "Was a great flight with my daughter pilot! Lewis Hopkins."

A business colleague, Steve, won my award for originality in a biplane cockpit. On a fun sunset flight after a long, hard, frustrating day at work together, I watched from behind as he hung his elbow over the side of the cockpit, like a teenager riding down the main drag in town in his shiny new hot rod. The only things missing were a can of beer and a carload of babes alongside.

George, another colleague and friend, dog tired and jet lagged from his trek from London to Dallas, nonetheless agreed that it would be a sin for any Royal Air Force alum to crawl into a hotel bed instead of into Nanna's cockpit. Off we went on a hot July evening in relentless pursuit of the Red Baron. I do worry about the physical condition of my riders, frequently asking, "Are you feeling okay? How are your ears? Wind okay on your forehead?" By rights, George should have been a basket case before the first barrel roll. But we flew one after another maneuver, each ending with my query "More?" Invariably came the response, each full of more gusto than the last, "Yes, more!" On and on we went, doing more maneuvers than I had ever done with anyone else. "George, I worry that you'll be sick." Finally, I responded to his "Yes, More" with a "Sorry, pal, we've got to head back." The sun had already dropped below the horizon.

The next day, George admitted, "I must say that I was a touch queasy when I got back to the hotel."

Right-o, chap.

Special to me are pony rides that can never be again.

"I'm the healthiest dying man around," Paul told me climbing onto Nanna's wing. I had been reciting for him a string of disclaimers about my new skills. He turned his gaunt face and runner's body back toward me and said, "No need for an elaborate briefing. The worse that could happen couldn't be any worse than it already is." We flew northwest from Santa Monica along the Pacific coast. Both the route and flying a biplane were familiar to him. The day was warm, the breezes light. I was still a novice at giving pony rides, but I think he enjoyed his. Years later, half a continent away, his wife Joyce flew with me to my grass strip where we sat and spoke until sunset of Paul and their life together.

Sometimes when Nanna and I fly alone, and everything seems routine—same sounds, same sights, same feelings—I catch myself and laugh. How can I think of this as commonplace? What an ungrateful soul I am. True, I can never again fly in a biplane for the first time. Never again will I be surprised to sit in an airplane and feel the open air circulating about my legs or blowing my fingertips at the edge of my windscreen, or discover upside down at the top of a loop that nothing separates my head from the earth but molecules of air.

When I start having these feelings, I yearn for my pony riders. Through their unspoiled senses, I experience it all again for the first time. I watch their heads turning to soak up the world at our feet, see their hands rise to touch the wind, hear their giggles, squeals of joy, and awestruck words. They thank me for their gift of wings, not knowing that they have given me the greater one.

Grass Strip

This was how I had imagined it would be, lying under the wing of my biplane at a grass strip out in the country. All afternoon a breeze had been whistling through the wires. I felt the warmth of the sun and breeze as it blew around my bare arms, which stuck up in the air holding a book. My head and shoulders lay in the shadow of Nanna's broad blue-scalloped wing, the rest of me jutting out into the sunshine atop a blue canvas picnic cloth. Nevil Shute's novel took place long ago in lands thousands of miles away from this spot in Texas. It was the kind of book I liked to read here, one full of airplanes, pilots, and magic.

I was alone but for the butterflies flitting about, grasshoppers jumping and thumping on the fabric drum of a wing, and an occasional weakened fire ant that had braved the perimeter of poison I had sprayed some hours before. I had only to shift my gaze a few inches to look beyond the page and Nanna's top wing to watch circling hawks, contrails of mammoth jets ferrying busy and important people, or to gauge the speed of one after another puffy cloud moving to the southeast toward my home airport, that big sprawling, official place. Dozing beside that concrete runway would be out of the question—even to try would bring a truck with a flashing red light and a security guard. Here, though, it was a natural thing to do, and I had done quite a bit already, little touch-and-goes glancing off the soft edge of sleep.

I rolled my head toward a rumbling sound approaching overhead, another airplane. The sound grew louder, and I propped myself up on an elbow to search the sky. The plane, a Stearman biplane, crossed overhead with its great round engine roaring. It flew alongside the neighboring oat field and then slid down the invisible ramp to plop down on the grass and roll slowly by Nanna and me. Once in awhile, such a newcomer would roll to a stop and cut the engine, break the silence again with clacking metal doors or thumping footfalls along a hollow wood and fabric wing, and stop to chat. Today, though, the yellow biplane touched down on its main wheels, continued rolling along with its tailwheel still in the air, powered right up again, trundled toward the low wooden fence at the end of the runway, lifted off, and flew away, leaving nothing behind but the smile on my face.

I had come upon this grand outdoor reading room on a hot, sunny day, soon after we arrived in Texas. Nanna and I had been searching more than enough minutes for this favorite place marked on an aeronautical chart by a pilot friend. His note read "Beautiful Grass Strip used for training WWII pilots in the T-6. Great for touch/go's or picnic. Privately owned but taildraggers welcome." Circling the general area, I saw fields everywhere, most of them suitable for a slow old-fashioned airplane to land, but none had the telltale signs of an airstrip. Finally, a faded orange windsock on the roof of one of two large barrel-roofed metal hangars caught my eye, then a large, faded tetrahedron that pointed the direction for landing into the wind. I saw no airplanes. We circled again and then dropped in over the trees and fence at the north end of the runway, plopped down on the grass, taxied off through longer grass to a wooden tower with white paint peeling from its crossed timbers, and shut down. The day was quiet, very quiet, with not even a whisper of wind.

I climbed out of Nanna's cockpit and strolled toward a weathered WWII-vintage fuel pump and a small wooden office building that stood between the hangars. I tried the door. It was locked. Through the grimy windows, I could see that the office had been vacant for a long time. I headed for nearby trees tall enough to provide some shade and sat down on a weather-beaten bench with "Hartlee Field" branded into one of its wooden slats. I waited.

Soon enough, a red pickup truck, faded from years of sun, pulled up with two mixed-breed dogs racing alongside. A man dressed in work clothes, boots, and a cap opened the creaking door. He was the kind of man who looked like he could change from right friendly to darned gnarly mean in an instant. That day he was just curious. The dogs scampered about, yipping and panting, trying to get their master to pay them some mind.

I introduced myself and learned that his name was Jeff, and that he pretty much managed the ranch work.

"Would you mind if we landed here once in awhile? A friend of mine told me about you all."

"That'd be alright, I guess. Mr. Carter likes to see the old planes coming in." As he spoke, he looked toward the sea of long grass and Nanna against the blue sky, the kind of airplane I would want visiting this field if it were mine. From that day on, we always parked out in the open where anyone could see us from Jeff's little house perched high atop a nearby hill or from the dirt road that ran alongside the hangars and on across the pastures to the main house.

Over the years, Jeff stopped by to visit often when we flew in for an afternoon. We became friends. If he saw I was asleep, a frequent occurrence, he did not disturb me, but came back later. Sometimes he pulled up in the pickup. Other times he roared in on his motorcycle or he would be mowing the strip with a tractor when we landed. A time or two, he galloped up on one of the rodeo horses that lived on the ranch. He kept me informed about what was happening at the ranch and with the families. Only once did I feel unwelcome, and for good reason, the day of hay harvest, when bales all over the field blocked me from landing.

Once, I took Jeff flying. He flew Nanna like a cowboy worked a quarter horse, turning steeply and on a dime, charging low at a bend in the narrow, tree-lined river that meandered through the ranch, pulling back hard with his head cranked around for a longer look.

"There's a dead horse in the bend here somewhere." By gosh, if we had to stand Nanna on his wing fifty feet in the air, we were

111

going to find it beneath the trees that grew together overhead and obscured the narrow waterway.

"Where'd you learn to fly, Jeff?"

"Oh, I fly the King Air some." That was one of the ranch aircraft. I took this to mean that its pilots had tutored Jeff, but he had never trained formally. Like most things on the ranch, one learned on the job what needed knowing.

More often, I flew alone from the grass strip, my treat between chapters of a favorite book or desert after a lunch of string cheese and green apple. Sometimes Howard would be with me, and I would leave him behind relaxing or contemplating the oats that shot up through the dark soil of the field across the runway. We had watched the oats sprout year after year and then turn from youthful green to the pale gold of maturity. Each year, I plucked a stem and added it to the collection in a wooden vase Howard had turned for me. I have it still. I like to think that one day a scientist will develop a test similar to carbon dating. Instead of determining age of these oats, however, it will measure their magical content.

The day I lay reading Shute, the breeze blew from the south. I put the book down, stood and stretched, and walked around Nanna's wing. I climbed in and started the engine, shattering hours of silence. We meandered toward the strip through grass made a rippling, glossy sea from the force of wind from the propeller, then turned north along the mowed strip. On one side lay a wide bristly patch of weeds and on the other, the oat field. Through a blanket of vibrant orange wild flowers, we rolled and bounced, as crickets jumped up onto the wings and butterflies flitted among the wires. I swung the tailwheel around in an arc toward the aged wood fence that marked the end of the runway and prepared to take off.

I pulled back on the stick and held the brakes with my heels, like a jockey holding a horse at the starting line. When I released the brakes and eased the throttle forward, the fringe of grass behind the wings blurred as wide wheels bounced along the turf, and I could feel Nanna pulling against the stick, telling me that it was time to give him his head. As I did, he lifted his tail and his wings met the air at that angle and speed that made magic. We felt light on our wheels as the weight of bodies and engine matched the lift from wind over wing. We were off, climbing the rising road of air that other aircraft had traveled hundreds of thousands, even millions of times, since decades ago the government had claimed this air to train pilots for a long ago war. In this sky, no tracks marked their passing. No tread marks told of rambunctious youths peeling out fast. No earthly hint suggested that any traveler had passed this way before.

Again I became the lone observer of sights of the ranch, crossing above the farm-to-market road, banking left toward the river meandering from the north to south, reservoir to reservoir, and the oat field. To the southwest, on a small hill like the ones in my childhood storybooks, stood the small cottage where Jeff and his wife lived, beside it a workshop bigger than the house itself and a tall windmill standing guard, a marker for our slalom course in the skies above the ranch. A third hangar with one side open to the field was under reconstruction by Jeff, who sometimes could be seen dragging and welding metal, but not today. Beyond the hangar lay brightly painted and decorated hay barn, swings, and silos, designed for the grandchildren. The artist had spent months cutting out and painting huge plywood flowers to adorn the fence. A mailbox with wings attached and labeled "airmail" stuck out from one eave. A rutted dirt road ran along all the buildings, down a gulch, and across pastures sprinkled with horses and cattle. The road ended at a hacienda complete with helicopter hangar and pad.

Up we spiraled, the air changing from moist and warm to cooler and dryer the higher we rose. Along the way, we passed hawks and watched the ranch blend into all the other bunches of fields in patchwork greens and browns. Clouds above grew larger, but never came close. Reservoirs north and south moved in from the horizon to show their distinct shapes. All the while, the warmth of the sun crossed small bits of skin on my cheeks and the back of my neck not covered by my helmet. I looked around to be sure we were alone in our corner of the sky and it was safe to maneuver. At last, we arrived at our destination at the top of our invisible skyscraper, hundreds of stories above the field. And then the games began.

Wheeeeeeeeeee. Up and around we flew, first pitching Nanna's nose up and rotating his wings to paint a big lazy circle around the horizon. We moved through the sky like a corkscrew lying on its side, a barrel roll. We felt upright even as we hung upside down, as though the world turned about us, which is why I always start with this most benign of tricks; time enough for maneuvers that move a stomach sideways and slings ear fluids to confound my sense of "up." Next, I chopped the power, pointed Nanna's nose up to slow the flow of the air over his wings to a mere trickle, and pushed his tail rudder left to speed up the right wing's flight while the left wing floated lifeless on the inside of the turns. We made a corkscrew going straight down toward the ground. One, two, three turns were enough, so I broke our spin with a couple of brisk moves of stick and rudder, added power, and pulled level. Then I threw our nose up and back into a loop, a backward somersault. Upside down, we leveled off a bit to float over the top, and then as we picked up speed on the backside of the loop, I pulled hard against a force that made me feel over three times my weight to fly level and right side up once more. So went the shenanigans for about twenty minutes, long enough to blow all the dust and flotsam out of the cockpit and dislodge a bunch of floaters in my eyeballs, yet short enough to make we want more another day.

A thousand feet over the end of the grass strip, I pulled back the power and tilted Nanna into a turn to draw one final spiral down to earth, touching down when we had completed the circle.

When nobody was watching, we did these overhead approaches perfectly. We rolled back to the blue cloth stretched over the ground where we left it, and I arranged shadows of our wings with little jabs of rudder and turns of tail, like a host fussing over a party table. I cut the engine. Nanna was back in place as my parasol.

Stillness returned. I stood on the cockpit seat, looking over the top of the wings across the grass field to the oats I had watched being planted New Year's day, that had peeked up weeks later, and were thick enough now to hide the brown earth. I thought about all the pony rides that had touched down on this turf, giving my riders their first, and likely only, open-cockpit, grass field landing experience. I remembered the holiday photos taken here with Nanna in the background against the blue sky: once sprawled out on the grass with fluffy red Santa caps and another with poinsettia-adorned cowboy hats with me mounted on Champ, the bright-eyed, muscular gray rodeo horse, who pranced and tossed his head, throwing his mane and tail into the breeze.

I climbed down from my perch and walked back around the wing, tall grass whacking at my legs, to sit and let my inner ears settle. I looked around at the tall white tower that moviemakers had built as a camera platform years ago.

One evening a few weeks earlier, Don had visited me as I sat there. My feet dangled off the side of the high platform and my chin rested on a wooden rail. I had been watching the migration of color and shadow on the fields and trees as the sun drifted lower. Nanna sat close by, like a horse might stand quietly grazing as its master paused to survey the land at the end of the day. Don must have seen him. I turned my head at the sound of an engine and watched his truck kicking up dirt along the road that led from the ranch house. He turned onto the grass and bounced toward me. He got out and strolled closer, looking lean and fit, but walking a bit stiffer than usual.

"Glad to see you this evening," he said tipping the brim of his cowboy hat and then looking up, hands on hips. His white hair and smile stood out against a bronzed face. His expression was the confident one of a man who had achieved enough in business to buy whatever he wanted. The Don I knew was just a fellow who took pleasure in the simple things in life. I had once watched him work all day to weld and brace a wobbly hangar door.

"I appreciate you letting me come around to enjoy your place." I could tell he knew what I was watching and why.

"It's your place, too."

I smiled. Yes, it was my place, too, not according to any legal document filed in the county recorder's office, but according to some ledger kept by the recorder of the universe. There my claim was as strong as anyone else's was.

That had been one of my quiet evenings with Don—just the two of us. On another evening, there had been hundreds. I had seen a big tent from the air as I was setting up to land early in the afternoon. It sat in a section of the field usually overgrown with tall weeds, but recently mowed. Jeff had warned me a week earlier that a retirement bash would be underway starting around four o'clock. He thought it would be okay if I hung out and read until then. I landed and taxied farther up the field than usual to stay out of the way of the set-up activity.

Caterers arrived and began preparations for the barbeque. I leafed ahead in my novel and picked a stopping point. I was gathering my belongings when the buses pulled up and disgorged dozens of women with bejeweled, glittering blouses and big hair. Then came the helicopters, three of them, to give tours of the ranch. Jeff strolled over and told me not to hurry off, that Nanna added decoration. I began another chapter, but soon the noise and activity overwhelmed my reading room. Linda walked over and invited me to eat barbeque. I started to decline, but leaving without food in my belly was not an option Linda offered, and Linda was every bit the powerhouse as husband Don.

I packed my books, magazines, pillow, and water bottle into

the lunchbox and headed for the tent. Two friendly gals latched onto me at the end of the buffet line and led me to their table. "Don wants you to sit with us," said one. I had lost control of my life by then. I spent a delightful half hour learning about selling jewelry and household items to neighbors along the hollers and hillsides of Kentucky. The women were as cordial and down home as my farmer relatives in the South, and as generous. One insisted on giving me a gold-painted, rhinestone-encrusted watch from her inventory. It told time for just two days, but I have kept it in my jewel box and still smile each time I notice it there.

"I've got to leave, or it'll be dark before I get home," I told Don after saying my goodbyes to the ladies. He had just come in for his dinner after circling the ranch dozens of times giving helicopter tours. Another pilot had relieved him and the lines for the rides were still long. He looked like a happy kid, loving being the center of attention. Then he scowled at me like I was being a party pooper.

"Well, at least could you do some stunts on your way out?" He asked, shaking my hand.

"Okay, but I'm going to be so high that you'll hardly be able to see me. What frequency are your guys using?"

He told me and radioed to the other pilots to stay west. I would stay east.

Nanna and I maneuvered around the line of helicopters, took off in the fading light, and climbed high above the field.

"Now, show us what you've got, girl," I heard Don's voice, as happy as I think I ever had, coming across my radio.

I flew a couple of loops and rolls, then shot away home, landing in the last shreds of twilight. This had been Don's big day, a point in life where he and Linda could, if they chose, take it easy. I knew they would not. They were both perpetual motion machines, driven to start and finish projects. I looked forward to seeing what they would think of next. I was happy to have been a small part of their celebration.

That had been the busiest day so far. I wondered what it would be like here when it got busy on a regular basis.

"We're going to spoil it for you, you know," Keith told me the day following the party. He was one of two partners with plans to restore the field to an active airport. He had been mowing up and down the length of the runway when I landed. Now he pulled off to fill the tractor with gas and stopped to chat. I had already settled in with my tarp and book, enjoying the fresh-cut smells.

"I suppose I can share it." I sat up and gestured for him to sit down. "When will you all open?"

Keith sat down. "By fall, we hope."

"I see you've been clearing out the office." I glanced toward the small frame building. Through the dirty windows, I had noticed that the boxes and lumber stored there for years had disappeared.

"Yeah. We're going to hang a sign out front—Happy Bottom Riding Club." He gestured in the air with both hands as though unrolling a banner. "We'll put chairs out front."

"Good idea. People can rate landings and read. Maybe I'll donate books for a lending library."

Keith spoke like a man with a dream, which he was. I listened as he talked of hangar improvements, a new fuel tank, and other ideas for later. A few years earlier, he had left the Air Force, still a young man, and was eager to get back into an aviation business.

I never found out exactly what happened to kill Keith's dream, why Don and Linda had decided not to lease the strip to the fellows, why the Foggy Bottom Riding Club never came into being, no chairs out front, no hangars full of Piper Cubs, Aeronca Champs, and Stearmans. I surprised myself with feelings of disappointment. I would have the field all to myself for my remaining years in Texas, but I was sad that others would not know this wonderful place. After I was gone, who would bring their old airplane? Who would tend the soul of this magic place?

My ears had settled down while I sat and thought about those earlier times. Tired, I stretched out on my back to watch the sky as it reversed from a bright field of blue with only a few clouds to a field of graying clouds marbled with few blue spaces. I picked up my book again and read. The forecasted mild front began approaching from the northwest. I arose and snapped the black canvas cover over Nanna's two cockpits in case it rained. A downpour would have made my earthen bed soggy and forced me to retreat into a hangar, but none came. Instead, a brisk wind blew from the northwest, moving the front rapidly through and away toward home. I pulled back beneath Nanna's wing, wrapping one edge of my cloth over my legs for warmth, set my book aside, and watched the front pass as the day waned. A few sprinkles drummed the fabric wings. I began planning our flight home, facing one of the many weather decisions needed when I traveled with Nanna. Should I take off before the front passed or wait and allow just enough time to reach home before dark? Would the winds at home be stronger across the runway if I waited or hurried? How low was the layer of clouds? In the end, I waited.

That day ended at my grass strip as all days there did. Without hurry, I stood and stretched. I gathered the boomerangs that I had brought but not thrown, books, magazines and a makeshift head pillow into a mesh bag and walked through the grass around Nanna's wing past the cockpit. Into the lunchbox I packed the bag alongside the cockpit cover and a spare quart of oil. I shook the blue canvas and picked off a few burs, then folded it several time, rolled and tied it securely, and tossed it into my cockpit, where I would lash it to the back of the front cockpit seat, ready for the time we happened again upon a place to sit and rest and find peace. All items stowed, I checked the oil. Then I turned around to drink it all in one last time: straight green air strip, field of magic oats catching the rays of sun slanting through breaks of cloud, hawks circling, aluminum hangars now glowing pink, tattered windsock telling me to take off to the north, dog barking and cattle lowing in the distance along with the whistle of a train passing a few miles south. As I slipped off the tethers that held me to this place to settle into the cockpit and strap myself in, the cutest of all airplanes ever allowed to fly, a Piper Cub, puttered in from the west, circled midfield and, wings rocking an aloha as I waved, departed in a straight shot east. I had never met this particular plane and its pilot, but I knew them well.

The engine cranked and exploded into life, shattering the calm. We taxied to the southern end of the field a few feet from the fence and road and swung around into the wind for customary safety checks. The evening sun warmed my left cheek as I eased the throttle forward. Nanna raced ahead and vaulted into the air. We leveled off low and flew a wide circle around the ranch, over the hay-barn playhouse, across the wooded pastures, around the ranch house for a wing-wagging goodbye to anyone watching, over the Texas state flag fluttering at the ranch entrance, slaloming around the paddle boats shaped like duck and swan in the fish pond, then in a straight line to swoop beside the windmill at Jeff's house, then diving low across the middle of the air strip, now deserted, to pass above the oats and on and on across river and trees toward home.

Where is this place? Any North Dallas taildragger pilot can tell you that Hartlee Field lies in the middle of ranch land northeast of the Denton skyline on a line a few miles northeast of the highway bend, or if you fly in from the north, on a straight line south along the fields from the westernmost edge of the dam at Horseshoe Lake. Drivers and cyclists on the county road bordering the south end of the runway would say, "Oh yes, that's the place where I stop and watch the old planes land and take off right over my head." The Federal Aviation Administration would say more precisely "Look at your Terminal Area Chart! Hartlee Field lies N33 16.4; W97 04.5". Most precisely, though, my grass strip is the same one adopted by all biplane pilots of all time, and they all lie at that intersection of eternity where the souls of airmen, mine among them, pause on their journeys to wherever.

Same Day, Same Sky

Imagine the headline "Biplane Pilot Sees No Other Planes." The hawker brandishes the newspaper in the face of each pedestrian rushing by his busy city street corner. Not a single person stops to buy.

What sells papers is news about airplanes in dangerous and crowded skies. "Midair Crash!" flies off newsstands and halts the TV channel surfer. I doubt that a single airplane has ever crashed and NOT been reported in the news. Even airplanes that do not collide make headlines: "Near Miss!"

Most action occurs miles above the ground where contrails mark the passing of airline and business aircraft. Some happens where planes cross through lower altitudes arriving or departing from sprawling commercial airports.

What happens in real life is different for a biplane pilot. I rarely see another plane unless I try to. The low skies are empty, empty, empty. Granted, around the small airports that Nanna and I frequent, one other airplane might takeoff or land when we do, but seeing one or two other airplanes out in the countryside during an entire month-long trip is about as crowded as our skies get. Because it is rare, another airplane nearby is cause for notice, even celebration. Ahoy, another sailor at the ends of the earth.

Flying in formation is a sure way to see another airplane. It also guarantees dealing with ex-military pilots at some point along the way.

Among military rivalries, none I have observed is livelier or more humorous than the one between Air Force and Navy pilots. While both would agree that neither march worth a darn, when the conversation turns to flying, feathers fly.

"How hard can it be, landing on a something a mile long? Heck, the runway doesn't even move!" the Navy carrier pilot needles the Air Force jock.

"Oh yeah. Well, you know how the Navy defines formation flying, don't you?"

The Navy pilot stands ramrod straight, says nothing, eyes shielded behind aviator sunglasses that reflect the smirk directed at close range. "Tell me."

"Same day, same sky."

I entered a quasi-military world full of these pilots for my first try at formation flying, hoping that a civilian like me might be treated as well as a neutral non-combatant. For weeks, I had been looking forward to my class, one that the Confederate Air Force was running for warbird pilots at a nearby airport. I called the organizer.

"My biplane is not a warbird, but could I enroll anyway?"

"Sure. We'll put you in with the primary trainers. If nobody else can fly with you, I'll haul out my Cessna and you can fly off me."

I was on my way.

By the time the Saturday for the class arrived, I had studied *Formation Flight Manual, 4th Edition* and felt confident I had the theory down pat. I would never go "belly up" on my leader. I would cross under when my leader pumped his arm. I would stay out of horizontal or vertical planes of aircraft close by, stepped-up or stepped-down. I would pick out a couple of points on my leader's aircraft and bolt Nanna onto it with that picture. Yes, I knew this stuff. Off I went with practical formation skills on a par with the novice snow skier who had read the how-to book on that sport. That is to say, I arrived raw and green. Nevertheless, I was eager to learn.

My first reminder that I was a fish out of water came when I taxied from the airport runway to the ramp where fellow students had parked their aircraft. I felt a little like the *Private Benjamin* character, the ditzy gal showing up in her natty outfit to enlist in the army. Ramp marshals bent, waved, and pumped their arms to direct Nanna and me down the row of aircraft. They were the kind of planes with nicknames like Texan, Mentor, Mustang, and Stearman. Parked on my left were a matched set of three heavy metal trainers, painted with Navy insignia. I think that made them SNJs instead of AT-6s, but I am never sure about such things. Their bodies squatted on monstrous landing gear that looked sturdy enough to withstand a drop from a multistory building. The riveted metal surfaces looked tough enough to withstand rounds of machine gun fire. As I zigzagged back to the right, I passed several big biplane trainers, Stearmans, one battle-gray Marine version, the rest the Navy's bright "Yellow Peril" versions. I was glad to see them, because they would fly slower than Nanna and were made from the same thin fabric that a determined combatant could decimate with a plastic knife. Still, they looked serious and official. Nanna looked, dare I use the word, perky, S-turning along, fanning his gorgeous feathered tail.

When the marshal had twirled me around into a parking spot, he drew a finger across his throat and I pulled the mixture. The engine stopped. When I got out, he walked with me.

"Nice job. Some of these fellows don't turn tight when I say and mess up the line. You did it just right." The marshal was a bulldog of a man in a jumpsuit much like mine, except his was a bright orange, mine navy blue. His longish white hair bushed out from his cap and made his face look more brown by contrast. He chuckled and winked, deepening the crinkles around his eyes and lines around his full mouth. "If they get ornery, I make 'em pull right back out and do it over again, heh, heh."

"Oh, I wouldn't dare disobey around here."

"One thing. Don't S-turn when we're guiding you. We won't run you into anything."

Doggonit. Nanna already looked like the odd man out, a prissy little fellow prancing through the valley of warriors. Now, everybody watching knew the pilot was a raw recruit to the military game to boot.

All day, everyone was friendly enough, but when assignments

came down, I was always last. Most of the pilots were experienced formation flyers, many retired from the military, as I had suspected. They were not taking the class to learn the basics like I was. Heck, most of them could teach the course, but they needed to get a competency certificate required to fly in air shows. I only flew twice the whole day. A third flight fell through when my companion plane, a low-wing, fabric trainer, sprayed a bunch of oil on engine start and was unable to fly.

My first instructor indoctrinated me well enough, but he seemed not to enjoy his assignment. I worked hard to do as I was told, but I could not seem to please him. For the first half of the lesson, I flew lead and another plane flew off my wing, first on the right, then crossing under to the left, higher than us, then lower. All I had to do was to fly straight and make a few easy turns, climb, and descend, things every pilot knows how to do.

When it was my turn to fly the wing position, I could feel my muscles tighten. I could hear the strain in my own voice. When I got too wide, my stomach knotted.

"No! Closer," my instructor shouted and I inched the throttle forward to pull back in, my heart racing as I saw the lead plane get too large, too fast.

"Not too close! Relax, relax."

Easy for him to say. Finally, with just a few minutes left before we would head in to land, something clicked. It was the feeling I had known before so many times learning a new flying skill. One second the task felt impossible. The next moment, it felt as if I had been doing it without effort my whole life. I could feel my back muscles relaxing, like a thawing roast. My grip on the throttle became a light fingertip hold. I stopped thinking so hard and relied upon a direct connection between my eyes and my hands, like typing. That last minute turned out to be day's high point. Before I was ready to stop, we were back over the airport, preparing to land.

"There's the signal. Count for the break. One…two…"

"Break right?" I started to bank.

"No! No! Not from this side!" He grabbed the stick and pushed to the left. He did not let go until he could feel that I was turning in that direction. I could see his head shaking in the cockpit ahead, disgusted.

My first session, which had held such promise just moments ago with my success at station keeping turned sour with that stupid mistake. I landed well and thanked the gods for that small consolation, given the army of observers.

The second flight was not in Nanna, but in a Texan, an airplane I had never flown before and did not expect to fly that day either. The instructor-pilot flew us from the ground through the ascent and positioned us on our leader's wing.

"You've got the airplane," he said casually.

Surprised, I hardly had my hands and feet on the controls when he let them go. I jiggled the stick to confirm that I accepted control of the airplane. Then I tensed up again. I was just a few feet from another Texan. With a flick of the wrist, I could generate one of those awful mid-air headlines. The thought made me fall back, leaving me in the position of having to pull in closer. I kept sawing in and out this way as adept with the controls as a drunken lumberjack. On I went, jerking forward and backward until I finally had to admit defeat.

"You take it," I said. I was so unhappy. I should never have begun this flight.

On the ground, the lead pilot asked my instructor, "Man, you sure were sloppy there for awhile."

My instructor did not respond, but dipped his head toward me.

"No, that was me. What a mess, huh? Sorry," I said.

That evening I thought about the day. I gave myself the nothing ventured, nothing gained lecture. I remembered how good that one short minute felt when holding position right on that forty-five degree line on my leader's wing finally clicked. I reviewed my many mistakes. I also remembered the kind words during a break when one instructor took time to sit with me on the grass beside Nanna to chat and express interest in us and why I wanted to learn.

Weeks later, I would take additional lessons, flying with another Great Lakes and an instructor eager to see me succeed. I would make a perfect join on my first try, starting a mile away from my leader and turning in a long gentle arc inside his wider turn that ended right where I needed to be, tucked on his wing. We turned, dove, and climbed together. On downwind to land, still in flying close formation, I heard a deep bass voice on the radio call, "Biplanes on downwind, that surely is one pretty sight."

The night of my poor performance with the Confederate Air Force, however, I was brooding. The phone rang. It was my dad. I mentioned what I had been doing that day.

"Flying formation is hard," I said, fishing for sympathy.

"For Pete's sake, Anne," he said in an exasperated tone. "It's easy."

When not flying formation, the next best way to find airborne airplanes is to fly near busy airports.

At the Oshkosh fly-in, Howard, Daddy, and I sat in the shade of Nanna's wings a couple hundred feet from the edge of the runway as an Air New Zealand 747 dazzled the crowd doing touch and goes. I had watched similar jumbo jets departing on overseas flights before. On those occasions, I had observed from a bench overlooking Los Angeles International Airport or from the bicycle path along the beach when one roared and lumbered over the sand dunes, filling the sky like a Hollywood B-movie monster. On those occasions, the plane was full of fuel and people and barely lifted off in the nearly two-mile length of runway. At Oshkosh, the 747 flew with little fuel and only the pilots, so it was nimble, quick, and ate up little runway. It reminded me of a hippo ballerina in Walt Disney's *Fantasia*. Bong, it touched.

Bing, it bounced away.

A few days after leaving Oshkosh, Howard, Nanna, and I were winging across North Dakota heading west. Departing from my usual practice of steering clear, I had decided to keep flying along a highway through a bit of controlled airspace, so I was talking with the tower controller as we transitioned his area. He had directed us to fly on a path that would take us a couple of miles south of the end of the runway that ran north and south.

"Northwest...heavy, cleared to land," the controller called when we were still several miles from the airport. I heard a similar call twice more and wondered why an airport like Fargo would have so much jumbo jet activity. I would have guessed that a few such planes could airlift the entire population of the city.

As our right wing crossed the extended centerline of the runway, I saw a whale of an airplane with the distinctive hump that could only belong to a Boeing 747. It was heading south, and it was on a collision course with Nanna. The pilot would barely be able to see us, a gnat in his windscreen. He grew larger and larger, filling the windscreen at an alarming rate. On the ground, such an aircraft is impressive. In the air, closing fast, it was a surreal beast.

"Two-Tango-Echo, aircraft one o'clock one mile is a 747 turning base for three-five," called the controller.

"Talley ho." Never have I felt more confident uttering the response that confirmed I had the airplane in sight.

To the jet pilot, the controller said, "...aircraft eleven o'clock is a Great Lakes biplane westbound, cleared for the option."

"Cleared for the option," the pilot confirmed. Without the controller pointing us out, I doubt the other pilots would have seen us (if they ever did), focused as they must have been on their takeoff and landing practice. Possibly, we were witnessing a check ride for one of the pilots. We all knew that the controller had us both in the big picture and was tracking us carefully.

The jet banked. The graceful arc brought him still closer,

now belly up. The great swept wings, in full view against the sky made me gasp. As the arc continued, the giant passed briefly alongside, grew smaller, and disappeared descending behind us on a diverging course to the runway.

If I tried a thousand times, I would not be able to recreate the perfect timing that brought our two odd-fellow planes together in a remote corner of the North Dakota sky. I am glad it happened in a bit of the sky with a protector watching and not in the wide-open spaces at the end of a bizarre chain of errors. I do so prefer exhilaration to terror.

The least certain, but most fun way to see other airplanes in the sky is to troll and attract their attention.

Kevin flew vintage airplanes for the museum at my home field. No one who met him off the airport would guess that he was a warbird pilot. He had the light hair and a pale complexion that made me cringe when I saw him standing on the ramp in the harsh rays of the Texas sun. His body was full and soft, like his friendly manner. Nothing about Kevin was harsh. He was a teddy bear.

To see such a man in the air was quite another matter. I always saw him flying one of two planes, the yellow Stearman biplane, and the gray AT-6 Texan with yellow stripes. With him would be a paying passenger out for a joy ride, usually a birthday or anniversary gift. Both of us went out of our way to up the odds for our chance encounters.

If I saw him ahead in line for takeoff at Addison Airport, I listened to his heading and took off in pursuit. If I caught a glimpse of a looping airplane around Lewisville Reservoir, we headed straight there. If I heard him call inbound to Addison, we tried to catch up to follow him in and duplicate his wide-turning overhead approach to the runway.

What happened once we sighted each other depended upon Kevin's passengers. Once in awhile, they wanted to remain upright and not try any aerobatics, so Kevin would join up with me to give his passenger a close view of Nanna. After we had become an informal flight of two for a few minutes, he would dive away and head for home. That was in the Stearman, a slower airplane. In the AT-6, slowing to Nanna's speed became too much of a challenge, so Kevin would circle past me repeatedly.

Usually, he carried an anything-goes passenger. What typically went were Cuban Eights (figure eights lying on their sides) and aileron rolls. We circled a safe distance from them as they maneuvered. After Kevin finished and the passenger was in a position to watch, we would perform our odd-shaped loops, more like a pinched letter "l" than an even circle, and lopsided, wobbly rolls. Then he would do a hesitation roll that hesitated precisely, followed by one from us that sort of hiccupped around. Kevin drew figures as even as mine were odd. One day, tired of being out-flown, I remembered something Kevin could not do in his airplanes because of the design of their oil systems. As he headed toward me, Nanna and I passed off to one side—upside down.

Another day, far from home, the first day of our first-ever summer vacation trip, the morning sky hung low and gray above us. The airport ramp was still wet from yesterday's rain. I watched as Howard and a lineman soaped, brushed, and rinsed Nanna. The flat tailwheel was gone, a metal jack took its place, and the replacement had yet to arrive. The bath filled dead time as we waited. I was eager to launch and kept looking at the automatic gate every time it tripped and clanked for a vehicle, hoping to see the delivery truck.

Yesterday's storm had been a grand and glorious boomer, a fitting end to our first day. The hot, humid air along the southern Mississippi River had collected into large flowerets of cauliflower well above our heads, and the clouds grew steadily darker and closer together. Afternoon light pierced the breaks like white-hot javelins thrown into the muddy river and moist green farmlands alongside. We flew a winding course upriver dodging the darkest spots first east, and then west heading for Twinkletown airport—we had selected it for its name alone and were quite proud of that first whimsical decision. Directly ahead, clouds closed into a single mass, choking off all light. Soon, lightning struck and thunder drowned out the voice on the radio, that of the tower controller at a larger field close by. He described the approach of a strong cell and the downpour already in progress there.

Convective, churning air began buffeting us about, adding to the other clues that we must concoct a new plan. Straight ahead was a deadly option. I looked at the chart.

"Let's land at Abide. I guess we weren't meant for Twinkletown tonight," I said over the intercom. Abide, I thought. What a good name for a home to friendly flyers hanging around to welcome us. We would land, meet great new people, and see wonderful old airplanes. I was eager begin the adventure.

Howard buried his head in the cockpit consulting his chart. "There's nothing there."

"It'll be great. Serendipity. Can't you just feel it?"

"Uh-huh." The sound was not a groan, but close to it.

The skies grew darker still as we approached Abide and landed on a damp runway of crumbling asphalt and encroaching grass. Quaint, I thought. The locals I had hoped would be sitting on a porch waiting for us must have missed the serendipity briefing and gone home. The place was deserted, everything locked. Town was pretty darned far on yonder down the road. Maybe this no-planning idea of mine was flawed.

As I gnawed a stick of jerky, the monster storm blew away and the sky lightened. We decided to launch and head north again. Perhaps serendipity was working better somewhere else. In the air again, radio chatter at the big Greenville airport made no mention of a lingering storm. Operations had become relaxed enough that an incoming pilot negotiated with the controller to place a long distance collect call to relay the score of a baseball game. Airborne again, we flew a short, uneventful leg to the larger airport. The recorded arrival information warned us not to land at a catfish farm nearby, which looked like a wet runway. We carefully selected our airport and splashed down upon what looked like a wet runway. It was. We wobbled to the ramp plowing a wake and hauling a sharp bit of something from Abide that had lodged in our tailwheel.

Our first-ever day on our first-ever trip to wherever-the-winds-may-blow-us ended. We were making up everything as we went along. A familiar pattern between Howard and me had begun to emerge. Given a choice, I would opt for the small, unknown, and potentially uncomfortable, Howard for the larger and more certain. The first day had been fun, seeing grand new sights, facing weather challenges. Yet, something had been missing. There had been no magic.

That was yesterday. Today we would head farther up the Mississippi, perhaps as far as Memphis and then turn east toward the Smokey Mountains. We did not know where we would land after we left the river, nor did we care. Our new rulebook stated clearly: "You Must Not Care Where You Go."

I did not expect to see another airplane on the morning of our second day. After all, we had not seen even one since leaving Dallas along the interstate, nor after we hung a left at the Mississippi. Why would we see one here? We had taken off and were running below a low blanket of clouds that would keep most other small airplanes on the ground, so the odds of encounter dropped even farther. What I did not think of was how Nanna's double wings with their dark blue edges stood out against the clouds when sighted from below.

The clouds grew lighter and thinner as the sun warmed the top, as though it plucked the batting from the top of a watery quilt. Nanna passed beneath the smooth ceiling like a minnow beneath the surface of a stream. The air was misty and moist, pleasantly cool, the dampness soft against my skin. It was a primeval sort of day, the kind of day that a pterodactyl might rise from the waters, screeching and diving alongside.

We kept the main channel of the Mississippi off to our left so we could explore the tributaries and irrigated fields to the east. The farms had been carved in rectangular sections like Texas. Within those even borders, though, crops were not like the straight corduroy ridges of beans and cotton at home, but irregular green silk moirés with watermarks that really were water, not just illusions of light.

Suddenly, I felt uneasy. I felt that something was near, but could see nothing. I rarely look behind when flying straight legs through open countryside, but this morning I did, "checking six" as the military would say. I had a feeling that someone was stalking us. I had become that minnow swimming with abandon along the surface of the stream as a great fat trout moved in to slurp me up.

In an instant I saw it, a low wing airplane, a Pawnee, closing fast from behind and right. The nimble plane was yellow, a color pure and vibrant against the bright green crops below. My heart beat faster, first with alarm, then excitement. How exhilarating! I smiled and waved. He slowed as he closed in and stationed himself effortlessly as my wingman.

What a wonderful surprise for both of us. Here was a pilot out for a day's labor of endless passes back and forth across the fields, dropping fertilizer or insecticide, dodging poles and wires, landing and refueling. Then, overhead, out of another era appeared a biplane, its scalloped wings and great rounded tail cutting a romantic figure above the fields where he worked. A decisive man, he made a split-second decision to follow before we could slip away into the land of what ifs. I had no doubt that its pilot had come to crop dusting from the military.

The Pawnee flew on our wing for a minute or two then wagged his wings, pitched up and dove away.

We had found the missing stuff. Magic.

I have three wishes for do-overs in my life, and one of them is that I fly those few minutes with him again. Instead of continuing straight ahead when he broke away, I would follow, to linger above and watch him at work, admiring the economy and precision of his flying. It simply did not occur to me at the time, new as I was to aimless aerial pursuit of bliss. My new friend had seized the moment, breaking away to taste a sweet morsel of life. Perhaps it is enough to know that he had broken the code. I am still learning.

Flying M

The white, high wing airplane had been droning back and forth in the blue skies for several minutes. Its shadow passed beside me and over dozens of other people standing along the wide grass strip tucked into the piney woods of eastern Texas. The aerial comedy was playing again as it had many times yesterday and would again today before all the incoming aircraft landed for the weekend gathering. For the fourth time, the plane passed directly overhead.

"Look down—now," pleaded the volunteer directing traffic from a handheld radio. I stood near the base of his semi-official control tower. I had just strolled over to learn how the private airstrip had turned into something a bit more official. "You're right over the field. Look for the Cub on short final from the north."

"Got it. I have the field," the pilot said, his voice sounding happy that his frustration and embarrassment would soon end. "Cessna three-bravo-zulu, turning left downwind, landing to the south, full stop." The director, having put that one to bed, turned his attention to two more radio calls from inbound airplanes still a few miles from the field.

The airplane overhead had been one of many flying in for the gathering that Saturday morning whose pilot did not recognize the airstrip when it was in plain sight. These amusements— amusing only to those on the ground—had been occurring for more than a decade on the same weekend in October. Dave and Judy Mason had once invited a few friends to fly in and camp out for the weekend. The weekend had been enough fun that, same time next year, the friends invited a few more friends. A mailing list and notices in flying magazines had swelled the attendance even further. The event had peaked with over three hundred airplanes from all over Texas and beyond. This was my first year at the fly-in, and more than a hundred aircraft had already landed by the time Nanna and I arrived.

Dave and Judy must have spent much of the year and no small amount of money preparing for the event. They had stocked the pond with fish, mowed acres of grass, and built barbeque pits, picnic tables, and benches in a stand of pines to accommodate mass lunches. In the hangar, they had installed temporary cafeteria facilities. Various pilot organizations would put on the weekend meals as fund raising events, but the aftermath fell to the proprietors. Dave and Judy were the only couple I had ever met who owned a bunch of portable latrines.

On the ground that first Saturday, many people observing the lost soul overhead wore shirts with the event logo, a large circle with a slim wedge of blue sky between a corridor of tall dark green trees that swallowed a red, radial-engine biplane as it descended to the lighter green runway. "I found the Flying M Ranch, Reklaw, Texas," the lettering around the graphic read. I had just registered and bought my own shirt and smiled now at my fellow flyer as he turned onto his base leg. I had been luckier arriving. I saw wings glinting in the sun as another airplane turned onto downwind to land, so I just followed him in, assuming I would see the field at some point. Otherwise, I would have suffered the same little embarrassment. Less than a mile away, even with the location pinpointed on my chart and all the airplanes parked in the meadow, I had not sighted the field. From the air, it looked like all the other fields around cut from the forest.

The perky, yellow Piper Cub touched the grass with a gentle thump and rattle when its bungee-cord landing gear took the weight of the light craft and began bounding across the uneven grass. Its wings rocked from side to side like a happy puppy racing back into its litter. The plane continued rolling, dwarfed by the trees along both sides of the turf, past dozens of airplanes—ancient and modern, bi-wing and mono-, high wing and low wing, fabric and metal—that had backed into camping spots beneath the trees along the runway. The Cub turned toward the grass corridor that led to more parking and camping spaces in a neighboring meadow. A fellow holding a garden hose sprayed water on the worn track to keep the dust down. Soon, the lost Cessna touched down on the runway with the louder, metallic clanking common to that breed.

I walked back toward Nanna to drop my new shirt inside the tent that I had pitched behind Nanna's tail. Chuck, a veteran of this event and my friend from a favorite grass strip near Dallas, had seen me land and helped me find my spot. We had tied Nanna down along the edge of the meadow backed up to the edge of a pond. Small chocks behind the wheels kept him from rolling downhill. My tent stood farther down the gentle slope.

Children stood along the bank fishing as I unzipped the tent flap and tossed the shirt inside by the sleeping bag, backpack, and book. The throbbing roar of radial engines grew louder overhead. I stood to watch a flight of two biplanes in formation buzzing the field. A cool breeze rustled the trees and blew the clean smell of grass and pines over me as I zipped the flap and walked forward to Nanna's wing to begin my explorations. An electric cart raced toward me.

"Welcome," the driver said rolling to a stop a few feet away. "Hi, I'm Dave Mason." He stepped off the cart and rounded the wing, smiling, hand extended. I told him my name as we shook hands. Dave wore the open, eager expression of the host come to be sure his latest guest felt welcomed. His shirt buttons pulled at their buttonholes in the familiar progression of mass added with successive years of retirement from airline flying. Neither handsome, nor sophisticated, he was the kind of man whose whole being oozed friendship.

"This is your place, then," I said. "I just met Judy at the desk." Judy Mason was the organizing force behind the event, managing logs, issuing tags to identify pilots and passengers, and selling meal tickets and shirts. She was heavy-set with a cap of soft curly hair and a no-nonsense manner of speech. "How kind of you all to put up with such a gang."

"We love doing it. This must be your first year—I'd have remembered the Great Lakes."

"Yes, we're newbies. This must take a lot of work." I scanned the packed meadow before us as I spoke. Everywhere, people were strolling, surveying, and inspecting parked airplanes. Airplanes were taxiing to and from the field. Dogs were romping, their barks blending with squeals of children and the roar of airplanes flying low passes along the runway.

"Everyone pitches in. We're just glad we didn't have rain this year. One year we had to close the runway it got so bad."

"I'll bet." I could imagine how muddy the touchdown areas would get with the drubbing of just a dozen planes, let alone hundreds—sort of like an elephant wallow.

We chatted for a few moments more about Nanna as well as Dave's planes, which he had pulled out onto the apron in front of a large metal hangar across the pond and runway from where we stood. The hangar had become a large social and dining hall with people milling around.

"See you at dinner." He started the cart rolling forward and headed for another row of airplanes where another recent arrival was tying down.

"You bet," I nodded. I strolled into the meadow, where row after row of airplanes were lined up like kernels of corn waiting for me to nibble. I discovered a choice nook of the meadow where campers had arrived early the day before to stake out their favorite campsites. Non-campers tied their planes down in the middle and bussed back and forth from nearby motels. Dozens of trailers and campers had driven in and clustered at one end of the field.

When I returned from exploring that afternoon, I became a hit in my row of airplanes. I discovered a few fire ants and began spraying around my tent and Nanna's wheels with a large can of insecticide I always carried—a necessity for anyone who spends time sitting or lying upon Texas grass. Soon, my neighbors, who had been lounging in camp chairs watching all the activity, noticed an ant assault on their little plane, as well. A trail of ants had marched up the wheels and landing gear and had begun exploring the cabin. I sprayed and they mopped the tiny remains until peace returned to their camp.

As the afternoon wore on, fewer planes arrived, but more flew out and back, taking off and landing or forming up and passing over the field, some with decorative smoke trailing behind. The docile wind had shifted so that planes touched down in front of the hangar where spectators had begun to gather for dinner. The runway was not flat, but more like a plateau with a little bump and then a down-slope, south to north. The overall texture was not smooth, but clumpy and uneven, typical of a private grass strip. When an airplane came in too high over the trees and touched down a little long or with too much speed, it would roll to the bump, vault back into the air like a ski jumper, then bounce or dribble before rolling to a stop.

I would have been content to sit forever and watch other airplanes and pilots, to smile when one hit the jump and bounced, and to marvel at a particularly skillful pilot like my friend Chuck. He flew a slow, light plane, dropping effortlessly below the tree line, touching down right at the start of the runway, and rolling to a stop before even reaching the bump. As the sun sank lower, I decided to join the few remaining pilots in the air. So many people appreciate watching biplanes flying and the evening was mild and awash with color. I took my chances that I might be one of the comical landing performers and prepared to make a short flight.

Nanna and I had spent nearly all our time together far away from spectators. Now we had an audience. Even rolling to the spot where we would take off, I could see people's heads turning as more and more people strolled to the runway. Nanna was unfazed. I managed to put them out of my mind, except as obstacles in my path. I pushed the throttle forward and the engine roared with the propeller whapping and pulling us faster and faster along the grass. We hit the bump, catapulted into the air, and kept climbing. I let Nanna stay low to the ground to build up a bit of speed, and then gave him his head. He popped up like a balloon held underwater and then released. From the rear, I could imagine how the angled wings looked, their broad, scalloped surface gleaming in the rosy light, each rib shadowed where the fabric stretched and dipped along the twenty-seven foot expanse. Still climbing, we rolled into a left turn and flew the pattern. We wound up a little high turning from the base leg onto final, so we shed altitude with a slipping maneuver, which skewed us sideways and produced a dramatic rapid descent. We dropped close to the treetops, cut the engine to minimum power, and floated quietly to earth, kissing the grass and then rambling along a short distance. I added full power again and in a heartbeat, Nanna leapt back into the sky. We did it again. On the second landing, we suffered a little leap at the bump, but only a small bounce before rolling to a stop. Satisfied that I had not embarrassed myself and happy that I had been able to add to the fellowship of flyers, I tied Nanna down for the night. As I walked across the runway into the hangar for dinner, I looked back over my shoulder. Because of the sloping bank, I was looking down on him. His wings glistened at the edges as though lined with a golden silk braid. The sun dropped below the horizon, but the sky shone between the wings like a glowing curtain swirled with pink and purple.

Dinner was a down-home sort of affair with plastic plates and paper napkins, long rows of table rumbling with conversation and chirping with laughter. The main ceremony of the weekend followed—the sort or program common to such flying events with awards for youngest and oldest pilots, farthest traveled, and many other excuses to clap and carry on. Gradually, we all disappeared into the black night and slumber, noises from distant corners of the meadows growing more and more faint until there was nothing but silence.

I slept soundly until the dark night turned gray. My eyelids let in enough light that I lay at the edge of waking, yet I was reluctant to give up sleep. The air was cold and damp upon my face, but snuggled in my sleeping bag on a foam pad, I felt warm and cozy. Silence slipped away with the murmur of distant voices and the clanking of a latrine door. Then the event's alarm clocks, engines starting, shattered the quiet. Startled, I remembered where I was, opened my eyes, and chuckled. My tent faced east toward the runway, so I opened the flap to see a line of Piper Cubs directly across the pond and runway. A man grasped one propeller and pulled it through several times, each rotation sounding a little click and then a clunk.

"Contact!" the starter shouted, then kicked his leg forward and back as he pulled the tip of the propeller through and backed away. The engine caught and the starter moved down the line to repeat the procedure. Soon the peppy little airplanes, engines warmed, rumbled down the grass, and lifted off with morning mist still rising around their wheels.

I rolled over and smiled. I gathered my frigid clothing and stuffed it into my sleeping bag to warm up. By the time I had wrestled into my clothes and climbed out of the tent, the Cubs had invisibly linked themselves together somewhere in the distant skies and flew low overhead. The fly-by consisted of several planes in close formation, a gap of a few seconds and then another group and then another. Before the Cub fleet made its second pass, I had crossed the field and was standing outside the hangar with my sleeping bag draped around my shoulders as a shawl and my palms wrapped around a hot cup of coffee.

Soon other planes had joined the formation game and the skies were abuzz. One pilot, who could not attend because he was working, participated for a few seconds by roaring over the runway in his corporate jet—we onlookers wondered who else

143

was aboard. Soon after, a pair of yellow Stearman biplanes in close formation swooped by the breakfast crowd, then shot up together like a two canaries chased from their perch by a pouncing cat. A bunch of us early risers stood together with our heads tilted skyward, watching it all. We said little, but smiled a lot. These Sunday morning awakenings and dawn patrols became my favorite events at the Flying M.

Before breakfast, the number of takeoffs equaled landings for these short, fun flights. After volunteers had served the last plate of pancakes and an impromptu work party had folded and stored the last of the tables and chairs, though, takeoffs began overwhelming landings at a rapid pace. Houston was forecasting low visibility and rain later in the day, so pilots heading south left earliest. The Dallas route forecast promised good weather, so I could safely linger. I packed away my tent and then carried my book and cloak to a gazebo by the pond and sat on a bench to watch. At first, aircraft were on the move everywhere, engines roaring. They rolled along the grass like a choir marching down the aisles of a vaulted cathedral, a resounding chorus of engines. The choir moved in a line in front of me, each awaiting its solo opportunity to roll onto the end of the runway, voice its crescendo of cylinders, race ahead at full throttle, and surge into the air toward home. After a couple of hours the choir had dispersed and the line disappeared. I remained bundled in my sleeping bag, reading in the sunshine, and looking up every few minutes to watch solitary airplanes taxi, turn, and take off. It was like sitting at the grass strip near home and reading, except there in a whole day I might watch only three or four planes flying by, perhaps landing. In a few hours here, I had enjoyed a month's worth of my grass-strip Sundays.

By late morning, at the end of a chapter, something strange caught my attention. I looked up and shut my book. There were no sounds but those of birds chirping, leaves rustling in the breeze, and one electric cart humming as it approached the gazebo. I looked down the runway and out across the meadow. Nowhere did I see a bit of trash, a discarded can. Nothing suggested that hundreds of people and airplanes had been here just a few hours ago. I saw the only remaining airplane in the meadow—Nanna. He sat in the crisp air, facing away from the pond and toward our home. I stood to leave.

"You must be relieved," I said to Dave as he pulled his cart to a stop beside me.

"Yeah, no big problems this year. It sure seems empty, though," he said. "It's always a little sad when everyone is gone. It was a good event, wasn't it?"

"It was terrific." I waved a hand toward Nanna. "Would you like to take a hop before I go?"

"Maybe next year," he said, looking around the grounds.

"Deal. I'll be back."

The following year when I returned, Dave begged off flying with me again, but encouraged me to keep after Judy. "She'd love it," he said. All weekend long, I looked for lulls in activity to ask Judy to fly with me. Like the mother hen that she was, she always found some little detail she needed to attend to so her guests would feel more welcome or more comfortable.

"If we can't fly this weekend, we'll be sure to next year," she had said after one of my invitations.

"Judy, I'm not leaving here until we fly," I said.

"Okay, I promise," she said. Finally, midmorning on Sunday when most of the crowd had departed, her children took over all her chores. She had run out of excuses.

As I briefed her on climbing in and helped her adjust and latch all the buckles around her ample body, Judy reminisced about the years past when she had flown her own small biplane. How she had enjoyed her time in that little gem, how much it had meant to her. We took off and made a couple of low passes by photographers to be sure she had a record of her flight. Then we flew north to a reservoir well away from the Flying M. She looked out of the cockpit as though the rushing air carried all the old memories back to her.

"You fly," I said. I felt her take the stick and the additional pressure of her feet on the rudders. "You've got the airplane." I felt the stick shake and let it go.

"I have it," she said. Back and forth along the water we flew, turning, climbing, descending, and feeling the sun warming our face and bodies.

"Shall we try some acro?" I asked.

"Yes, let's do. But, you take it."

We spent several minutes climbing for altitude and flying sweeping turns to clear the area for traffic, then many more drawing circles and corkscrews in the skies, downward in spins, sideways in rolls. From the front cockpit, I heard the giggles and gasps that I knew meant she was enjoying our romp. We flew back to the Flying M following power lines and roads. Judy spotted the field long before I did. We flew another low pass, roaring by Dave, waving wildly, and then pulled around and landed.

After we rolled to a stop and peeled off our helmets, I waited for Judy to speak. "Anne, that was such fun. Thanks for keeping after me to go," she said.

"Carpe Diem."

During all my years in Texas, Nanna and I returned to the Flying M every year on that last weekend in October. It was an event that, but for family emergencies, I would not miss. Never did Dave fail to show up to greet me, usually when we first arrived.

The last time we attended, the year we arrived late and were able to stay for only a couple of hours and not overnight, he had missed our arrival. I had looked for him, but had not been able to find him. I was becoming anxious about getting home before sunset and would soon have to leave. As we taxied out to take off, I saw Dave racing alongside us in his cart and motioning for us to stop. We pulled over closer to the trees, swiveled our tail around to turn our wings out of the way of any passing planes, and I cut the engine.

"Glad I caught up with you," he said. "Aren't you staying?" I noticed as he moved toward my cockpit that he still limped and walked with his cane.

"Unfortunately, not. I just stopped by on my way home to Dallas."

We spoke for a while. He reminded me how much Judy had enjoyed our flight the year before. He caught me up on his life for the recent difficult months, since the last time I had seen him here on a cool, damp, overcast January day. There were not hundreds of planes that day, just a handful. Nor did any of us camp overnight. By the time I arrived and tied Nanna down, a few dozen people had already gathered beneath the pines, a place Judy had loved, and where I had first met her as she signed me in, set me up with everything I needed, and became my friend. The wind was stiff and the needles whistled and shouted as they swayed high above the congregation.

Dave Mason stood before us that January day, leaning on his cane, and spoke. He had been in the terrible automobile accident, too, but he had survived. The memorial service that followed was quiet, moving, and simple, much like Judy herself had been in life. Low overhead, a formation of airplanes flew in low from the south. Abeam the pine glen, one aircraft pitched up and flew away from the rest.

Judy was gone, and the Flying M would never be the same.

The Vapors

"Is he done?" I asked the mechanic over the phone from my office. I had been expecting the call to pick up Nanna and taxi him back to his hangar after maintenance on a landing strut that had begun weeping a sticky, pink fluid.

"No. Something's happened," he said.

"What's up?"

"Can you come over?" The strain in his voice told me that he had bad news and that no further information would flow across any telephone wire.

"Sure. I'll be there in about half an hour." I braced myself for news that the repair was not the minor one suspected, but a major expensive project, probably lengthy as well. Whatever it was defied description and required pointing at broken and worn parts that would be hard to find. I was used to such conversations, as were all owners of aircraft.

It was late in the business day and I had no further appointments, so I tidied my desk, drove the short distance around the airport, and pulled into the parking lot behind the maintenance hangar. The late-May afternoon was warm and humid. I could feel perspiration beginning to form on my brow, and my long-sleeved, silky dress began to cling uncomfortably.

I entered the back door and made my way forward toward Nanna, ducking wings and weaving between aircraft wedged into every available space. All eyes studied me furtively as though I was the lioness strolling beside a herd of impala. I noticed none of the usual casual glances and smiles from the men at work. Whatever the problem with my airplane was, it had already made the rounds.

"What's wrong?" I said to the young man who had been working on Nanna. I had reached the group standing near the engine with their backs to the open hangar door. I looked down

149

at the strut, suspended by a rope instead of sitting on its tire, which had been removed.

Nobody said a word, but they all began to look up, as though striking a group pose. My gaze followed theirs from the strut, up along the hoist to its tall arm, to the edge of the upper wing. There I saw the reason everyone had been looking so strangely at me—the leading edge of the wing was crushed.

"Oh my, oh my," I gasped. My hand rose involuntarily to my throat as though I was a weak-kneed, fainting belle. "I do believe I have the vapors." I paused for a few seconds to calm my breathing as I took in the gravity of the situation.

"I guess I'm not going to the biplane fly-in this weekend, huh?" I looked from face to face at various expressions, some appropriate for a funeral, others like someone was about to get a whipping. I willed my hand to drop from my throat and stared at the gash.

"I feel awful. The rope broke and the wing dropped on top of the hoist arm," said one of the mechanics.

"The rope? Just one?" I tucked my chin for solid eye contact over the top of my glasses. I willed myself not to cross my arms and tap my foot. I was livid.

"Yes. We should have had another one on, too. I'm so sorry. A gust of wind blew in." He pointed hopelessly toward the open hangar door. "I can't tell you how awful I feel. I'm so sorry."

I raised my open palm, shaking my head, not wanting to hear any more about the combination of errors that had led to the disaster. The young mechanic was more distraught than I was, but if I hung around to stew, anger might overcome me. I took a deep breath. "Okay, now what?"

"What" turned out to involve removing the wing and shipping it back to the original restorer for repair. Nanna sat for three months of the summer flying season like an invalid under a plastic tent in the hangar corner, doing nothing more strenuous than collecting dust. Once the repaired wing came back, the mechanics hoisted it up into place and twisted on the flying wires to approximate the original rigging. Nanna was ready for a test flight. It was early September, and I was planning to fly him to San Antonio the upcoming weekend.

"Maybe we can get Kevin from Cavanaugh to test fly it," Scott, the owner of the maintenance business, suggested the day before the repairs were to be completed. Because I had flown less than a hundred hours in Nanna, I had decided to find a pilot with more experience for the first test flights. Kevin, who flew the museum's Stearman and other taildraggers on a regular basis, sounded like an excellent choice to me. I had not met him yet, but had seen him flying.

"Great. Let me know when. I'd like to watch."

Days passed with no word.

"Anne, Kevin's coming over tomorrow, but we're having trouble getting any of the insurance policies to cover him," Scott sounded exasperated when he finally called.

"Shoot. I'll be there. Maybe we can work out something."

The next day was cool and overcast with a damp wind, the kind of day that showed up in movies on an English moor portending doom. Kevin had already looked Nanna over and was prepared to fly if we solved the insurance problem. Scott was still working on a few angles.

As I looked Nanna over, I felt the frustration from being stalled well up inside me. "Scott, I'm just going to take him up myself. We could futz around for weeks on the insurance thing if I don't."

"Are you sure?" He looked surprised, but not mortified. I took that as a sign that I had been overly conservative to begin with. After all, Kevin had never flown a Great Lakes biplane before, and I had, many times.

I nodded and began poking and prodding Nanna, checking ailerons and rudder carefully to be sure they traveled in the right direction when I moved the controls. I tugged extra hard on the engine belt that had been sitting idle, pulled the oil stick out a couple of times to check the fluid level, and did all the other items on the preflight checklist with extra care. The additional time helped me to reassure and calm myself as much as to prepare Nanna. Anne, the test pilot, then came up with a plan.

When I finally belted myself in, heard the familiar engine roaring or purring as I pushed and pulled the throttle, saw the prop turning, and felt the rudders yielding to my prods to turn right and left as we S-turned along the taxiway, I began to settle down. Five minutes later, Nanna and I sat alone in the run-up area by the end of the runway, completing the checklist. Everything was working fine. I ran through my head again the standard takeoff procedures, how we would proceed if everything were normal. Throttle full open, ease the controls forward, right rudder to stay on the centerline, and fly off. I had already trimmed Nanna to maintain proper climb speed. "But, what if the wings weren't set right, maybe that speed would not work and we should fly faster and climb slower. Should I push the trim forward a bit now? No, I would push the stick forward if necessary." I was still debating with myself. I forced myself to concentrate on the basics of takeoff and stop inventing any more disaster scenarios.

"Okay, Nanna, this is it." I said aloud. Then I called the tower for takeoff clearance, adding "…staying in the pattern for test flight, full stop landing." I paused, then added, "There's a greater than zero chance that I'll abort the takeoff."

"Affirmative. Two-tango-echo, cleared for takeoff." The controller's voice was a familiar male one, calm and reassuring. I should have been so calm.

I had prepared a list of things that would cause me to abort the takeoff, a longer than usual list. I ran through them one last time as we pulled out onto the runway. The sky was still gloomy under a layer of clouds. The back of my neck felt damp and cool. I took a deep breath and shrugged my shoulders to make myself relax. As I pushed the throttle forward, I tapped the rudders to straighten out. My back pressed against the seat as Nanna picked up speed and lifted his tail. My left hand cradled the throttle, with my thumb hooked on the mixture knob, ready to pull it back in a hurry. I scanned the airspeed and engine gauges, which all read normally. The control stick felt lighter and lighter in my hands, just like it always had. I looked left and right at the wings. They were still on, they looked parallel, and all the wires were holding. Suddenly, magic happened. Nanna flew.

I felt only a little stiff and unfamiliar flying the single pattern. The landing was a good one. I pulled off the runway delighted and headed back to the hangar so Scott could inspect Nanna again before we headed out to do air work and check the rigging. I shut down the engine.

"Well?" Scott asked, looking expectantly at my face for clues.

"Everything worked fine. No problems." I said it the way all pilots do when disaster does not strike, with a practiced nonchalance to suggest that I was a pilot with nerves of steel who could handle anything.

Two days after that and one more test flight, Nanna and I were back in the air together, living a normal biplane life. We had missed the summer season together, but I had found a lovely little Piper Cub to rent to stay current in the meantime. We soon made up for our lost time together, exploring our new state, Texas.

The crushed-wing incident had occurred only a few months after Nanna's initial restoration. I would have several more occasions to get the vapors, twice more in a hangar at the hands of mechanics unfamiliar with a nose-heavy taildragger. Both times, Nanna nosed over, his prop striking the ground and lurching to an abrupt stop that required that the engine be torn down to assess any internal damage.

It would be years later before I myself became the culprit, inflicting substantial damage on Nanna with my own prop strike and hitting the fence at Timber Basin—all within a single six-month period.

During these five outages, each one cutting between two and five months out of Nanna's flying life, I have had ample time to brood about the stress and bother of owning an unusual airplane and venturing to strange and out-of-the-way places. Life would be much simpler if Nanna and I operated more conservatively. We could spend more time sitting and thinking about flying. We could restrict ourselves to wide, paved runways. We could introduce all those constraints and more. Life could become more predictable and certain, less of a hassle.

But that would not seem much like life.

Good for 120 Knots

"Dab some o' that clear on." Joe Cragin stood on the dirt floor in Nanna's hangar, looking up at the patch of fabric on the top wing and me hovered over it. I stood in the front cockpit bending forward, holding a glass jar half-full of clear dope in one hand and a narrow paint brush in the other, a rag draped over my shoulder. Joe had warned me, "Always keep you a rag when you're working—to catch drips."

"How thick?"

"Oh, you know, just brush it on pretty good."

I dipped the end of the brush in the jar and applied what I judged a pretty good amount and looked back over my shoulder at Joe for confirmation or correction. He nodded. Joe was a slight man with a friendly smile and gentle manner, the kind of man who might blow away in a stiff wind but would stand rooted like an oak in a crisis. Everybody at the airport knew Joe or at least knew the "Cragin Aviation" hangar that sat off a taxiway near the south end of Addison Airport. Joe had sold his aircraft maintenance business and officially retired, but he still kept his hand in, working at his own pace doing what he loved to do. At the time, he was building a custom war bird for an old customer. I had seen the trainer about half-way finished and could tell that it would be a showpiece.

I had met Joe when I was looking for someone to repair a spot on Nanna's top wing. The butyrate dope had begun to peel. Joe had said no, he was not interested in taking it on, but fabric work was not hard, and he would show me how to make the repair. I was getting my first lesson that mild Dallas afternoon, a day when temperature and humidity fell within the range needed to do dope work.

"That looks about right. Now let it dry."

I climbed down and covered the dope and brush with plastic

film. Twenty minutes later, I brushed on a second coat.

We spent about two hours together that day, doping and waiting, doping and waiting, chatting all the while. Joe laughed at my enjoyment of the work, said he had never known anyone to get such a big kick out of it. I had always enjoyed craftwork—knitting, crocheting, sewing, woodworking, and those homey sorts of things—but this was my first foray into the mysterious crafts of aviation.

The following day conditions were still good, so we sanded and applied more dope, this time with the cream color to match. Within days, I had built up layers and sanded them until the top surface looked smooth and as good as new. I felt happy about my new skill, and thanked Joe for encouraging me to learn it. You never know when the next repair opportunity might come along.

Two weeks later, another strip of dope pulled free and flew off the top wing somewhere over the fields of Texas. After landing, I poked around the edges, and more lifted. I peeled inch after inch as panic set in. The whole airplane was molting. I consulted Joe. Then I phoned the specialist who had done the original fabric and dope work two years earlier. Nobody knew why this was happening or had any ideas how to stop it.

Several more episodes occurred over the next few months, all on the top wing surface. Each time, I confined Nanna to his hangar and took the few days to make the repairs. The last time, exasperated, I peeled huge patches off until I reached edges so bonded to the ceconite fabric that only sandpaper could dislodge the dope. Months passed after that final repair without further problems, so I packed away my dope cans, bottles, and brushes. It was time for the summer trip.

We had been out for about ten days and had left St. Simon Island that morning heading for our usual destination—no place in particular. Below lay a flat expanse, irregular green and gold patches of reeds and rushes cut apart by swirls of silvery water, the tidelands of the southern Atlantic coast. The calm, moist air and languorous scenery had lulled me into a pleasant stupor. Overhead a scattered layer of clouds dragged a shadow over my cockpit. Howard's camera popped into sight. I dipped a wing to expose more of the graceful swirls and watched as he framed his shot. A flickering above Howard's helmet caught my attention. An edge of dope had begun lifting off the top wing. The flake fluttered violently and broke away. I watched the wind work like a potato peeler for the rest of the morning, enlarging the bare patch bit by bit. Soon the smooth edge of the fabric tape that held down the sheets joined the rising tide, ballooning inches above the wing.

We landed at St. Augustine around midday. Howard left to telephone some old friends. I hovered over the wing surface, pondering what to do. I believe this was the moment, two years after I had bought Nanna, that I decided that he never needed to look perfect again. If we were going to explore, scrapes and scars and scratches were bound to be part of our life.

"Do you have any duct tape?" I asked the fellow who had set about changing the oil.

"Sure." He left and returned with a heavy, new roll of that shiny, gray, and stretchy stuff that has become the favorite emergency repair material of choice from the earth to the moon. Today in the heat and humidity of Florida, it was also gooey.

"Put the roll on my bill, please."

I pulled apart the Velcro on my pocket, fished out my Swiss Army knife, and opened it to the wimpy, but priceless, scissors. I cut half a dozen foot-long strips and hung them like fringe off the trailing edge of the top wing. I peeled off loose scabs of dope until the attached edged refused to lift. One by one, I laid the strips of duct tape until I had built a foot square patch. I wondered if the adhesive would be strong enough to hold.

It did, mostly. For the remainder of the trip, I replaced strips when a corner dried out, lifted, and the wind seized it. When a strip finally flew off, it happened so fast that I rarely saw it go. I would look up and notice the gap. Next stop, I would chop off another strip of tape and rub it in place. Sometimes I found escaped strips holding fast to wires or leading edges of tail surfaces.

Soon I had refined my technique so that a patch lasted all day. I rounded the top edges of tape so the wind could not pick up a square edge. I laid the strips like ladyfingers lining a mold, edges touching but not overlapping. Using this technique, a single errant strip could fly off without pulling another one loose. The patch had proven that duct tape over fabric or dope was good for our top speed on those legs, about 90 knots.

On every trip since that first one, the duct tape has ridden along in the lunchbox with spare oil, tie downs, and wheel chocks.

We were on the Four Corners Trip. The black desert night would not hint of the coming dawn for another half hour. I dressed quickly and headed out into the cold air toward the airstrip where I had tied Nanna down the day before. My legs were shivering now, but I knew I would be comfortable in the heated cockpit. I had added an extra layer of exercise tights, even though I would look goofy walking across open ground from the airstrip to the restaurant after sunrise. After my awful landing yesterday, I was sensitive to being recognized as the goofy pilot.

I walked downhill along a road between canyon walls faintly illuminated by light from casitas and maintenance buildings along the way. Ahead, everything else hid within the blackest void. I watched as a picture slowly emerged like a developing photo, a dark purple glow pushing the black sky up from the horizon behind the landmarks of Monument Valley. Minutes later I saw Nanna's wings silhouetted against the awakening sky and framing the rock outcroppings. The black and purple bands had risen farther, giving way to brightening violet. I hurried to prepare for a takeoff before the sun broke the horizon. As we lifted into the sky, darkness evaporated and liquid orange flowed over everything from the tiniest leaves of the desert plants falling away under our wheels to the grand volcanic plugs ahead. Even a mitered edge peeking around the outermost rim of Nanna's lower right wing shone gold instead of silver—duct tape at sunrise.

The tape was there because I had scraped Nanna's wing on an earthen berm the afternoon before. The scrape followed a bizarre dip of that wing as we touched down. This was the first time I had landed Nanna on a one-way strip, this one an uphill stretch of gravel and pavement that ended facing a sheer rock wall. I knew the trick to making such a landing was to forget the cliff and watch only the runway centerline and a few feet on either side needed to land. Whatever else surrounded that critical strand of real estate did not matter. That was the logical, analytical truth and my focus as we rounded the bend to final. The edifice grew so big and so tall and so close that it fairly slapped me in the face. My mind turned to Jell-O. In that moment, I jerked the stick and the wing dipped.

Only on the ground did I learn what had happened in that moment. I had not felt a bump or strike. Howard had left to find water as I walked around Nanna checking for gravel dings. Then I saw fabric, ragged like a kid's scraped elbow.

When I do something boneheaded like this, I probably look stoic to those around me. I save little emotion for external display. All the action is inside my head, where I stomp around, kick the dirt, and berate that stupid, idiotic pilot who makes such dumb, avoidable errors. The internal outburst is so violent that it passes quickly. Then I set about solving the problem, today, fabric scraped off the rounded bow of the wing.

I lay flat on my back on the ground and brushed off the dirt. Nothing looked bent. I removed the inspection plate to check the ribs and spar. Everything looked normal. To prevent any further tearing and additional drag, I decided to make a field repair.

I opened the lunchbox. There, buried in Nanna's overnight bag of ropes and corkscrew anchors sat the roll of duct tape, half the weight when purchased two years ago in St. Augustine.

Since then, as new sections of dope had lifted from the top center section of the wing, I cut, shaped, and applied strips of tape. Periodically, I would remove the tape, reapply dope, and a new cycle would begin. Instead of original dainty silver squares that covered just the bare area, repairs soon employed great long strips that wrapped around the leading edge all the way to the trailing edge of the wing. The strips hid the graceful curves of the scallops, but who the heck cared. More mechanically secure, the duct tape withstood much greater speeds without frequent re-taping, at least up to aerobatic speeds of 110 knots. (Another year would pass before a problem with a leaking fuel tank would necessitate a remanufacture of the center section, at which point the lifting dope problem disappeared.)

I crawled back under the wing, decided on my covering strategy, and began cutting strips, hanging each along an undamaged edge of the wing. It struck me how much smaller the roll had become. During these two years, duct tape had become a permanent enough feature that I had begun to worry about ultraviolet exposure to the underlying fabric. I also wondered if colors more closely matched to Nanna's cream and blue tones were available. I had called the manufacturer.

"Does duct tape block ultraviolet light?"

"Not much. Why do need UV protection?" The engineer spoke in a pleasant, but businesslike, voice.

"I am using it to patch biplane fabric."

Pause. "Well, it's designed for ductwork." He paused. "Inside. In the shade." His voice had changed, as though he was unsure he was speaking with a rational being.

"Does anybody really use it for that?"

"Uh-huh."

"Does it come in any other colors, like off-white or dark blue?"

Longer pause. "We have colors in a similar tape, but the UV value is less than the silver."

"Okay. Thanks."

Click.

Silver it remained that day in Monument Valley, as I lay on my back under the wing with my arms stretched upward, pressing one after another of the strips onto the scraped wingtip. As I worked, a tour plane landed and parked, and I saw a pair of uniformed pilots approaching. Two of the shiny black shoes stopped close to my shoulders. Soon, the pilot was squatting. He observed my little surgery before he spoke.

"Great stuff, duct tape. Good for 120 knots."

Story Time

"When do you think it will fly?" I asked without looking up. I continued stripping shreds of fabric from the horizontal stabilizer.

Cliff Patty sat on a metal stool in a small workroom carved from one side of the cavernous metal hangar he had built long ago to house his El Dorado Zeppelin Works. The heater hissed, putting out enough warmth to keep my fingers from stiffening as Kansas winter seeped in around doors and windows. Cliff was holding a template over a sheet of metal. Son Brent, who now ran the aircraft maintenance, repair, and refurbishing business, had just fixed Nanna's heat exchanger. He was out in the cold hangar re-installing the device. For several days, Nanna had been sitting there, stripped of inspection plates and engine covers, undergoing such repairs as part of his annual inspection.

"Don't know. Maybe a year or so." Cliff did not look up as he spoke, but moved the template and ran a calloused forefinger over one edge. Apparently satisfied, he set the template aside. His movements were the economical, unhurried ones of a craftsman. He might as easily have been a gourmet cook turning and inspecting a filet, before deciding where to cut.

When he did look up, the shiny spot of light from the bare bulb overhead slid down his balding head to a bulbous and porous nose. His complexion had that pasty look that comes from spending long, dismal winters indoors. His beard was full and mostly white. He was a big man with a soft body and a waist broader than his shoulders, the kind of man who probably never considered embarking upon an exercise program. The clothing he wore was similar to what he had worn nearly thirty years earlier as the first employee at the Great Lakes biplane manufacturing company not many miles from where we now sat: comfortable shoes, slacks, and a short-sleeved shirt with pockets stuffed full with an engineer's tools, pencils, pens and a notebook.

Cliff had shown me plans for the ancient biplane he was building, plans that he had convinced an able researcher to retrieve from a dark corner of the Smithsonian archives. From these he would fashion tooling and parts. Already, along the wall that separated the workroom from the maintenance hangar hung dozens of ribs, panels, and other parts, plus assorted jigs and patterns used to produce them. Cliff had been working on the project for years.

"When do you think you'll be ready to start assembly?"

"It depends. I may quit making parts for a while to put together the fuselage. Did you see the wheels out there?" Cliff pointed to the double doors leading to the hangar.

"Yes, they're beautiful. I wish I could use the big old ones like that on Nanna."

"They came from…" Cliff told the story of the wheels, who had owned them, to what aircraft they had previously belonged, and all the other details. Every bit of his airplane-to-be came with a story, and I am sure Cliff had told each one to several other people. Now, having shown an interest in the wheels, it was my turn to listen. I remember less about his descriptions than I do about the eagerness in his voice, the animation in his face, the way he would pause and look up as though he was describing a search-and-rescue movie playing right there before his face. Talking about his airplane project seemed as important to him as the doing.

Over the next couple of years when Nanna and I flew into Patty Field for Brent's repair or inspection services, I saw Cliff. Parts still hung on the hangar wall, perhaps a few more than before, and he would be working on still others.

"How long before it flies?"

"Oh, maybe a year or so. See this panel?" He tilted it toward me from the familiar metal stool. "We're looking for an original compass that fits here…" Cliff continued the story about the

166

piece just completed and his hopes to pull the missing instrument from some dark, forgotten corner of the ancient airplane universe. As I listened, I thought that Cliff's pleasure would not be less, if he never finished that airplane.

Once during those years, I flew Nanna to San Antonio and landed at Kardys, a small airport farther away than Twin Oaks, the field where we usually landed when I visited my parents. There beside a wide grass strip under a metal shade roof sat the Skybolt, a biplane about the size of mine. Roddy Stitz had invited me to stop there so we could fly his newly completed project.

Roddy was a lean, compact man with a deep, soothing voice, and the style of a southern gentleman. He spoke softly, yet I had no difficulty imagining his voice carrying above the din of the aircraft engines he maintained for the Navy during World War II. His hair was pure white above a gentle face. Whenever I saw him, he looked pressed and polished, particular about his appearance and his possessions. Therefore, it was no surprise to me that as he briefed me on the airplane that cool January day, he spoke about how unhappy he was with his partners.

"They haven't done much to get it fixed up," Roddy said.

"You'd just a soon do it all yourself anyway, wouldn't you?"

"That wouldn't bother me so much, but they can't fly worth a hill of beans either. You'd think an airline pilot would be able to handle this airplane, but, Anne, I'm telling you he scares me to death."

"Oh?"

"Comes in high and fast, doesn't flare worth a darn." I had heard this complaint before about airline pilots. Bringing in a jet aircraft weighing hundreds of thousands of pounds from a seat dozens of feet above the runway is a different task from landing a featherlike thousand pounds of biplane from only a couple of feet.

"Oh, that's too bad." By then I was climbing into the cockpit and worrying that I had best flare well in a few minutes. Soon we were in the air.

The intercom was a portable afterthought, and the quality was little better than two tin cans attached by a string. The wind interfered awfully with our attempts to communicate. I announced to an Air Force tower that controlled the airspace right next to our field that we would be working in the pattern. The controller said something that I hoped was agreement, because I could understand not a word of her brief response.

"Roddy, we're going to have to stay in the pattern. We can't go roaming around with the radio like this."

"Okay____throttle___keep____five___over____fence." Roddy tried to remind me of speeds and settings, but only a few words made their way to me unmangled.

"Say again?"

"_____teen hundred____seven____the fence."

In the end, I just felt my way around, picking trim settings and speeds that felt right to me. The Skybolt handled much like Nanna. I flared at just the right time. The Skybolt settled down on the dry grass, quickly picked up speed along the hard Texas ground, raised its tail, and roared back into the sky. Once in awhile, Roddy tried to say something, but the radio seemed even weaker and more garbled than before. It did not matter. We were happy to listen to the wind and enjoy the feeling of flying with someone who enjoys it as much as we each did.

After a few circuits, we taxied back toward the shade ports. With the propeller slowing to a stop, Roddy said, "Nice job." As he climbed out, he called to my dad who had been watching from the side of the field, "She's a good stick, Lew." I felt as happy for Roddy that I did well as for myself. Except for the radio, which is really an optional luxury for an old airplane, his baby flew just great.

A few months later, Roddy and I met in the lobby of the building where my parents lived. He looked crisp and dapper dressed for dinner in a blazer and neatly pressed slacks. After a progress report on his Skybolt radio, and a few new tales of woe about his partners, he paused. His bright look faded and his eyes dropped. "My wife and I were so close. It's really hard without her." I think he was remembering how he might have been telling this story to his wife, who had died some years before. It was the only time Roddy ever mentioned her to me.

About a year later, I saw Roddy. He had left the Skybolt partnership and had begun building an experimental airplane, his alone, a single-seat biplane modified to have a forward cockpit.

"How's it going? Will you make Oshkosh this year?"

"About two more weeks. I've got an inspector coming out next week before I cover the last section. Come out and see it."

"I'd like that. How about next time I'm down?"

He smiled and nodded.

Three weeks later, I was back. The day was overcast and cold as Roddy, my dad and I drove out to the field. A staunch Texas wind blew across the flat land of the airport, an assortment of small metal hangars with a few homes of die-hard aviation enthusiasts sprinkled among them. We rounded the corner of one house and saw a biplane sitting out on a concrete slab covered by a tin roof.

"Looking good, Roddy. How long before it flies?" I hopped out of the car's back seat, zipped up my parka, and headed toward the plane.

"About two more weeks," he said, and began reciting a list of work items remaining. The list sounded to me more like a month's worth of labor, but I said nothing.

"Come look at the new cockpit. I had to cut this…" He exploded like a cannon blasting out the saga of a redesigned fuselage. I listened and asked questions at encouraging intervals. Roddy looked happier then than he had all day.

Surely, he was happier here than he had been at Kardys Airport. Here he could share his enthusiasm for airplanes with fellow builders. They gave one another advice, commiserated when obstacles arose, rejoiced when they hoisted wings in place or mounted an engine, and listened. We met his landlord, who was building airplanes and cars just a few feet away inside his hangar. We drove around the airport and met another friend who dropped what he was doing and opened a hangar full of enough projects to last a lifetime. How wonderful that Roddy had found a place like this, I thought, although nothing could fill the empty spot where his wife used to be.

A couple of months later, I heard from my dad that Roddy had finally finished his airplane and it would soon fly.

Howard and I were on our way home from the Four Corners Trip. Nanna had been performing flawlessly and would have been content to continue until dark, but Howard and I had enjoyed enough of West Texas for one day. We had flown through El Paso, across the Guadalupe Pass, and across mile after mile of flat and desolate ground that sprouted little but scrub grass and metal grasshoppers pumping oil. We decided to land at Odessa for the night.

We fumbled about deciding which of the several runways to land upon and finally picked the one right beside the tie downs and airport office. Out front, a handful of fellows in dusty jeans, boots, and cowboy hats greeted us as we set about our evening chores. They helped fetch water for Nanna's sponge bath, reserved a motel for the night, and generally entertained us with their West Texas drawl and down home point of view on restaurants and the local sights ("Drive on by the Tee Pee Motel, heh, quite a place"). After about thirty minutes, we finished and piled our backpacks onto the torn upholstery of the back seat of the ancient airport loaner car and started to leave.

"Ya' need to stop in the mornin' t'see the Fokker a fella's buildin' back roun' there," a tall lanky fellow said, pointing to the south hangars.

"We'll be leaving pretty early, but thanks." Howard started the engine and we started rolling away.

"Aw, we'll be here."

The next morning when we pulled into the airport and parked the car by the front door of the office, I looked at the tie down area felt the beginning of panic. Nanna was gone. Nobody was around. We rushed inside, where the locals had gathered. The men were drinking coffee from paper cups and a near-empty donut box lay near the pot. One of them must have read my concerned expression, because he signaled with his head and led us through a rear door into the hangar. There sat Nanna, carefully parked away from anything dangerous, surrounded by some of last night's bunch and a couple of new faces.

"No need sittin' out all night. We though it'd be better off." People at a metropolitan airport would be afraid to touch an airplane without an owner's permission. If the dust storm blew through, well that was the owner's darn fault, her problem. Here, though, an airplane was no different from a straggling calf separated from the herd. Any fellow would sling it across his saddle and bring it in.

"Thanks." I liked these people. No doubt, if we sat and talked politics for long, I would find some real disagreements, but as long as we stayed on the common ground of airplanes, we were safe.

"I hear you're interested in seeing my Fokker," an old man in a dark blue jumpsuit and baseball cap said, stepping forward. The words came as a casual inquiry, but he could not hide his eagerness. I guessed that he had made a point to be here just for us and would be disappointed if we said no.

Howard and I looked at each other. We had not considered lingering this morning. Our sketchy plan for the day would get us home by that afternoon. Since neither of us signaled a veto, we followed him in the loaner car along the rows of identical metal hangars. Near the end, he stopped and pulled one open.

The hangar was small, which made the three wings of the Fokker looming above appear even grander than they already were. My head did not even touch the bottom of the middle wing. No fabric had been applied to the wooden skeleton, yet even without rich red dope or a single black iron cross it was recognizable at Baron von Richtofen's favorite. At a glance, the workmanship and attention to detail were obvious. What a showpiece this would be one day, a gem of aviation history risen from the dust of West Texas.

"It's wonderful. When will it fly?" I asked.

"I'm movin' pretty slow. Have to on social security."

I was flabbergasted. How could anyone afford to construct something like this on a shoestring budget? Why, just maintaining an already-built airplane was like feeding a ravenous teenage boy.

"Come 'roun' here," He motioned me around the front of a man-eating radial engine and gleaming prop carved from laminated wood, tipped with brass. The engine rested above tall, thin wheels.

He motioned me to climb up and sit in the seat inside the frame where the cockpit would be. My legs dangled down to the rudder bar. Already, the beginnings of the machine gun lay within my reach. Someday, some lucky pilot would fire bullets through the propeller arc timed so that every shot would miss the blade. My new builder friend noticed me handling the weapon.

"You know how that works?"

"Not really." I did know in principle, but I recognized the look on his face. It was the story-waiting-to-be-told look.

"There's a gear...," and he began and pointed.

The stories flowed about one part or another for nearly an hour.

For most of my life, finishing something seemed to me the only reason to start it. A project or initiative had to be conceived, planned, embarked upon, and, by gosh, finished, and the faster the better. Got a business problem? Study it, collect data, concoct a solution, test it out, execute, and, wah-lah, success. Move on. Need a new Christmas sweater? Head off to the store that minute, pick out pattern and yarn, cast on that night, keep those needles knocking every evening during the television news and weekends watching movies, and steam the finished garment before Thanksgiving. Tired of flights grounded by weather? Fix it. Get that instrument rating, study and fly, study and fly, every day, every night, weekends, too, then zip back to work, certificate in hand. Whew.

About the time I met these airplane builders, though, I had begun developing a taste for the unhurried journey. I found myself setting fewer pointless deadlines for myself, caring less where I was heading on a flight or when I would return. I sat more, doing nothing, alert for whatever chance brought my way. I am unsure if this change is due to wisdom or age—probably both.

Cliff never finished his airplane. He died first. Roddy finished his biplane, but crashed it on an early flight, killing himself. If the Fokker triplane ever flew or its builder lives, I do not know.

One thing I do know. If there is a heaven for airplane lovers, it is a hangar full of half-started and half-finished flying machines, sheets of metal, fasteners, tubing, butyrate dope, and bolts of grade A cotton. Among the parts and carcasses lay plans, manuals, and scraps of paper with pencil drawings of assembly diagrams. Over in one corner sit metal stools, a dusty couch, and chairs that do not match.

There sit Cliff and Roddy and all the others, hands in the air, gesturing, poking fingers into holes debating how to join two parts. Then they see a neophyte like me approaching. Their faces light up. A listener.

Story time.

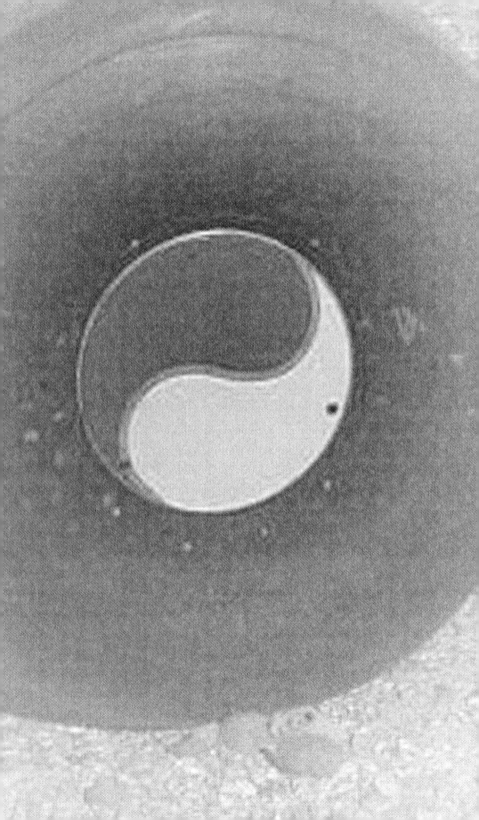

Yin and Yang

The Great Lakes factory had originally, back in the 1920's and 30's, been in Cleveland, Ohio, but rights to the aircraft design had passed to others since. In the 1970's and 80's, Nanna and his fellow biplanes were manufactured at a factory in Kansas, and then ownership passed to the Patty family. Cliff Patty and son Brent lived and worked at Patty Field, a hangar and grass strip east of Wichita, Kansas, known as El Dorado Zeppelin Works. Nanna and I flew the route between Dallas and his old home many times.

We flew up for annual inspections, specialized modifications, or tricky repairs. On one Saturday late in January, we headed up for his annual. I remember well that flight—and the return.

The alarm music blared tinny and harsh, piercing my sleep and shattering the dream I had over and over—I flew with my face into the wind, both arms outstretched like wings and then along my sides, steering with twisting hands or torso, as though body surfing. I was so nimble and skilled that I could fly around the neighborhood trees, poles, wires, clotheslines, and swing sets. The window from which I launched was above the grape arbor on the second story of a white clapboard house that reminded me of one I lived in as a girl. It was while living in that house that I learned to climb large oaks and maples and to eat tart-sweet grapes. I sat under the arbor with purple-stained fingers squeezing the skins to shoot them into my mouth.

I liked this dream so much, that I was annoyed when it ended unnaturally, as it did that January morning. Without opening my eyes, I knew it was still dark, and remembered why I had set the alarm on a Saturday morning. I hit the off button, slipped out of bed quietly, and shut myself into my bathroom before turning on the light. It took only minutes to complete my morning routine. Along with the customary flight tools already zipped into the pockets of my flight suit, clothing I needed for the flight lay on the counter: long underwear, woolen socks, sweaters, neck warmer, face mask, gloves, ski jacket.

The forecast was for mid-to-high thirties with clear skies into southern Oklahoma, then a chance of scattered showers, maybe patches of low ceilings and steadily deteriorating visibility as we approached El Dorado, Kansas. With any luck, the weather would clear as we flew north, and I would be down, warming myself, and listening to Cliff's stories before lunchtime.

At the hangar, I hurried through my packing and preflight chores. The sun was shining. Even so, the wind turned the damp cold into icy barbs. I slipped down into the sheltered cockpit and felt better. Soon, the engine sprung to life, turning the propeller a thousand times a minute, each beat adding to a swirl of frigid air flowing back around an extra fleece collar that protected my neck. Engine heat blew into the front cockpit and, trapped by the cover, continued back toward my legs and lower body. By the time the heat rose above my gloved hands and waist, though, it had mixed with too much outside air for me to stay warm. By putting my hands low in the cockpit and crunching my body forward to trap the heat before it could escape, it was possible to maintain a reasonable temperature. It was tough to see and fly in this position, though, so I reserved that technique for moments of dire need. The race was on to reach warmth on the ground a reasonable distance ahead before my cold-soaked body cried Uncle.

We took off and turned north, keeping railroad tracks to our right and two reservoirs to our left, then letting go of those landmarks to grab Lake Texoma, a big damned-up section of the Red River. The water looked cold enough to freeze. We ran out of chart just as we ran out of Texas. The route spanned only three small sections of two aviation charts and ran straight north, so I never had to refold, only swap one chart for the other. This made cockpit chart operations simple with no diving turns while fumbling with paper accordions.

So it went across most of Oklahoma, a game of hopscotch between landmarks, following a country road north to Madill, then the railroad, watching it angle out and back again near Ada, picking up another road until it crossed a river, matching airports in the distance with circles on the chart. All the while, we dodged communication towers that dotted the countryside, ready to snag an airplane like a prairie dog hole might trip a horse. Tower dodging was a skill we had learned in north Texas. Unlike hilly terrain where most towers sat on high spots and were easy to find and see, in the flats a tower could pop up anywhere. We used three techniques to avoid hitting them: finding a tower on the chart along the route and flying around it, flying high enough to make hitting it impossible, or flying well below it so that it stuck up above our nose, clearly visible and as unlikely a target for us as a telephone pole beside a highway was for an auto.

We needed to stop for fuel once along the way. By that time, my face was stinging, my fingers were numb, and my limbs were aching from dampness, cold, and the strain of bunching together every part of my body to share whatever warmth my body or the heater produced. Clouds now blocked the sun and the ceiling had begun to drop. Maybe we could get all the way through, maybe not. A telephone conversation with the weather service would answer questions about if, when, and how.

Off to the northeast about fifteen miles, lay dozens of orderly white dots, the oil tanks east of Cushing Airport. I had wondered about them many times in passing, but had never stopped to satisfy my curiosity, another reason to do so now. As we drew nearer to the airport, tendrils of cloud drooped lower and lower. We had to land, and soon. We flew the pattern at half the normal altitude, landed, and dragged off the runway to the fuel pump.

"As soon as we heard your engine, we knew we'd see you down here directly. Looks like you have a flat tailwheel, too." The local operator who had appeared to help looked at me as if I were a bedraggled mutt with an injured paw whimpering at his back stoop.

Soon I was inside a warm room drinking hot chocolate, working to thaw myself inside and out. I kept all my clothing layers on for a long, long time. Any hope of continuing that day disappeared as the weather briefer at the other end of a telephone line painted for me a picture of the Midwest. It was enduring a wintry low, abysmal weather stretching hundreds of miles in all directions useful to me. I arranged to stay overnight and got the tire refilled. How it had gotten so low so fast would remain a mystery. At the motel, I continued thawing in the tub, replenishing the hot water several times, as though defrosting a frozen turkey in a kitchen sink.

By early Sunday morning, the ceiling had lifted, and parts of the sky showed through breaks in the cloud. Nothing had changed about the cold, though, so another hour or so of frozen discomfort lay ahead. North of Wichita the weather continued to look dicey, but chances were good that flyable conditions would hold all the way to southern Kansas, although not much beyond that.

The engine started right up, but the oil temperature gauge held on the coldest reading. After a few minutes sitting on the ground, engine purring, the needle crept up, and soon we were off. Nanna dashed up into the sky like a sleigh horse eager for a warming trot, and the clock started on my willingness to endure the cold and damp. The trip would be short, so I savored the early morning flight across the countryside. On and on below rolled fields of brown dirt, old gold stubble of crops harvested long ago, and crisp white mounds from dustings of snow and frost. Pickups and cars belched whitish clouds behind them as they rolled along the shiny black roads. Rivers and reservoirs were a choppy gray, as though the wind and cold had sucked any brighter color from them, too. Though the clouds bases stayed high, we hugged the land's rolling contours, fields with stands of trees, and farmhouses with chimneys puffing smoke, proof of life within. Nothing stirred in the fields. Farmers were absent, and cattle stood still with their tails into the wind. We stayed clear of the many small towns along the way, far enough that I could not read the names on water towers, but close enough to guess that the length of the names looked about right.

This bucolic peace continued until we were about thirty miles from Patty Field. Then, as had happened the day before, conditions overhead attracted my attention. Bottoms of the clouds grew more ragged, like wisps of a hairdo falling loose, mussed by a hat or a child's grasping hand. For about ten miles farther, the conditions held and required no plans beyond the standard one of being prepared to turn around. The next ten brought the clouds down low enough that we would be unable to climb higher and remain in the clear. Within a few miles of my destination, I faced a decision which, made wrong might spell disaster. If the conditions got much worse, we would have to land close to wherever we happened to be. We had plenty of landing options in the terrain we were crossing. Familiar with the route, we hugged the road that passed beside El Dorado Airport. The low ragged clouds stayed put, so we passed up those runways and cut the corner south of town. At the sight of the familiar water tower, we circled back toward Patty Field. We made one low pass to let Brent know we had arrived and to see if the grass field looked puddled or otherwise unsafe for landing. We pulled up into the pattern again and descended as lowering clouds began licking at the water tower.

We landed. Down and safe, I relaxed. I looked forward to seeing Brent again. He was the kind of man who would put work aside on a spring day to play ball with his kids. All us pilots could call up on one of those days to moan and groan about needing this repair finished or that part shipped, but by gosh, Brent's family came first. He kept his priorities straight. He also had the knack of keeping me humble. "Maybe Anne should get herself a second Lakes," he suggested to Howard after one short period full of mishaps and repairs, "One to fly and one to break."

As we touched down, Brent waved at me from the back door of the hangar, motioning me to meet him around the front. Then he disappeared inside. The sodden grass tugged at the tires as we pulled around the corner. Cold drizzle, no longer blown back by rushing air, began dripping into the cockpit and penetrating my clothes. We rolled onto the cement pad and the hangar doors slid open. We pulled up close, and I shut the engine down.

Right away, I lost control to Brent and Cliff. They swiveled Nanna around and pulled us tail first into the hangar. Inside, we melded into the jumble of custom tools and jigs for Great Lakes manufacturing and repair, wenches, pumps, and an assortment of biplane pieces: wings in long racks, fuselages suspended from the ceiling, handcrafted parts hanging on the wall. The place was a grandmother's attic of aviation. To me it looked a tangled mess, but I could not argue that the hangar was disorderly. Too often, I had watched Cliff or Brent move directly to a hillock of stuff and retrieve precisely the tool they sought. The door rolled shut as I rose from the cockpit and pulled off my silk facemask.

"I think you like to fly in foul weather," Brent said, shaking his head. "The water tower was socked in, wasn't it?"

"The ceiling didn't drop until thirty miles south of here. I could see the tower just fine—sort of." I had enjoyed the peace of being a solitary traveler when everyone else was sheltered indoors, just as I had once enjoyed running on snowy nights along empty roads, the only noise the sound of flakes crunching beneath my soles, the only other humans vague forms behind bright-lit windows. I felt exhilarated with a sense of accomplishment. I had stayed alert to risks, balancing them, prepared to stop if safety dictated, but to press on otherwise. Engage with danger, hold it close, Lindbergh had said. I think I knew what he meant.

My plan to help with the annual inspection for the week and then fly Nanna home when we finished fell apart when Brent discovered a small crack in an important piece of metal in the tail. The fabric would have to be removed to make the repair, then re-covered and re-doped, a lengthy process. I went home alone without Nanna. Many weeks passed before the repairs were complete and I could fetch him.

The weather for the flight home to Dallas that day was as merry and spring-like as it had been harsh and wintry on the way to El Dorado. I had not flown in the meantime and was eager to be playing again in the skies. The sun shone bright at midday when Nanna's wheels rolled along the turf behind the Patty's hangar, their yin and yang symbols spinning faster. Tires pushed and wings pulled. We lifted into the zephyr winds that danced with us for dozens of miles as we skimmed above trees, heading south. Now the risks of weather problems were nil. Whatever dangers existed would be of my own making.

We flew low, below communication towers that I tracked on my charts and well above power lines, for as long as plentiful open fields promised safe options for emergency landings. We passed dozens of farmers preparing their fields for the spring planting and lingered to circle a few. When we neared farmhouses and barns, we swerved away, like a colt skirting around an outcropping rock. We flew wide of roads to stay clear of cars and trucks. Drivers might have felt a shadow passing over and watched it move ahead like a speeding car, puzzled about the source until Nanna and I showed ourselves playing a favorite game of shadow tag.

Ahead lay one of the several rivers we would cross that flowed from the Rockies to the Gulf of Mexico. Many times before on this familiar journey, we had dropped low above the water and run a few-mile stretch that ran east and west before we turned again on course. We had never seen people along the shore or boats on the river, and judging from the many sand bars, it was a shallow stretch. That day I saw it approaching and craved a longer river run. I glanced at the chart to check for obstacles along the next stretch after it turned south. Finding none, I decided to keep skimming along beyond the bend.

Turning right onto the wide river, we became less a plane, more a hydrofoil speeding along a cushion of air. Just below, glassy water reflected the trees rushing by along the shore. At that moment, I had not a care in the world. We rounded the bend of the river with this heightened sense of life and well-being.

Something ahead flashed into view. One split-second there was just an impression of manmade straightness across our path. The next, without any conscious thought, I pushed down Nanna's nose, bringing his wheels closer to the water. My heart raced, and the adrenalin rush nearly overwhelmed me. As quickly as it had begun, it ended, no more than a few seconds. Whatever I had seen, we had passed below it. We climbed, and I looked back. Nothing. I searched the chart again. No power lines appeared along that stretch of river. We might have gone back to inspect what we might have hit, most likely wires, how low they were, how much clearance there had been between wires and water. But, I did not want to scare myself any more that day. I have never gone back to look. I like to think it was just my imagination.

Whether real or imagined, avoiding danger would have been so easy, just a quick first pass at a couple of hundred feet, as simple as a racing driver taking a practice lap before attacking a course at full speed. It helped that I had read so many accounts by pilots who have flown toward wires, by mistake or on purpose, and written, "Dive. By the time you are close enough to see them you will never climb fast enough to miss them."

When we landed at Addison Airport later, my sense of joy and freedom from the flight had returned.

I remember those two flights between Patty Field and Addison Airport as flights of sheer joy, the first heightened by the adversity of weather, the second flipped for a few heartbeats to pure terror. I wonder if I would hold either so dear without the contrasts.

Being There

As a kid, I looked forward to a history program on television. Every week, as I sat cross-legged in front of our huge twelve-inch screen, the announcer assured me that the episode I was about to watch would be "…filled with events that illustrate and illuminate our times. And," he paused and lowered his voice, "You Are There." What followed was primitive by today's production standards, but it did let me eavesdrop on people and events in a way my third grade history book did not. I watched outraged colonists toss tea overboard in Boston Harbor and defenders of Ft. Sumter prepare for battle. In a similar way in my biplane, I pass above historic sites and watch lingering apparitions recreate their acts for me, according to my recollection.

All over the South, the hardships endured, sacrifices made, and conflicts overcome to build a country show up. On the Dixie trip, we flew east to the Mississippi River at Vicksburg, a city under siege and ravaged during the Civil War, its bluffs now fully healed, graceful with shrubbery cascading to the edge of the muddy river. We circled above a riverboat paddling downstream toward New Orleans as tourists waved from the boat. We flew low and level with the portico of a hilltop plantation home. I imagined the front door opening between the white pillars and a southern belle dressed in gingham stepping into the doorway, swinging her hoop skirt to pass through, banana curls bouncing at her temples, ruffled parasol in one hand, and a fan in the other beating against the humid air fragrant with honeysuckle—and the slaves tilling a garden nearby. Pressing on north, crisscrossing the river as afternoon thunderclouds began to form, barge after barge passed below, plying the watery artery that had long attached the heartland to the rest of the world.

The next day we flowed like a cork on a winding stream around the emerald hills and valleys of Tennessee, and I thought about the frontiersman, my childhood hero, who might once have hunted there, right down there. Our custom was to sing a representative song when crossing a state border, but I could not restrain myself from repeating the one for this state. I sang, "Born on a Mountaintop in Tennessee / greenest state in the land of the free / raised in the woods so he knew every tree / kilt him a b'ar when he was only three. / Daveeeeeeee, Daveeee Crocket, king of the wild frontier."

Days later, after crossing the Appalachians we ran like fallen rain to the wide rivers and bays of the Atlantic coast. Trees and the stockade of Jamestown Island fell below our wing. The first settlers arriving here at the end of a torturous ocean crossing had entered the mouth of the James River with no idea what lay beyond, that expanse of rivers and mountains that we had crossed in the past few days, and more beyond. Their wood and stone settlement looked tiny, fragile, and as imperiled as a lost toddler wandering along a highway. Whatever drove people to abandon their homelands on such journeys to this unknown land, must have been unbearable.

Farther north we came upon the red bricks and white trim of colonial architecture and orderly tree-lined streets—Williamsburg. Here, the action had been indoors, delegates arguing points of law, principles of government, matters urgent to an emerging nation, and I felt none of the visceral connection I had felt to Jamestown's open-air stage. The farther we progressed through the suburbs growing out from the nation's capitol the more my connection slipped away from the famous players inside the old buildings.

Sailing away from that city and back down shallow coastal waters of the Atlantic, we came upon Kill Devil Hills, the ancestral home of all airplanes. Before landing, we circled the monument on the same hill Orville and Wilbur had climbed year after year to launch gliders into strong winds, recording data to perfect their wings for the next season, and the next. Nearby, along the flat sandy soil where the brothers had laid out a few simple tools and a rail for launching, monuments now marked the distances of the first sustained, controlled, powered flights. Later that day, after landing and touring the museum, I watched from the sky visitors strolling among the markers. They looked up, hands shielding their eyes from the sun, as a descendant of that first Wright Flyer roared up and banked sharply from the airstrip near by to reenact, albeit higher and faster, the first flight.

The next few days we traced the shoreline along the Outer Banks above the pastel greens and aquamarines of shoals that had wrecked so many ships, abeam lighthouses, bold-striped and whitewashed, that had guided so many others to a safer course, then along the marshes of the Carolinas into Florida. Coast, shoals, ports, marshes, rivers, forts, and lighthouses—for days we had became like generals and admirals standing above a scale model, surveying and comprehending a whole theater.

We approached the point at Cape Fear where bright sand paled and then darkened beneath the aqua and blue of deepening waters. Arriving at the tip, I watched a scene that had played out all around the world where any land jutted out into an unknown sea. A human, alone and still, stood at land's end, looking out across the water, pondering what lay beyond.

Once in awhile we turned inland to explore one of the forts that guarded the entrance to a river. We circled to inspect the walls and cannon, formidable from land or water in their day, but from above, the defenders were as vulnerable as hogs in a slaughterhouse pen. All the forts sat along the shore or on a channel island in position to fire upon and stop hostile ships. But the most massive, St. Augustine, was nowhere to be seen near the river's mouth. We turned upriver and finally spotted it much farther inland, close to town. Spanish military, we learned later, traded the safety of isolation for the proximity of a pub.

At another time, most of a continent away, I had been flying for days above cultivated fields and ranging herds of animals, the battleground in nature's war between hunter-gatherers and farmer-herders, the Great Plains. The fields and herds became for me nature's enduring monuments to that struggle, great in expanse, vast in scale. Far to the western end lay Little Big Horn, the site of Custer's Last Stand, a boundary skirmish in that greater war. How small and inconsequential the buildings, burial ground, footpath, and cemetery looked, human monuments on a meager scale. We did not linger over these trinkets of man, having savored nature's crown jewels.

The Black Hills lay ahead, home to tribal spirits and more human monuments. An invisible rope of protected airspace cordoned us off from Mt. Rushmore's carvings. Long finished and admired, the heads of four presidents captured little of the spirit of the surrounding land that a nearby granite outcropping did. As we approached Crazy Horse, it seemed as though he summoned nature to push us away with rising winds and dangerous clouds around the peaks that surrounded his home. Even distance could not diminish the proud chief, a blasting and chiseling project that has been going on for most of my life, a testament to perseverance and enjoyment of the journey rather than the destination.

No historical spirits look up and shout louder to flyers than Meriwether Lewis and William Clark, Charbonneau and Sacagawea, and the rest of the Corps of Discovery that explored the northwest two centuries ago. I have flown only bits of the route from St. Louis up the Missouri and across the Rockies to the mouth of the Columbia River, and at different times. Always, the ghosts I imagine are headed outbound, everything ahead unknown.

How easy it was to look at calm waters along unspoiled stretches of the Missouri and imagine their boats laden with papers, ammunition, and trading goods, as the men push, paddle, or sail upstream. The Yellowstone River looks as promising as the Missouri did—which way? See the grizzly racing along the shore in pursuit of hunting party. They keep turning to shoot, yet the bear keeps coming. One desperate hunter hurls himself from the cliff into the water and the bear follows as a final crack of gunfire sounds, mortally wounding the creature. Look, there is the white pirogue out of control and in peril of sinking on choppy waters, Charbonneau shouting above the storm for divine intervention, as a calm Sacagawea plucks floating papers off the rising water, so The Corps' precious words could become ours forever.

As our flying machine lifted our eyes above the first ridge of the Rockies, I thought of the long hard climb that lifts theirs. They hope to see a navigable river running through a gentle land to the western sea, but find instead ridge after dispiriting ridge of the most rugged mountains. We turned south through Judith Gap, and left the explorers heading into the mountains. How difficult it will be for them to reason which drainage leads, ultimately, to the sea. What despair to come upon narrow rapids, sheer cliffs, and have to turn back to find another way. Years later on the Timber Basin trip, when we banked east from the Pacific coast into the mouth of the Columbia River, we see their boats again, now racing toward us, Clark shouting "Ocian in view! O! the joy!"

Like many flyers, I feel connected to them across time and space—they explored the surface in the early 1800's, we fly above them in a flying machine a bit more sophisticated than an early 1900's model, and in my cockpit sits a 2000-era device that speaks every moment to a satellite whisking along miles above. Beyond the satellite, an observer in 2100 will gaze back through a telescope on the moon's Mount Marilyn to see the earth's Judith Gap and ahead into deep space toward the next place to be named for a loved one.

And—We Are There.

One Man Watermelon Band

I do not remember his name, the man on the riding mower on a mountaintop in Tennessee. Call him Pete. I do not remember what Pete looked like, either. What I do remember is how he made me feel during the hour or so I spent with him one summer afternoon.

Earlier that day, Howard and I had been flying Nanna across the state, the long way, west to east. We had started out south of Memphis, bobbing and weaving up the Mississippi high enough to miss hitting bridges, but low enough to see details of barges, riverboats, and Mud Island. The day had started out in dim light with a low hanging overcast. The sky grew lighter as the clouds melted, thickening the air with humidity. Past the city, we turned inland. We would miss our muddy, meandering river companion, but there was much to see elsewhere. Surely, we would find the Big Muddy again in our travels. I watched its coppery twists and turns continue north without us.

Ahead, the moist air turned the green-green hills progressively more misty and mossy green until those on the horizon looked gray and pale. It was our custom to avoid flying over cities, but we cut straight across Nashville, not a huge place, thinking we might spot the original Grand Old Opry building. We hardly had to search. The dark red bricks and white trim showed up off our right wing with no fuss at all, simple as a country song. Nashville would be the last city of any size we would see for days. From there we meandered along a highway toward the Smokey Mountains.

"We need to stop in about an hour." I opened a typical negotiation about where we should land for fuel. The chart strapped to my leg showed dozens of possible airports on our general—albeit aimless—path. I knew Howard would pick a big old airport with amenities like a restaurant, a choice of purveyors of fuel, and wide concrete runways. I would look for something more modest. My choice might have soda and snack machines. Its runway would be asphalt, most likely with sprigs of grass pushing through cracks. With luck, the runway would be nothing but grass, but that rarely happened. Grass strips seldom pumped fuel.

"Can we make it to Knoxville?" Howard said after a brief pause with his head bowed over his own chart. At that big city airport, air traffic controllers would direct traffic for two huge, long runways. They would sell jet fuel, too.

"That's a stretch. How about Rockwood? Four, five inches to the west." I could not point out Rockwood for him on his chart. Our two cockpits were like little sovereign nations. Only occasionally did we send an item back and forth beside his seat, typically some dropped item that slid back under my feet. I would hand it back as though passing a baton.

After another pause, he found the small magenta circle with the little spokes signifying the fuel for sale. "Well, okay. Doesn't look like there's much there." The airport sat far from any town and a mile or more from any highway.

"It'll be great!" My assertion was only a hope stated boldly.

"Uh-huh." The tone of his voice was skeptical. My ideas did not always live up to my expectations.

We flew across the greenest hills in the land of the free, the valleys similarly hued and lush, each with a gray thread of a stream or thicker twine of a river with steel bridges marking towns along the bank. The forests were thick and lumpy, jutting out into lakes and rivers like the heads of green serpents drinking.

Instead of gazing at rivers, towns, and roads that caught my fancy, now I began searching for the specific ones on my chart that would guide me to the destination, Rockwood Airport. I shifted from aimless meandering to purposeful seeking. Just ahead lay the town with three towers to the left of the highway. Farther in the distant haze stood a ridge a thousand feet taller than the rest. We followed the interstate through a gap in the ridge. Emerging to the east, I saw the hint of an airport, a slash through the relentless greenery atop a hill, a straight pale mark angled in the same direction as the runway on my chart. We kept flying along the highway until I could see the runway off my left wing, surrounded by trees. I noticed no significant structures nearby and began to worry that this might turn out to be one of my poorer airport choices.

To land surrounded by forest or cornfields—or any other uniform growth—is like descending through the ground into a ditch. The treetops or tassels alongside form what looks like a solid green field, just as clouds below an airliner look a solid white blanket. In setting up to land at Rockwood, I ignored the taller surrounding forest as though it were nothing more than overgrown grass. This runway was like all others and the pattern that led me to it would be the same, as well. This intellectual trick, theoretically, would allow me to land on a slab of concrete suspended in the air, as a gymnast would land on a three-inch beam high above the ground by imagining that the beam was just an outline drawn on the floor. The mind game ends, as it did that afternoon in Tennessee as I watched the far end of the gray runway to judge my rate of descent and glimpsed tree branches out to the side moving from our wheels, to our wingtips, and then far above as we sank into the ditch. The jolt of reality thrilled me, being surprised in that moment we broke through the green canopy, like a child turning the crank of a jack-in-the-box, savoring the suspense, surprised when the clown pops out.

We rolled along the runway in our green maze, seeing nothing else but a bit of taxiway at the far end leading out. We slowed to turn through the break in the trees and saw a paved area surrounded by lawn. A couple of airplanes were tied down on the ramp. Separated from pavement by a weathered gray rail fence sat a plain building, red brick at the bottom with corrugated walls and roof, and a shade porch propped up by metal poles running the length of the front. Atop the porch, large block letters spelled "ROCKWOOD." A man puttered around the lawn on a riding mower. He looked up, stopped the machine, and strolled our way.

We pulled up in front of the fuel pump and shut down. Air that had felt moist and pleasant swirling about us in the open sky, descended on us like a steam bath.

"Thanks. We'll pump it ourselves," Howard said, as the man started pulling the grounding wire from its spool. To put fuel in the tank built into the center section of the top wing required special care. Only with practice had we learned to fill it without gas gushing over the rim during the last few seconds.

"Suit yourself. I'm Pete," the man said nodding once as he clamped the wire onto Nanna's exhaust pipe.

"Anne and Howard," I said and nodded back.

Pete stood by as Howard stood on the ladder, holding the nozzle in the fuel tank. Pete and I watched the vapors rising as the gas flowed.

"Don't let us keep you from your mowing," I said.

"No, no. I've got plenty of time for that."

"Any drinks inside?" Howard, already drenched with sweat, climbed down and headed toward the office.

"Oh, sure." Pete and I followed.

Inside, I leaned on the counter drinking the cola Howard offered. As I paid for the fuel, I looked around the small room. It was like so many other airport operations. On the walls hung signs posting rates for fuel, airplane rentals, and instruction, a poster for an air show that occurred years ago, photos of aircraft, some famous, others belonging to local flyers, and an inexpensive plastic wall clock. Pilot supplies and magazines sat on the counter and within the built-in glass display case. One other person, a younger man, lounged on the sofa that had seen service elsewhere before landing here.

"Great rates," I said, eyeing the wall chart.

"I'm the instructor. Don't need all that much to get by."

"Let's see, you maintain the place, pump gas, instruct,"

"Mechanic, too. Oh, I do just about everything that needs doing here." Pete said it in an easy way that made me think that

I had come upon one of life's charmed voyagers. He had found what he wanted out of life and saw no need to look for anything better. "Say, we just got a watermelon, first of the season. Would ya'll like some?"

"Sounds great to me," Howard said. I nodded.

"It's out on the picnic table." Pete handed me my credit card slip and led the way outside. The air smelled fresh from the new-mown grass. It was quiet but for the chirping of birds and crickets and the screen door banging shut. There on a concrete table sat one of the South's prettiest sights on a hot humid day. The watermelon lay cut open lengthwise with a couple of slices already missing. The pink surface glistened. Pete picked up the long-bladed knife and sliced through the flesh. The rind cracked apart with a twist of his wrist. He cut the slice in two and handed us each one, juice dripping down the cut surface onto our fingers.

"Mmmm, good," I said after my first bite. "Thank you so much. What a treat." Howard, mouth full, nodded in agreement. We had not eaten since breakfast and the liquid sweetness perked us both up.

We stood and chatted awhile about the area as we bit off one mouthful after another, spitting out seeds, letting the juice dribble onto the ground. Pete did not eat another piece, but gave us pointers about what lay ahead on our route into the Smokey Mountains. After awhile, he said, "Eat all you want," and sauntered back to his mower.

The silence died with the rumble of the motor. He had stopped mid-row when we arrived. Now he slowly picked up the task, eating through long blades of grass to the end, turning in a graceful arc to head back in the other direction. He looked like he was having fun making his swirling patterns.

As I watched, I envied him. In my working world, I lived among specialists. Here lived a one-man band, as fit for this spot of Tennessee as his ancestors had been, doing everything for themselves, self-supporting.

His simple life was good—so was his watermelon.

Solitude

"Want to stop soon?" Except for the constant droning of the engine and a propeller slapping at the air twenty-one hundred times every minute, it was the first sound I had heard since we intercepted the Rio Grande. The relaxed voice belonged to Howard, my most frequent passenger. I watched his shoulders shift as he squirmed to stretch his muscles within the cramped forward cockpit, a feat he could more easily have accomplished in a straightjacket. The air had been smooth all afternoon with only occasional buffets from puffs of heated air rising from the sun-soaked earth, like bubbles blown through a soapy ring by a child lying on a flat boulder along the river below.

We had been flying for ten days on the trip that would take us over four thousand miles around the southwest and in the end name itself the "Four Corners" trip. That morning we had left Arizona, passed west of Las Cruces, and now headed north, skimming the river with a stiff wind at our backs. The water sparkled, rushing in the opposite direction around sandy islands. The river valley exploded with greenery—crops, grasses, shrubs, and cottonwoods. The highway lay off to our left, rising and falling along the higher parched slopes through which the river had carved its course. In every direction lay mountain ridges separated by wide valleys.

Tomorrow, Howard and I hoped we would stand on the ground and watch the skies fill with the hundreds of balloons gathered in Albuquerque. Now, we were alone together—Howard more alone than I, because he could not even see me in the cockpit behind him. I can always see my passenger, or the empty space where a passenger might have been. I can watch a head nod, shake, turn, or even bob off to sleep. I can see fingertips creeping out beside the windscreen to touch the sky or sense a cool, damp wisp of cloud, or whole arms braced against the wind holding cameras. Ahead I see all this like a silent film. With a passenger or without, I can become as solitary a traveler as I chose.

The trip had brought busier, chattier times when departing or landing required me to speak to Howard about checklist items. Carrying on a conversation between one windy, noisy cockpit and another, even assisted by intercom, is difficult and unsatisfying. Words are sometimes clipped and easily misunderstood. What on the ground might be casual banter becomes a difficult listening exercise in the open skies. Even a first time passenger, who starts out chatting as though we are on the ground, soon learns without coaching to restrict talk to the necessary or compelling.

Sometimes no need to speak existed, but a sight was so small or interesting to require pointing out, lest the other miss it. "Look, there's a flock of geese" or "Glider, nine o'clock low. Pretty." Mostly, though, on long stretches, I escape into my own head to absorb images of the countryside passing beneath, or to let the land become a subtle background canvas for thought.

I have always enjoyed solitude. I have gone for days without seeing another human being and enjoyed the time alone with myself. Those closest to me know this about me and do not feel hurt or rejected. I do not carry a mobile phone, and I doubt I ever will. The thought of anyone anytime on a whim disturbing me is as unbearable to me as being out of touch is to others.

"It's about time for us to leave. I think you're ready to be alone," my daughter had said after she and her sister had been visiting me. For days, we had laughed and joked, shared pleasant meals, gone to shows, and spent every hour together. Her observation was a simple statement of fact that Mother had reached her togetherness limit. No feelings were hurt.

This craving for solitude is one aspect of my nature that has bound me to Nanna. Alone with him I have experienced my life's most peaceful moments—and a few of the most terrifying. To fly alone with Nanna is to be in the world and away from it at the same time. Once clear of airports, I have turned off the radio to push the rest of the world away, yet still experienced it and its people held at a distance. Sometimes the people are in great social herds. Other times one person stands alone. Still other times, humans are absent, but artifacts of their presence linger for me to discover—an empty boat on a remote shore, an abandoned fire ring, a car parked at a trailhead.

New Year's Eve was still over two days away. I had spent the holidays with family, caught up on news of the diverse clan, and indulged in the family specialty when we get together—overeating. I looked forward to feeling hungry again—and being alone. The weather was unseasonably mild with no significant weather forecast between Dallas and the Gulf Coast. Nanna was in tiptop shape. I looked at the Texas sectional charts. Within striking distance lay a long winding line, the Rio Grande, beckoning. Nanna and I had crossed the river at El Paso on my way to live in Texas, but had not seen it since.

The following day we flew straight to the Gulf coast, and then along the shore to the mouth of the Rio Grande and upriver until time ran out and we made another straight shot for home. Where we ended marked the starting point for future day when we would follow the rest of the river to the source. Like most pilots, I engage in quest-like thinking—devise a pointless task and become obsessed with it, things like landing at every airport in a state, landing in every state, every country. We have yet to complete my quest to fly every inch of the Rio Grande, but it remains on my list of unfinished business. We lack only the segments from the Taos to the source and another from Fabens, near El Paso, to the railroad track east of Presidio.

That day we flew to the Rio Grande, I arose at first light. Morning is the best time of day for solitude. Overnight, my mind sorts through and stores all the untidy thoughts from the previous day like a mother picking up a playroom after the toddler scampers off for bed. Chaos builds afresh with every new day. Before it has a chance to take hold, when the mind is clear and able to imagine everything and nothing, that is the time I like to be alone.

Within half an hour of rising, the sun had broken the horizon and cast a long shadow in front of the hangar. I rolled open the door and pushed Nanna out into the morning chill. I thought about the trip, curious as to how it would turn out, how far we would get upriver before all the sand fell through my imaginary hourglass. I strapped my backpack into the harnesses in the front cockpit and fueled up. We lifted off into a partly cloudy sky, skirted southeast around the Dallas airspace. To fly over the Dallas would have meant talking to controllers, climbing and descending to specific altitudes, and engaging in The System— none of that smacked of the solitude I sought. We took up a heading that would put us in Corpus Christi by afternoon. Clear of the airport we crossed over numerous interstates full of holiday traffic. Soon, neighborhoods and factories disappeared. I turned off the radio. The farmland below, once an ancient seabed, changed subtly, sloping gradually to the Gulf of Mexico. We steered clear of Waco, Austin, San Antonio, and Houston, navigating along the narrow farm-to-market roads, using distant city skylines as signposts. I used the radio twice more that day, once to stop midday for fuel in Smithville, east of Austin, and again at Robstown, a small airport west of Corpus Christi. All the hours that day and the subtleness of the land we crossed provided a backdrop to clear my mind at year's end.

That evening, I checked into a motel as well appointed as a child's cardboard playhouse and walked the few paces to one of many family-owned barbeque restaurants in Texas that claim to be the best—and they all have framed newspaper reviews to prove it. After dinner, I set the alarm for sunrise and flipped channels looking for a movie. I ran across a local news story about a serial killer on the loose in the area. Then I found the TV movie about another serial killer and watched that. About half way into the movie, I considered that nobody who cared about me knew where

I was and I fretted about the fragility of the chain on the door. By morning, I laughed at how easy it was to scare myself when I was alone.

The day had broken bright and crisp again, with only gentle breezes and small decorative clouds. By midmorning, Nanna and I were flying a low pass along a runway at Corpus Christi Naval Air Station heading for the shore of South Padre Island. The Gulf lay just ahead. I knew we would turn when the water fell under our wheels, but I have never flown to the edge of an ocean without thinking that I could keep on going out to sea alone, taking a flight so many others have taken over open seas in open-cockpit airplanes not so different from Nanna. I think the ghost of Chichester stows away in the front cockpit whenever we near any shore. Given enough fuel and decent weather, I think I would like such a flight very much. Approaching the coast that day, I saw a dark armada of cloud shadows sailing away on the green water, leaving me behind.

Once we hit the ocean, we did turn. Padre Island was the spare sort of place I love to fly alone. It was long, narrow, and sparsely populated. The air smelled like the salt air and seaweed I had learned to love when I lived as a child on New England's Narragansett Bay. This sand looked as inviting as the sand behind our quarters, where I dug down with my toes into its wetness for clams and quahogs with my father, and where I caught and released thousands of horseshoe crabs with my older sister. The Gulf's water was lighter in color and calmer here than I remembered in the windy, choppy northern bay. Long stretches of the flat sand lay empty except for long-legged birds skittering along, poking beaks into the sand looking for food. An occasional car had driven out onto the sand and parked, its owner lying or sitting on a blanket enjoying the brisk day. Others drove slowly along the shore, solitary people sharing a moment in time with a solitary flyer.

The tasks of flying there in a calm wind were simple. I had

only to follow the shoreline and check the gauges now and then. Otherwise, I was free to think, or not. The engine droned on smoothly, mantra to a flyer's meditation. Here a few hundred feet above repetitive scenery, I found it simple to clear my head, to relax and think of nothing for long periods, "...the spaces between the leaves" Castaneda described, the emptiness between thoughts according to others.

I engaged with my surroundings and civilization again when the masses on the beaches and buildings of Port Isabel appeared. There we flew lower along the waves, wagging wings and turning away from the path of another aircraft towing a banner. The sun was high and made the calm inland waterway shine bright and sharp.

After a stop for fuel, we started to hunt for the mouth of the Rio Grande. It had seemed like an easy enough task when I stood on ground, looking at the definite blue line on the chart. In the real world, though, someone always forgets to draw the blue lines. We left the shore and began zigzagging back and forth along what looked like ponds and peninsulas. We must have hit that blue line somewhere. As we continued inland, the confusion ended. A single channel began its twisting journey to shape the Texas border and then cut in through New Mexico and on into Colorado. Farmland and orchards soon fell under our wings. I let my eyes sweep as far in the distance as possible as we turned with the river. Somewhere out there, I thought, are the grapefruit that my mail order supplier would pick and ship to me. It was only a failure of knowledge that kept me from flying to the very orchard, the very tree, and looking upon its single limb and the tiny speck of the grapefruit I would eat in a few weeks. These sorts of notions pop into my head as I fly alone in Nanna. I love these thoughts—simple, meaningless, fun. Okay, whacky.

That day, I came to love not just the river, but the Mexican border as well. My previous experience with it had been mostly on foot or in an automobile crossing at a border checkpoint with a crush of humanity. So much of the borderland we flew across was unpopulated. The river was narrower than I had imagined, such a thin thread of a border for a huge countries like Mexico and the United States, nothing like the thick Mississippi and Missouri Rivers that divided only states like Tennessee and Arkansas. The water did not run fast, either, but slithered along its twisting course like a snake in no hurry. Nor did the banks show dramatic cliffs. The soil and foliage along the way reached down to waters edge along gently sloping ground.

We flew a line straighter than the course of the Rio Grande for most of my journey, but never out of sight of the water. On stretches where I could see far ahead, I tested myself, flying low along an imaginary centerline, turning sharply at every bend so that my wingtips never touched a bank, a little like a slalom course. If I did well along a long stretch, I quit while I was ahead and straightened my course line again. When I did poorly, I also quit for a while, refocused, and tried again. If a cluster of buildings or small village appeared ahead, I popped us up higher like a hurdler, and then tucked back down low on the far side.

Along stretches of sparsely populated land, I noticed few differences between the two countries split by the river. Both sides had dirt and paved roads. Both had ramshackle wooden sheds, lean-tos with rusted, corrugated roofs, and more substantial ranch houses in the distance. The differences lay in the cities and towns that straddled the border like two pieces of fabric, one, a vibrant print, stitched to the other, a length of muted tweed. The shocking pink and cobalt blue buildings with bright white doors and trim on the southern side popped into sight and separated into distinct structures before the more subtle buildings of pale adobe tans and browns to the north. In the larger towns, the economic links of the two countries declared themselves with factories that lay along the borders, and highways leading away to the north.

To my right lay a level land, a horizon unbroken. On my

chart, rectangular sections noted unobstructed, safe-to-fly altitudes of only hundreds of feet. To my left the flat horizon turned fuzzy and irregular, and then painted a jagged edge across the sky as mountains rotated above the curvature of the earth as it spun toward me and we meandered toward it. I relaxed a few accordion folds of the chart to peek beyond the immediate southern flats of the Rio Grande to see "Sierra Madre Oriental" in large print along a range with a peak over twelve thousand feet. As the river turned us northwesterly to Del Rio and the falling sands of my imaginary hourglass turned us north toward home, we left the mountains behind. Another day, we would return.

North of the Rio Grande, we crossed some of the most isolated land in Texas. Where I expected to see roads, there were none. Where I saw roads, they had no power lines running alongside. I saw no buildings or fences at all. The gray and chalky land had a deserted, ghostlike quality. Vegetation consisted of shrubs and other tufted plants. There were no large trees. The ground undulated and made gentle turns to contour the shale-like rocks. We came upon a road heading in my general direction and followed it. When minutes passed without encountering a car or truck, I pushed Nanna lower to enjoy the rush of flying close to the earth. Soon we were rising and falling with the road, flying above the pavement, more like a car than an airplane. A pickup truck surfaced over a crest a few rises ahead. The solitary driver was like me, rolling along a timeless, empty land, alone with his thoughts or, perhaps, listening to a country and western radio station. I slid out a distance from the road as though pulling into a passing lane and we flashed by each other. Something about the easy way he waved told me he enjoyed, as I did, our moment alone together in the wilderness.

I flew other segments of the Rio Grande alone over my years living in Texas, sometimes traveling upstream, sometimes down. The segment from Las Cruces to Albuquerque, I flew in both directions, but not alone. Howard came with Nanna and me.

The following fall, Nanna and I started up the river again at Del Rio. Riverbanks steepened beyond the Amistad Reservoir and we followed along the river's loneliest, uninhabited stretches. By the time we reached the point where the river turned southwest toward the mountains of Big Bend, the river banks had become cliffs. Gorges cut back from the river, making an endless row of fingers grasping for the flat, green riverbed forever out of reach below. On many of these isolated points stood primitive shacks that showed no hints of modern utilities or conveniences of any kind. There were no towns close by and no roads, only dirt tracks leading inland.

Away from the cliffs, small beige hills shaped like gumdrops covered the otherwise even land. Stripes of darker and lighter layers of sediment from the ancient eroded seabed decorated each pale gumdrop like its neighbor, as if a confectioner had turned out thousands of molded candies onto a baking sheet and dusted them with sugar.

I returned to these gumdrop hills a week later from the opposite direction. I had left Nanna in Alpine for a week for a minor repair and returned to resume my river run. We lifted off as the rose light of morning lit the peaks and then descended the mountainsides around us. We flew south in their shadows, the wind cold and sharp, as we followed a deserted railroad track through a gently sloping valley. The track continued through Presidio and crossed the Rio Grande into Mexico where we left it and the mountain shadows to turn toward the warming rays of the morning sun. Around us, the mountain peaks had lost the pink tint and glowed gold with deep shadows still defining the ridges. The river flowed through a variety of beds. Some places were wide and full of sandy banks and vegetation. One such stretch continued inland to a small airport. Others were steep-walled, barren ravines where we dared not enter. We flew above the narrow cuts that dropped straight down and felt the buffeting winds that would have brought danger along the walls had we flown just a hundred feet lower.

I have enjoyed other solitary flights far away from that great river. Nanna and I crossed the Mississippi River one bright morning in early summer on our way home from Pensacola. I had been flying since sunrise over marshy, forested Mississippi and the bayous of Louisiana. For a change of pace, I decided to follow the river upstream. I sensed no winds blowing us one way or another, nor did I feel any pockets of air warmed by the earth and cut loose to buffet us as we passed. The river shone smooth and glassy along the main channel, betraying its speed only along the banks and sand bars where rocks and logs rippled the water.

The stretch of river looked deserted. No barges or riverboats motored or paddled toward us. No towns lay along its banks. Whatever houses there were lay hidden in the trees that stood thick along the shore. We could not see them from above, because we flew below the treetops and only a few feet above the water and sand bars, nearly kissing them with our wheels where open sand lay flat and looked firm. I pulled back on the stick to climb a few feet and leaned my head back to feel the sun on my face. I could have been Tom Sawyer on my raft that day with not a care in the world.

The route I flew alone the most connected Dallas and San Antonio. I always opened the charts, but never needed them. I could have flown by sight alone as easily as walking to a corner store. Despite the flatness of the land and similarity of rivers and highways, reservoirs along the way had distinctive shapes and lay close enough together to follow as easily as steppingstones across a stream. Once beyond the Dallas skyline, two reservoirs pointed me south between a long snake-like reservoir and another smaller one shaped like a "V." Nanna and I continued on to the west of Waco's border waters past a gang of tall towers to the tip of a dammed lake shaped like a Chinese dragon. Immediately south of Temple, lay another tadpole of a dragon, its twining tail trailing off to the west. The next was the hardest to spot, a smaller "S" shape thirty miles farther along. Soon after crossing it, the skinny northern tip of Lake Travis showed up to lead us along that large playground of boats and lakeside homes. Half way to Canyon Lake and out of sight of any water ahead lay only one east-west road. From Canyon Lake slipping into San Antonio was a simple matter of angling west to intercept the only interstate nearby and following it along until the last minute turn toward Twin Oaks or the larger airport just beyond.

Flying alone along a familiar route like this one gave me some of my best meditation time. The flight lasted between two and four hours depending on wind and rarely required a fuel stop. Once out of either of the major cities at the ends of the route, my only flight concerns were monitoring Nanna's simple systems and dealing with whatever weather presented itself. If conditions were good, I could relax and let my mind graze along the prairies of Texas. Here, too, I could tilt my head back, smell the clean country air, and feel the sun warm my face.

As much as I enjoy sharing the joy of flight with passengers, I prefer solitary flight. Passenger flights require attentiveness to another's thoughts, another's pleasure, and producing another's smiles. They bring me great satisfaction and a shared sense of discovery.

Solitary flight brings me peace.

'Twas a Pleasing Fear

Howard and I took off from the plateau above the eroded cliffs at Bryce Canyon. Thin air lengthened Nanna's take-off roll along the high mountain runway, just as it had made our landing the afternoon before faster and longer. We flew more comfortably in the calmer morning air, unlike yesterday's puffs of heat that buffeted us like popping corn. Within seconds, the level ground fell away into spikes of earth jutting straight up, each one casting an orange-fired shadow of morning across the pyre behind. Our pale wings glowed copper as we flew above the rugged terrain. As we banked, I looked straight down into a pincushion ready to impale us. My muscles tensed, and I thought, as I always did at such moments, of what a silent engine might bring us. Beyond the army of spikes marching down the mountainside, though, lay a valley full of flat spots. Our escape would require only a short glide. My tensed muscles relaxed. We headed west.

Midday, we drew up beside rocky pillars of Zion that pierced the bluest sky like spires of a stone-age cathedral washed bright by the sun. The jutting rocks we passed looked like short outcroppings until I dipped a wing to follow their faces hundreds of feet farther down to the narrow river ravine. I felt my hands tense on the stick and my shoulders tighten. That narrow winding road along the river through Zion provided scant hope of anything but a bone-crushing landing, should the engine seize or fall silent. This time, I saw no flat valley within gliding distance. We flew on straight toward the next tall pillar. As we closed the distance to its jagged cliff and swerved to fly alongside, I saw a pale saw tooth trail climbing one edge. I thought about what it would be like to hike on such a path and knew I would panic after the first few traverses. I cannot stand by a precipice or drive along a cliff-hugging road without tensing up—I am afraid of falling. Zion, as stark and biblical a place as I have ever seen, prodded from my childhood memories the Old Testament scripture about walking through the valley of the shadow of death. The sheer cliffs ended where the river escaped through gentler terrain. I felt my shoulders melt back into working human parts, no longer steeled against that aerial bogeyman that whispers of imminent disasters. We departed south to cross that other monumental wilderness, the Grand Canyon.

By the time we arrived at the canyon, the earth had captured and released enough of the sun's heat to transform the air into an invisible rumbling river. We ran these rapids high above the canyon, watching the carved buttes and mesas, the scouring river, the cliff-hugging trees through thick and hazy air, muted like a Chinese silk painting. The vast wilderness stuck in my mind, and I can close my eyes and see it as clearly today as a photo on an album page.

I paid the price of ecstasy that day in fear and that night in total exhaustion when I slept.

Years later, flying in Idaho, I learned how to banish the fear without giving up the ecstasy of such flying. We had crossed several mountain ridges east of McCall and dropped into the drainage of Big Creek that flowed into the Middle Fork of the Salmon River. The air was warm and calm—no dangerous or tricky winds swirled across the ridges that morning. Still, the familiar tenseness gripped me as we penetrated farther and farther into the mountain wilderness.

"Hug the slope," my instructor called over the intercom, tipping his head toward a mountain that rose above us as far as it fell below. "Leave plenty of room for someone flying the other way."

Everything on the slope—the boulders, trees, fallen logs— grew life sized as I sidled in closer, thinking he would tell me to stop any second. He did not. Soon, just a couple of wingtips away from the rocks, I was close enough to notice details of objects on the slopes—a cracked boulder here, a rotting log there, gravel and dirt broken loose to fall down the slope, a young tree struggling to grow old. Together, these elements made a mountain, but they were more like individual people yearning to be heard than an angry mob out to get Nanna and me. We had become a part of the landscape, as much as any hawk or eagle. Close enough to see and enjoy the parts, I lost my fear of the whole. The feeling of freedom was like riding a bicycle without training wheels when my father let go of the seat the first time. My natural balance clicked and my fear of falling disappeared.

"I'm moving up north," said my aerobatic instructor.

"Oh, Poop," I said. Roy had been my fourth teacher in the few years I had been looping and rolling around the skies. He was a good teacher and we had grown comfortable with each other. I was learning stuff and he had learned to put up with my idiosyncrasies. I did not look forward to trying to find and break in someone new.

I had the basic skills I needed—I recognized and could recover from squirrelly situations—and I had good books describing how to do additional maneuvers, so I decided to teach myself when Roy left. I already could do spins, loops, and a serviceable slow roll, which is like rolling a pencil between your palms with the airplane skewered on it like a marshmallow. The roll I had not yet tried, the barrel roll, was different, more like the corkscrew on a roller coaster, except the airplane did not need rails. Everyone had told me it was the easiest and most comfortable roll to fly. That should have been my first clue.

The night before my first attempt, I lay in bed with my instruction manuals propped open on a pillow. The Great Lakes owner's manual devoted twice as many pages to aerobatic maneuvers as to systems and operating instructions. Two pages explained the barrel roll, one beginning right side up and the other inverted. "...diving the airplane to a 110 MPH speed while simultaneously turning to an entry point approximately 45 degrees off a selected reference heading...gradual pullup...after 45 degrees of turn, the airplane should be positioned in a 90 degree bank and the nose at its highest point." I read the couple hundred words a dozen times. Thank goodness for the illustration. I lifted my hand into the air and set my feet onto imaginary rudders as I tried to marry the words to the movements I would make.

I opened the second book. It had fourteen pages and many thousands of words on how to fly a barrel roll that might last five seconds in the air. Stuff like, "...the nose is coming up and around the circle on the horizon. Use just enough aileron in your roll so that the plane will be knife edge when you are at Position Two...nose is 20 degrees above the horizon...the highest the nose will be during the maneuver, but not the highest altitude..." This was like trying to learn from a manual how to do a cartwheel. Words could not replace another human being saying, "Watch how I do it. Follow me on the controls." No matter, I thought. It would all be easier and more intuitive once in the air. All I needed to do was to remember the sequence of stick and rudder inputs and talk myself through them during actual practice.

Within a couple of hours, I had flown the barrel roll dozens of times in my head, flawlessly. My heels slide over the sheets making rudder inputs, my hand moved effortlessly and properly on the stick, and my eyes watched the line on the bedroom wall that served as a horizon. I had memorized the line that said, "...most pilots do not pull hard enough in this first quarter of the barrel roll..." When I pulled up the first time the next day, I was sure I would fly it well. I turned off the light, fluffed the pillow, and drifted into sleep, gratified and exhilarated from my imaginary training.

The air was cool the next day. A front had passed through leaving the sky clear. The winds had subsided. Conditions were perfect for sprightly engine performance. I had slept well. At the airport, as I completed my preflight inspection, I imagined the new maneuver. Anyone watching would have seen me rising on the balls of my feet, arms outstretched like wings, running forward, and swiveling around bent backward. Confident, I climbed into the cockpit, taxied, and took off toward my practice area north of the reservoir.

I set the propeller to twenty-five hundred revolutions per minute, the engine to twenty-five inches of manifold pressure. I trimmed the nose to fly at the altitude I wanted. I checked my harness and seat belt again. I banked Nanna sharply looking for other aircraft above, below, and behind. I did it again in the other direction. All preparation was complete. My heart began racing.

I pushed Nanna's nose over to pick up speed. When it hit one hundred and ten, I pulled back on the stick, firmly. I watched the nose. Seconds ago, it had pointed down at the highway running through the trees and across the river that fed the reservoir. Now it roared skyward as the green horizon fell away. I nudged the stick and rudder to begin rolling upside down.

Something was not right. I lost sight of the horizon. The engine roared louder, straining. I could see the airspeed indicator needle racing through the yellow arc toward the red line. When the horizon reappeared, the road was not straight ahead, but off at a right angle. Ahead was water, and we were rapidly diving toward it with the left wing down. I pulled back on the stick as the airspeed needle crossed the red line. I lost my peripheral vision as I watched the needle reverse direction and move back across the red line and into the yellow. I pushed the stick right and the wings leveled out. My heart pounded, keeping time with my rapid shallow breaths. My head felt light as my vision cleared. I looked at the G-meter needle. It had passed six. Finally, it occurred to me to pull back the power, the simple move that would have helped greatly had I thought about it seconds before.

After climbing back up to a few thousand feet above the road,

I flew straight, thinking about what I had done and what had gone wrong. The fourteen pages had stressed "think loop and roll, all at the same time." I remembered the caution that most pilots pulled too weakly at the start. That must have been my problem.

I began again. When I pulled up, I added a little extra force, and started to roll. Again, the engine roared, too loud as the nose dropped. My airspeed was accelerating too fast and the needle raced again through the yellow arc toward the dreaded red line. I pulled back on the stick, this time remembering to ease back the throttle as well. Heart and lungs lurched through the same terror drill, but my eyesight stayed clear. The G-meter only registered five on this attempt. I was making a major mistake, but did not know what it was.

That was enough excitement for one day. I could only terrify myself so often. For another twenty minutes, I flew the aerobatic maneuvers I already knew. How satisfying it was to spin around two and three times, nose spiraling down toward my road, then stop it with Nanna's nose heading straight along the centerline. What fun it was to pull up hard with wings level and look out over my left shoulder to watch the horizon turn upside down as I grew light in my seat, momentarily flying upside down, then throwing my head back to watch the earth reappear as we dove down the backside of the loop and pulled up to level again. These maneuvers I could do effortlessly, intuitively. Before starting, all I needed to do was think through the sequence briefly, and then let my senses take over from my brain. I felt like two people at once, one moving the controls, the other riding and enjoying the feelings of exhilaration.

Back home, I opened the manuals and flew the barrel roll in my head until I knew what I needed to do. Days later, I flew again. No barrel roll resulted from my efforts, just more new and inventive ways of scaring myself. I studied harder and tried again. For months, I felt that the harder I tried, the worse I got.

Still, I kept at it. At the beginning of every practice, I would try one or two barrel rolls. One day, I told myself, it would click. At least the consequences of my errors were lessening. I saw fewer excursions toward the red line and stresses less than four times earth's gravity.

It was winter and colder when Nanna and I completed what I could call an honest-to-gosh barrel roll. I had swapped my canvas helmet for leather, added a sweater beneath my flight suit. The practice session began with the usual failed attempt. As I struggled again to think through what I was doing wrong, I decided to quit thinking so much about it and just imagine tracing a large circle on the horizon. I had nothing to lose, practiced as I was in recovering from mistakes and living with fear. As I began, I did not pull up quite as hard as I should for a loop, just enough to get the nose heading up the circle. Then I began laying Nanna over on his left side. Like magic, he rolled over the top, his right wing dropped as his nose fell through the horizon, and suddenly we were back where we started. I checked all the gauges. We had lost too much altitude and the circle we drew probably looked more like a misshapen egg, but the airspeed never hit yellow and the G-meter moved only slightly. My heart did not throb, nor did my breathing pick up. It was a start.

We flew a half dozen more. As I finished each one, I laughed. I was that kid again, training wheels off, riding my bike through the neighborhood like a big girl.

"Winds two four zero at fifteen, gusting to twenty," the Dallas briefer said.

Perfect, I thought. The winds would be a direct crosswind at the airport where I would practice and right at Nanna's published limitations, with the gust sometimes a little more. I had not forgotten my horrible crosswind landing at Destin, Florida, but had sworn to myself that I would never repeat it.

On that awful day, Howard had been flying as we crossed Florida, east to west, approaching the panhandle.

"There they are," he said.

"Yep, we're about at the Gulf coast," I responded, looking toward the summer afternoon buildup of cumulous clouds offshore. I had been daydreaming when I felt the first buffets warn us of what lay ahead. To continue meant missing a long stretch of scenic coast and flying farther inland. "Too early to stop, don't you think? Want me to take it?"

"Sure," Howard said, releasing the controls.

Instead of a scenic adventure that afternoon, we would have a weather skills adventure. Then perhaps the following morning in calmer air, we would be able to fly long stretches of coastline on the way to Mobile and New Orleans.

So far, we had encountered little weather on our Dixie Trip. That afternoon, to the north the skies were friendly and blue with a few dollops of white, but to the south lay the thick, tightly curled clouds of the gathering storm. The adventure started as the kind of flying challenge I love. I could test the edges of the weather over friendly, flat terrain, experimenting with altitudes and winds. If anything started getting dicey, we could sidle north out of its way, or turn sharply to outrun it if necessary. The trick was not trapping ourselves between the solid southern squall line and any surprises that might develop to the north.

The sky changed constantly as clouds grew or disappeared, blew closer or farther away. A few clouds to the north began to appear larger. Warily, I kept my eye on them as we passed through a wide canyon where the winds picked up at first, then died. All the while, I kept my eye on the many military routes and practice areas along our course as well as locations and heights of communications towers.

"That next one looks pretty nasty," Howard said with his head turned at an angle to the south. I could not see his face in the front cockpit, but could hear an edge of nervousness in his voice.

"Sure does," I said and banked to the north, having just passed a culprit in that direction that no longer presented a challenge. I looked at the ground below, picking out my next emergency landing spot as I let go of my road to the south. We continued dodging for a while until the inland clouds disappeared and only those well offshore remained. The turbulence settled out and a more consistent head-on wind hit us.

"I'm pretty tired." The sort of flying we had been doing was wearying. I had been on edge, gauging the danger posed by each obstacle along our path, making constant decisions. I worried about Howard's comfort level, too.

"Let's stop at Destin," Howard said, raising his head after studying his chart.

I spotted the airport on my chart. "Works for me."

We flew along the coast, low and far enough offshore that the sunning crowds along the way would see us but not be overwhelmed by our rumbling engine. At Destin gusty winds prevailed. They blew generally across the runway, but in erratic ways that would make a landing tricky.

As we flew the downwind leg of the traffic pattern, I grew eager to be on the ground. I needed to rest. On final, I knew I was in for a real challenge. One moment the wind would be strong and steady so that Nanna's lowered wing and opposite rudder kept us tracking along the centerline heading toward the runway. As we descended, the winds became gustier. I could not keep us heading straight. My hope that the wind would calm down close to the ground disappeared as we neared touchdown. Things did not look good. I pushed the throttle forward. We stopped descending and began climbing with Nanna's wings rocking back and forth from the vagaries of the wind.

"Going around," I called over the radio. I knew of no other traffic landing or departing. I wished that we were not either. I was concerned about the combination of my crosswind skill level and growing fatigue.

By the time I reestablished Nanna on downwind, my concern had grown into a fear that I might make a very rough landing. The winds blew stronger and choppier as we neared the runway for the second time. The final descent felt a bit smoother than the first, everything was looking good and stable enough, although I had to move the controls continuously to compensate for buffets. My feet pushed the rudders like circus performer balancing a board on a ball, trying to maintain equilibrium. How I hoped that I would not need to go around again. I was so tired. I felt like any landing, no matter how ugly, would suit me fine.

Within a few feet of touching down the landing fell apart. A gust of wind pushed me sideways so that when the wheels touched they were heading sideways as well as forward. The right wing dipped, nearly touching the concrete. We swerved far to the right, heading off the runway. Soon, Nanna was rolling along the grass that sloped away from the runway. I yelped like a horrified roller coaster rider, amazed at what was turning into my worst ever landing. I corrected with too much left rudder and careened back toward the concrete, Nanna's wings bobbing back and forth like a berserk seesaw. Terrified, I felt myself giving up. Whatever happened next would have to happen. I could think of nothing else to do to stop the gyrations that multiplied with every action. It was too late to add power and fly off for a third try. I felt like the Sorcerer's Apprentice, beating off one water-carrying broom, only to see two more arise. Then, miraculously, it was over. We were back on the runway, rolling slowly toward the parking area. My muscles felt as stiff as frozen meat. We stopped and I climbed down from the wing, waiting for the adrenaline to settle.

"I had my heart in my mouth for you," said the first of several spectators to rush toward us, a sunburned local pilot with a sagging waistline and baseball cap, "but you pulled it off okay. We come out to watch when it's windy like this." (One rule of flying states that all bad landings will be witnessed.)

Later at the hotel after I had settled down, Howard held me by the shoulders, looked me in the eyes, and said, "You could have really hurt us."

"I know. I'm sorry." I was exhausted and still terrified at what I had almost done.

That landing at Destin was why, on a windy Saturday in Dallas Texas, just before the cold front passed through the area, I took Nanna out to practice crosswind landings. We flew alone. The sky was overcast, the low clouds moving east at a rapid pace.

Two larger, more stable planes were already in the pattern when Nanna and I arrived at a barren Frisco Airport. Someone had once made grander plans for hangars and businesses there, but those had fallen along the wayside. Only a couple of structures and weeds rose among unused concrete taxiways. A high-winged Cessna fought the winds and bounced twice on the runway, barely under control as we joined the pattern ahead of another aircraft, a low-wing Twin Comanche. Here we were, three gluttons out for punishment.

"Great Lakes biplane, left base, three-five, low pass." I announced my intentions to the pilots on the airport frequency and listened to the calls of the two other planes as they turned each corner of the traffic pattern.

"Going around," the landing pilot radioed, aborting his landing attempt. Hmmm. If his airplane could not handle the wind, Nanna would not stand a chance.

I did not plan to land on the first pass anyway. Instead, we would fly a few feet above the runway to feel how the winds blew. Gusts might be slight or heavy, strong in one spot and weak in another. Before attempting to land on the second pass, I needed to find out how difficult the landing would be. The runway was long, so I could choose to land on the calmest section. If I could not handle the wind, we had plenty of fuel and time to retreat to another airport with a runway facing more directly into the wind, or we could fly around until winds died down. I took a deep breath and shrugged my shoulders to try to relax. Everything I could do to reduce the pressure had been done.

The Cessna ahead of me climbed away from the runway as we turned onto final approach and continued our descent. If the winds had been straight with the runway, Nanna's nose would have pointed straight ahead. They were not, so I pointed his nose nearly forty-five degrees the left to compensate for the crosswind and keep us tracking in a straight line toward the runway. Pilots call this crabbing, named for that creature's sideways motion. The feeling was like side slipping down a ski slope, facing in one direction, and traveling in another. If I kept pointing this way until the wheels touched, they would hit sideways instead of rolling onto the concrete and Nanna would lurch forward and probably flip over on his back. The next trick was to dip the left wing down while pushing the right rudder to swing the nose around straight. If pushing the rudder all the way to the firewall did not swing the nose straight with the runway, then I knew the wind exceeded aircraft limitations. There was another technique I could use to stretch those limitations a bit, but that took another skill, one I hoped to practice that day.

About a quarter mile from the beginning of the runway, I pushed the rudder to the firewall. Nanna's nose swung right, but stayed cocked to the left a few degrees as we leveled off a few feet above the runway. I pushed the throttle forward to keep us from touching down and tried to fly Nanna right above the centerline. The first gust of wind popped us up higher and farther right. When it passed, we sunk a bit and I had to adjust the controls. We passed the windsock at midfield. It looked like an orange log perpendicular to the runway instead of a limp fabric tube. Nanna and I struggled together like a quarter horse and rider cutting a heifer from the herd, changing our balance and direction to keep the wind from pushing us away. Where a farm-to-market road marked the northern boundary of the airfield, I saw a car slowing as we closed the short distance between us. I pushed the throttle full forward and Nanna shot skyward.

The second time around, I decided to try for a landing. I could feel the tension building in my stomach and shoulders, my teeth clinching. To give me better control of the landing, we would approach with extra speed and touch on the windward main wheel first instead of on all three wheels at once at a slower stalling speed. As we flew downwind, I had to point Nanna's nose away from the runway, or else we would have drifted back to it like a boat carried toward a dock by the current. I reduced the power and moments later turned toward the unforgiving line of concrete with the wind at our back. It pushed us so fast that I had to turn onto final right away. As we turned, the wind kept blowing us away from the runway until I got Nanna's nose pointed back into a sharp angle into the wind. The runway grew larger and closer as I fought to crab on a straight track toward the number painted at the start of the runway.

I dipped my left wing and pushed in the right rudder. The wind was too strong. I would not be able to land with the basic crosswind technique. Nanna did line up straight with the runway, but began moving away like the boat now drifting away from the dock. I had to dip the wing even farther to struggle back to centerline, but had no right rudder left to swing the nose straight. Seconds later, we were just a dozen feet off the runway and I had to decide whether to attempt the landing. If the wind weakened at all closer to the runway, we would be okay. My fingers tightened on the throttle. The fear of another Destin landing gripped me and I shoved the control forward. Nanna roared and his wheels leapt away, never touching the hard, unforgiving surface. My heart raced and my breathing quickened.

This was not going to work. I was not good enough to land in these winds. I thought about going home, but the runway direction and winds there were nearly the same as here at Frisco. I might as well keep practicing flying the windy patterns and holding a straight line right down the runway until the wind changed. Either a weaker wind or a change in direction would improve my chances of landing. I felt relieved. Nothing about the new practice plan terrified me. We would not touch down. The flight had become fun again.

Around and around we went, crabbing, dipping wings, pushing rudders, and moving the throttle forward just before touch down. The wind ceased being a mysterious adversary and became a sparring partner. I looked forward to the surprise of a surge here, a little gust there. I loved the way Nanna exploded skyward over the road at runway's end like a puppet yanked up by the strings. The wind direction did not change, nor did the strength with which it blasted the windsock at midfield.

We had been flying for thirty minutes. On downwind again I pulled back the power and banked once toward the runway, then again onto final with a perfect crab in place. We descended to within a dozen feet of the runway before dipping a wing. I pushed the rudder a bit harder than before. I felt calm, relaxed, knowing there was no chance that we would land hard or careen off the runway, because I did not intend to touch down.

Yet, there we were in perfect position to land. My fingers touched the throttle lightly, ready to push it forward again. I sensed the sides of the runway rushing past straight and true. Our airspeed was a touch faster than normal landing speed, just right for such a crosswind landing. Nanna's left wheel was poised no more than a foot above the concrete. Without thinking, I shifted my fingers ahead of the throttle, ready to pull, not push. I let Nanna's left wheel touch. I heard the chirp. I held the stick firmly toward the wind and eased it forward to keep the tail in the air. We rolled along on one wheel until gravity pulled down the right main wheel. I pulled the throttle back, we slowed, and the tailwheel dropped as all surfaces stopped lifting. As we rolled, I felt the wind pushing and easing, pushing and easing along my side. I pulled off the runway.

"Biplane, clear of the active," I radioed to nobody in particular.

The other two airplanes had flown away long before. (Another rule of flying states that the best landings will never be witnessed.)

I let my head drop back against the headrest. Above, the clouds raced east as they had all afternoon. I sat for a while and watched them. I listened for the monster that had tried again to terrify me—he was gone.

A bogeyman will always lurk somewhere ready to reach out his boney fingers and grab me. I no longer check under my bed for the one that once lived there. He left my bedroom when I was still a girl. He moved into deep, murky water of lakes and rivers where he grew long fangs to nibble at my toes if I fell from my water skis. The one that ran alongside my bicycle, once I banished him, may have sprouted wings to lie in wait for me in the skies. My bogeyman belongs to an endangered species with a shrinking habitat. No longer can he thrive in hostile terrain, around the edges of bad weather, or within aerobatic envelopes. Nor may he crouch beside windswept runways. He will confront me again, no doubt, but not in those places. He may loiter around power lines on an Oklahoma river. He surely hibernates near Timber Basin.

I will have to go looking for him.

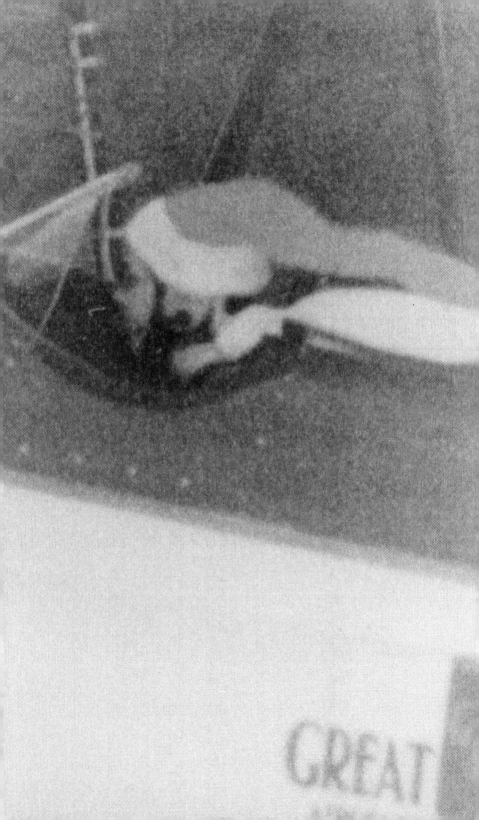

GREAT

Holiday Greetings

The tradition began innocently enough that first year. My annual holiday greeting card would picture Nanna. He was the new baby, by far the most colorful news item of my year.

The restoration was complete, but his bright and glowing paint had not yet met the wind aloft, grounded as he was awaiting government paperwork. One afternoon in December, I loaded Santa Claus caps and a dozen red poinsettias in their shiny foil-wrapped pots into the Jeep and drove the short trip to Santa Paula. Howard and I pushed Nanna out to an uncluttered spot on the taxiway with the golden hills in the background and began placing the red flowers in various configurations. By the time we lost the afternoon light, we had dozens of shots from which to choose. The project had been a simple, fun outing.

The second year was nearly as casual an undertaking on a mild late fall day. We had moved to Texas and discovered our favorite grass strip, so we set Nanna out grazing in the grass, long and green from recent rains. We relaxed in the foreground with holiday headwear and sweet grass dangling from our mouths.

The next year, the project began expanding. We enlisted Jeff, the foreman of the ranch on which our favorite grass strip lay to assist us by supplying a farm animal. The early fall day we were set to shoot, we climbed out of Nanna in our blue jeans and cowboy boots with colorful bandanas around our necks as he came galloping up on a gray horse with long mane and tail blowing in the wind. I attached a large velvet bow to Champ's halter. Jeff maneuvered him into position in front of Nanna, and I mounted up and adjusted the poinsettia on my cowboy hat. Howard stood on the ground. Champ, a rodeo performer, turned his head to show off the bow. This photo had begun the problem.

"Mom, everyone at the restaurant loved your card again. They can't wait to see next year's," Allison said as we spoke over the phone on Christmas Day.

"Uh, I don't think we'll top Champ."

"Of course you will. You'll think of something. We're counting on it."

The pressure was on. Family and friends had begun commenting how much they enjoyed the card and that they shared it with their friends, who had begun asking if our card had arrived yet. Nanna's holiday card was being passed around like a letter from the front.

By the following March, I had begun considering possibilities. So far, all the photos had shown Nanna on the ground. This year, I would try for an aerial shot. What had involved just a casual afternoon with a couple of people and a tripod had expanded to include a third party and an animal. Now I was facing an even larger project involving major logistics.

"Sure, I'll fly the photo plane for you," said Chuck. He had seen Nanna parked and me lying on my blue cloth reading at our favorite grass strip. Chuck had just landed his unique Bird Dog in the precise way he always did. He touched down right at the end of the grass strip, dead on an imaginary centerline, and rolled out only a short distance. Chuck was the kind of man who took a quiet pleasure in the skill and precision of his flying without requiring an audience or adulation. His high-wing plane was mostly fabric, the military version of the ubiquitous, perky yellow Piper Cub, but painted olive drab with Italian Air Force insignia. Such aircraft had been the most feared by enemy troops during wars past—to see one poking along on patrol overhead meant that deadly, heavily armed brothers would be along soon to pick off them off.

"That'd be great. I'll recruit a photographer."

Recruiting Bruce as photographer was easy. The flying bug had bitten him when he flew in Nanna, and he had begun taking lessons. The prospect of flying in another different airplane drew him immediately to the team. Getting photographer Bruce, pilot

Chuck and his plane, Nanna, Howard, and me together in the same point in space at one time with decent weather and good light proved more difficult. By the time we all stood together on the grass getting ready to launch, months had elapsed. I had begun to worry that the shoot would not come off in time, I would have to send out store-bought cards, and a raft of disappointed recipients would call, "Gee, we were expecting another airplane picture."

"You just fly straight and level and I'll maneuver around you," Chuck said. He had latched open the window and door of his airplane so Bruce could shoot unobstructed under the high right wing.

"Right. I plan to fly around the swampy north end of Lake Lewisville. Try to get that deep red stuff for background. What speed?" We agreed to fly a speed slow for Nanna, the faster plane, but good for the Bird Dog to be able to maneuver. As we spoke, I attached Santa hats to both brown leathers flying helmets with large safety pins. I pulled mine on, tucked in loose bits of hair, and around my neck double-knotted my white silk scarf. The bulging round ears of my headset protruded beneath the fuzzy white band of my cap and the cord dangled from my hand. Judging from the grin on Chuck's face, we would achieve the desired effect.

As I handed Howard his scarf and Santa helmet, he finished briefing Bruce on Robo-Cam, so named because of its automatic and foolproof nature. I hoped it would perform as expected. The sky was a bit cloudy, so lighting presented additional complications. My recent nightmare was that we would complete the aerial shoot and find all the shots blurred, poorly framed, or with Bird Dog wing struts running through the middle. A second attempt in time for this season would be impossible. My confidence was waning as we prepared to takeoff.

Once airborne, I released the ends of my hat and scarf into the slipstream. I had worn a scarf once before, so I was not surprised when it tugged at my throat, choking me mildly. The pointed tail of the Santa hat yanked at my head. I strained my neck to keep my head in a more natural forward position. Suddenly I saw something flash by on my left side. It looked as though it had come from Howard's cockpit.

"What was that?" I asked him over the intercom

"I lost my scarf." He had failed to tie a double knot.

"I'm glad I didn't give you the silk one, then. Shoot, we'll only have one now." The shot I had imagined, with the two perky scarves and Santa hats blowing was not to be.

We flew for about an hour, the Bird Dog bobbing and weaving around us over farmland and reservoirs as we headed for patches of light breaking through the layer of clouds. I tried to position Nanna over colorful backgrounds and against clouds. Finally, Chuck called over the radio that we had shot all the film. We flew back to the field and landed.

When the prints came back a few days later, several shots looked workable, but one was an excellent candidate but for a single uncorrectable flaw. It showed Nanna from the top down flying over the reservoir which made the overall photo a peaceful one in shades of blue, highlighted by two wooly red hats with white bands and pom pom tips straight out in the wind. Enough sunlight had broken through the clouds to show the ripples in the water. A bit of land showed in the lower corner, but could easily be cropped out. My scarf flowed artfully against the fuselage behind the back cockpit. The problem was that Howard's scarf flew like a pennant from the wires on Nanna's tail. Most of if blended with the light paint, but some of the end jutted out into the blue of the water.

"No one will ever notice it, Anne," Howard said.

I sighed. "I hope not. As Mother would say, 'You'll never know the difference on a galloping horse.' Let's hope she is right."

I mailed the cards and waited for the reactions.

"Wow, Mom. You came through. Everyone at the restaurant

loved you card. We can't wait for next year."

"Allison, I really don't think I can keep making this more spectacular, so don't expect too much next time."

"Oh, sure."

Others said about the same thing. Again, we heard stories of recipient's friends asking to see the card. Thankfully, not a soul mentioned, if they noticed at all, the runaway scarf. I scolded myself for being such a worry wort.

Later that winter, I flew to the grass strip at El Dorado for Nanna's annual. No sooner had I pulled up to the hangar door than Brent Patty walked outside, wiping an airplane part with an oily rag. I shut down the engine and pulled off my helmet.

"Hi," he said moving toward the cockpit. "We enjoyed your card again this year. Howard lost his scarf, huh?"

I have given up the notion that my holiday cards will be perfect or that ratcheting down expectations regarding them is possible. When packing for our flying vacation in Africa the following year, I tossed in the Santa hats. They did look stunning on us beside the rental airplane as we petted the trunk of a large bull elephant with others of the herd in the background. I failed the year after to convince the White House to let Nanna park near Air Force One's nose at an airport in Texas while the President was visiting his ranch. Instead, I borrowed Roy, a neighbor's longhorn steer, for the photo. He looked loveable beside Nanna with a garland around his neck. Not once did he try to gore Nanna.

A Short List of Very Important Rules

"Seat Belts?"

"On."

"Door?" Howard arrived at my little role in the preflight checklist.

"Closed and latched," I responded as I bumped hard against the metal door that opened onto the wing. I sat in the right seat of the Mooney. A few moments earlier, I had performed another task, watching the fuel flow from the belly drain and confirming to Howard that the flow stopped and the dribbling ceased when he closed the valve from its floor position in the enclosed cabin. My assistance as the outside observer meant that he did not have to climb outside again to look. Those tasks were the extent of my obligations when we traveled from point A to point B in Mr. Mooney, leaving Nanna behind in his hangar.

Howard did all the rest. I felt secure knowing that the weather had been thoroughly considered and every detail of the route had been planned. From the right seat, I helped with tasks upon request, such things as dialing radio frequencies and transponder squawk codes. I also watched for other airplanes in the sky. Typically, I saw an airplane long before he did, if he saw it at all. Howard was the one who labored over a flight plan precisely documented in a folder assembled for that specific flight. Weather information printouts and notes from the weather briefer conversation earlier that morning had been assembled just so. He had called the airport where he knew we would land. Somewhere ahead a rental car agent would have filed our paperwork, and Howard would know the agent's dog's name. A hotel reservation system would know the day and hour of our arrival.

The man left nothing to chance. To arrive at the precise moment noted on the last line of the flight plan brought a smile to his face. To have predicted accurately the amount of fuel consumed evoked a mental thumbs up.

When we fly Nanna, the preparation job is mine. In good conscience, I could not describe what I do as planning.

"Let's try the Southeast, take up a heading and turn left at the Mississippi," I said, kneeling before a map of the United States spread before me on the carpet. My finger sketched a line, and then meandered about a few states and paused on the few specific places we had in mind to stop, like Kitty Hawk. My finger proceeded along the Atlantic coast to Florida and along the Gulf of Mexico and back to Dallas. I picked up a sectional chart and noted which charts we needed to buy to cover my finger's journey. That did it for route planning. All the summer trips have used this method.

Weather checking was a day-to-day activity. If a briefer painted a foreboding picture in one direction, we headed another. If the weather was foul in all directions, we found a pleasant place to sit and read until it improved. Most times, unless the forecast was dire and widespread, we launched and looked, traveling as far as the actual weather conditions allowed. We never wound up turning back to the airport where we started the day. Most weather briefers did not know how different flying low and slow in a biplane was from flying higher where clouds and visibility present many more problems, so they often gave me an overly conservative picture. I chuckled when they warned me "Icing above ten thousand" or "VFR not recommended" and painted a picture of cloud layers starting two thousand feet above the ground, an altitude I rarely reached.

To set out on these trips with only a set of charts and a rough heading required a shift in mindset from regular life, particularly for anyone who was analytical, disciplined, and driven by objectives like me. To satisfy my right brain, I have listed a few very important rules.

Decide how long the trip will be. A trip must last at least two weeks, preferably a month. Anything shorter will introduce anxiety and stress and not allow enough time to decompress from whatever you do the rest of the year. It is time available that determines the geography covered, not the other way around.

Buy charts. Get all the ones covering specific areas that look interesting and a few more of others nearby in case you change your mind. Buy duplicates if carrying a passenger.

Count socks and underwear. Carry about a weeks worth. A washing machine will always pop up somewhere before you need it. Pack light and only for probable weather. Amazingly, you can buy most anything else along the way in a pinch. All suitable clothing is cheap.

Work on the airplane. Be sure that the craft is in tip-top condition. Get all the little nagging things that might turn into big deals taken care of before launch.

Do not turn a flying adventure into a tourist or social event. If you drop in on friends and family, it is hit or miss. Mine have grown accustomed to it. This rule I developed on our first "Dixie" trip, which included three stops to visit family and wound up having us spend too much time on the ground. Since you cannot appear everywhere in bib overall shorts and grimy T-shirts worn day after day, and too many earthbound events will disturb your desired head-in-the-clouds mental state, don't get caught up in the idea that you need to see and do such and such "…since I'm so close by." If you have lived without seeing something for your whole life so far, you can live without out it this time, too.

Do not imagine a specific adventure. Do not let yourself care where you are going, even if you have in mind stopping at a particular place. When something goes wrong or some opportunity presents itself, and it always does, tell yourself "Okay, so now I'll have a different adventure." If you know where you are going to be more than a day out, you have probably goofed.

Do not look at pictures of areas you might visit. If you seek out these images, you will rob yourself of the thrill of surprise and discovery. Charts will give hints of what is to come, but they only heighten the anticipation without spoiling the experience.

What Are They Thinking?

I wrestled myself out of the cockpit. My face was salty, grimy, and slick with sunscreen. My bib overall shorts were crumpled and swiped with the oil I had wiped from the cowling that morning. My cropped hair, smashed flat by a canvas flying helmet, erupted in sprigs from beneath a baseball cap, a device I rely upon to turn chaos into order. In short, I looked a fright. Nanna, on the other hand, looked smashing, as he always does, even when dust dulls his sheen, mud and muck splatter his fabric wings, or grass trails from his wheels.

Together we stood on an airport ramp nestled among hills covered with mesquite and live oak with scrubby brush and grass in between, a stop on the way to the Big Bend. The main runway on which we had landed was paved and long, but a shorter crosswind runway cut through the brush. I wished I had noticed that one while still in the air. Nanna was the only airplane around, the only sound was a bird singing in the distance.

"Quiet here," I said to the airport manager who strolled from the office to assist in fueling.

"Should've been here yesterday. First day of hunting season. Planes in and out of here all day long dropping hunters off."

"Should I worry, flying low? They wouldn't shoot at us would they?"

"I'd be careful." He said it in an altogether serious way.

Another old aircraft, a high-winged Maule, pulled up besides us at the pumps. I struck up a conversation with the pilot, a local, as I puttered about checking oil, peering at tires, and finding a ladder. He walked around Nanna for a view from one angle, then another, and uttered a string of complimentary words. Like most others over the years, he chose to include "beautiful."

"He loves to be admired. Go ahead and take a closer look from the wing walk, if you'd like," I said, and as I walked toward the fuel pump, threw in, "He flies better than he looks." Out of the corner of my eye, I watched as biplane magic swept over my new pilot acquaintance. I knew what he was thinking.

Other times, though, what did people think, not pilots like the two of us on the ramp, but people who cared little or nothing about airplanes? When Nanna and I were away from airports, not close up and stationary like this with his chunky tires firmly planted and four wings locked parallel to the ground, but up in the air buzzing around, how did ordinary people feel about us and what we did, how we played?

Since I could not know, I wondered. Then, I fretted. Were people below disturbed, worried, or annoyed, even angry with us? Or did the sight and sound of a biplane overhead stir in them the same joy, the sweet taste of freedom that I experienced flying above, watching them? In the end, I chose to believe my own stories about every encounter, gay ones ending with smiles. To justify these stories, I sometimes had to seize upon the smallest shreds of evidence. Still, deep down, I worry that my gift of a noisy old flying machine overhead might not be welcomed, that I may have become like the child raising a pet rat toward a horrified matron and asking, "Grandma, wanna pet Stinky?"

Soon, we departed from the bumpy grass runway climbing an extra five hundred feet. I did not want to present an easy target for any lurking, trophy-hungry redneck with one too many brews down his gullet. The seat on which I sat was metal, but I did not think my otherwise wood-and-fabric cocoon would stop much of a bullet. The country below was rugged and parched, riverbeds dry, vegetation colored subtle grays and sage greens against pale and sandy soil. I saw few buildings, and the road we followed had neither power lines nor telephone wires. Before long, I spotted some pickup trucks and a camp. Three men dressed in camouflage stood as though talking and looked up as I flew by. What the heck, I decided, and made a diving turn back to circle them several times. All waved and raised their weapons of choice toward me—beverage cans. I wagged Nanna's wings in return. Thumbs up for Texas hunters.

I am not sure what farmers think of us. On another trip, flying south of the Milk River and Highway 2, west of Williston and east of the new airport at Malta, North Dakota, a yellow harvesting machine tracked back and forth across the amber waves of grain of America's great breadbasket. The day was mild and bright, and we had carved many more days from busy lives to wander about the big sky country. We turned away from the road and headed out to meet the driver of the big machine. The farmer's wake of short stubble on an even field looked suitable for landing should the need arise. Adrift and lonely in this ocean of wheat stretching far beyond the horizon, the farmer faced endless labor, a solitary soul lost is the details of his task and likely a hundred other concerns of a farmer's life. For a time the sound of the Caterpillar muffled our rumbling approach as we spiraled down around him. When our shadow flickered across his path, he raised his face, shadowed by the bill of his cap, and watched as we flew out of the sun low on the horizon and circled. He did not wave, nor did he smile. I like to imagine that he enjoyed the break in routine, that in the evening as the screen door of the farmhouse squeaked and banged behind him, he said, "You'll never guess what I saw today, Jennie."

More often than farmers at work in their fields, we see drivers and passengers as we travel low alongside their automobiles and trucks on freeways and country roads. My closest encounter with them came the afternoon I wondered if we were following the right interstate through Arizona. For confirmation, I pushed Nanna low over the highway median looking for a bold "I-10" on a green sign. Eastbound motorists saw a biplane dive in over their heads from behind, fly level for a few seconds, then pop up like a kite rising on a strong wind and inch away toward New Mexico. Drivers traveling in the opposite direction saw that same plane nose over as though coming toward them for a strafing run, hesitate at the bottom of the arc, then hurl its wings skyward and disappear in their rear view mirrors. Whatever stories they made up that day about us, I am sure that not a one was about a mother and daughter trying not to get lost on the way to grandmother's house.

Sometimes drivers and passengers know exactly what we are doing. In Lawrence, Kansas, after waiting overnight with a stranded flock of pilots for a stationery front to lift, Nanna, the plane best suited for low, slow flight made the first break for it. Visibility had improved beneath the lifting clouds. Aloft, throttled back even slower than our usual pace and heading toward Iowa, we radioed condition reports back to the pilots we left behind as we passed cars and pickups on the wet roads below. If the ceiling dropped farther instead of rising as expected, we might need a stretch of road to set down, so we followed the winding pavement like a skater tracing school figures. The vehicles we passed knew we were fighting weather, driving north just like them, only a bit higher.

Trains, trapped on a course, moving slowly, are great partners for a biplane. To gambol near one inching along a track is like playing a flute's sprightly counterpoint above the steady melody of an oboe. Whenever I saw the freight train that ran from north of Lake Lewisville toward Denton, we would swoop in from the front of the train, dive toward the track, pull up as the engine neared, and pivot overhead to chase alongside, wagging wings and waving to the engineer as we passed. For a passenger train rolling through the open New Mexico countryside, we flew from back to front low alongside, hoping to surprise the passengers with a "Biplane and Buttes" picture for their scrapbook of memories. I enjoy the thought that a passenger might have snapped a photo as we flew alongside, that Nanna might enjoy a bit of immortality among the world's travelers.

On airport ramps, picture taking is a common activity, and I coach photographers regularly. "Your best shot would be from behind and off to one side," I suggest, checking the sun's position. The first impulse of the man in Bermuda shorts and polo shirt with the camera had been to stand nose to nose. The angle he had chosen would show that the airplane was a biplane, but the wings would look like two uninteresting parallel lines. When the vacationer looked at the photo later, he would wonder why it looked so mundane when he remembered that the biplane had seemed so special. That photo would display none of the features that made Nanna unique: the blue-scalloped wings; the way the pale blue stripe accented the darker upper fuselage along both cockpits and curved up gracefully at the base of the rounded tail, drawing the admirer's eye; and the large, rounded blue feather with perky splits that filled the tail with wonder.

He snapped one full frontal shot and then moved around to the back where I had pointed. "Here?"

"Can you see the feather and do the wings fill the frame?"

"Yep."

"You got it. Trust me. I've tried all the angles."

This was almost the top-down, quartering shot I strive to present to photographers when we are in the air, as well, like the afternoon we flew along the Outer Banks. We had been flying above clear waters as the waves broke and pushed their foam toward pale, sandy shores. In the distance against the bright sky rose what looked like a lone stick rising from the flatness. I nosed Nanna over to drop lower. Soon, the pole grew into a lighthouse, broad at the base, tapered at the top, Nags Head. A mile away, it showed more details, black and white stripes swirling upward to a circular observation platform near the top. Closer, people appeared along the rail, and at last we saw their cameras, all raised toward us. We flew slightly above them and up close. Nanna's right wing dipped low, its natural position for the turn, as we circled several times. Howard clicked away at the people on the lighthouse as they clicked away at us. On departure, we pulled up sharply and at an angle, presenting the top-down, quartering pose.

One final wing-wag, and off we flew. Nanna probably generated more exposed film in those few minutes than he ever had or ever will again.

Most people take only mental pictures, though. People without vehicles at play out of doors tend to demonstrate positive feelings, like the Texas hunters. My guess is that Nanna's image lives on in their memory books, and that once in awhile, one of them will remember and say "Remember that day we hunted, you know, when the biplane came around?"

On open waterways, most everyone carries on like Nanna's long lost pal. Our favorite approach to powerboats and jet skiers on a reservoir is a stealth entry from behind and well off to one side on a calm day. If we can maneuver to shadow-tag them as we pass, that is even better. As they focus on the water ahead, arms and legs glistening wet, plumes of water thrown up behind, I watch until their heads turn toward the engine noise gaining on them. They turn and look up as we waggle our wings and bank so they can see my hand wave, too. Their arms sway in huge arcs, as though signaling us to rescue them from a desert island. We circle, and then straighten out. Often they race us, but soon guess correctly that the biplane never loses these contests, and they resume their original course and speed.

Sailboats gliding along and Fishermen parked above tranquil pools in plain little metal boats sitting high in chairs telegraph serenity and a desire to remain so, so I take care to pass them from afar. Other parked boats invite the most boisterous fly bys. They are the party boats of a summer evening, lashed together in three's and four's, young people in shorts and bathing suits climbing back and forth across vessels to find the optimum partner or another cold drink. To these, I give special attention, lots of circling and waving, and sometimes even a farewell barrel roll as we depart.

My favorite water encounter occurred on a Saturday. I had risen early to fly in the cooler, still air of a Texas morning. We crossed over the south shore of the reservoir, and I saw boaters pulling ropes, hurling life jackets, hauling coolers, readying their crafts for the day's outing. Few had yet escaped the marina to disturb the reservoir beyond the inlet, still a green-tinted mirror. Far in the distance, I saw only one craft, so we were free to fly a few feet above the water along the shore, without worry of safe or legal distances from anyone. Nanna's wheels whispered across the trees that lined the inlet as we banked right along the shore and watched a few golfers strolling a fairway, a couple of others standing on a green, the grass under their feet still glistening from a sprinkling at dawn. Beyond the golf course lay waterside homes certain to hold late sleepers, so we turned left to drag our noise away toward a deserted shore ahead. As we pulled up slightly to hurdle the trees of the breakwater separating the northwest finger from the main body, I saw the picture that made me smile. Alone, at anchor floated a large, high-winged amphibious plane. Atop the wings in a low chair lounged a bronze man wearing bathing trunks and a narrow-brimmed hat. He read a newspaper and sipped a beverage. As we drew near and circled, he looked up and smiled. We waved at each other, not the boisterous wave of boaters and skiers, but the easy wave of kindred spirits, acknowledging how good life was with our airplanes.

I wonder sometimes about all the other people I have only imagined were down there watching. All my life, I have read biographies of pilots who described a childhood experience about seeing an airplane overhead and knowing right away that they wanted to fly, too, when they grew up. Yet, I have never noticed such a youngster as we flew over. Some boy or girl must have been sitting along the bank of the Mississippi when we skimmed the waters for miles. Some kid at an airport must have stood at the fence as Nanna's belly crossed overhead. I feel good thinking that maybe in some unseen corners Nanna and I have planted that dream of flight.

There are others among the unseen that bring me a twinge of

241

despair, those who want to dream such dreams, but dare not. I had an overwhelming sense of this the early morning we were flying alone along the Rio Grande east of the sheer cliffs of the Big Bend at a spot where the riverbank spread out broad and flat. I felt absolutely, utterly, blissfully alone in the middle of nowhere. In the joy of the moment, I tucked away all dangling objects and flew a few loops and rolls, laughing at first at the thought of what any viewer would make of such strange behavior. Then I thought, no, anyone would understand that this was typical behavior of an otter of the universe playing, no purpose required. Why, anyone would smile, perhaps laugh at the sight. I finished cavorting and looked south toward the rugged mountainsides of Mexico. A glance at my chart confirmed that I saw several mines. How sad it was to think that someone laboring hard for little reward in this life might have watched such playfulness and despaired that some lucky person who happened to have been born across that river could buy such a machine, take such a trip, and just play.

All these encounters were anonymous. Nobody knew Anne and Nanna, nor did I know the people named Bob, Pete, Joanne, Sally, and hundreds of others with whom I shared a moment and place in time.

Once I did know who lay below. It was over a year ago—long before fanatics with box cutters bullied the world into fearing every airplane—an early January morning. Howard, Nanna, and I launched southwest from Dallas on a mission of great importance to us, our second try at finding a particular ranch house south of Lake Whitney, west of Waco. The day was unseasonably warm, the sun shining, and the winds gentle. We approached from the north, picking up the railroad track near Valley Mills and following it south until we crossed a west fork of the Basque River. Turning west so we could see any ranch buildings between the river gulch and us, we studied every structure, looking for an old wood ranch house and a fence we had seen on a television news broadcast.

It was easier than we thought it would be. Police cars had already begun blocking the roads. Restricted airspace shaped like a giant tin can would drop onto this spot in another three hours, so this would be our last chance for perhaps eight years to make this flight. All we were after was a glimpse of the ranch.

Suddenly, out of a driveway, rolling slowly came three vehicles, heading toward the road that led to a newer ranch house. Nanna and I tried our darndest to look playful and harmless as we passed over the creeping motorcade. Then we spotted him, a man who was still just a citizen, but president-elect of the United States, and a couple of his Secret Service men leading the entourage. "Dubya" had been a pilot and was, like all Texans, a diehard protector and lover of freedom. On this day, sunny bright, worn out as he must have been from his recent election ordeal, what could have been more appealing than a well-wisher's playful salute, an aerial "Hail to the Chief." When the formation of three men split, the bodyguards spreading out and looking up to determine whether we were friend or foe, my heart sank a little. Here we were on a mission of frivolity and joy, yet they thought Nanna was a threat. Still, as we sidled away to confirm our friendly intent, circled the old ranch house, and wings-wagging, dipped low to depart along the river gulch, I choose to believe that George W. Bush smiled, even chuckled to his protectors "How about that – isn't that pretty, fellas?"

Recently, on a bright Sunday morning, I wondered about my new neighbors who lived under our traffic pattern. What did they think when they heard Nanna's low growl overhead, looked up from their driveways, newspapers in hand, and spotted him, then watched him glide toward them and purr as I cut back on his power, prepared to land, and then disappeared below the desert brush?

We landed, and as I finished fueling, two men bicycled along the low wood rail fence that divided the road from parked airplanes. As they spotted us and headed our way, I pushed the concerns about airport neighbors back in my Dungeon of Things to Fret About.

The cyclists were aging men, but fit and full of questions as they balanced on their bicycles and squinted at me. They wore helmets and sunglasses, casual slacks and shorts, and not the clinging, boldly decorated attire of serious cyclists.

"Where are you all from?" I asked.

"Just over there," one said and pointed to the northeast to the air we had just descended through to land. "Are you the one who flies over us in this?" He nodded toward Nanna.

"Yes, it would have to be me. He's one of a kind." Okay, I thought, now they are going to let me have it, me, the dastardly pilot out to terrorize their neighborhood, frighten their dogs, and worry their children. I did not need a conversation sure to dampen my spirits, high as they were from a fine morning flight. I put on my mental armor. "You all picked homes close to this airport. I do worry that I might disturb you, but can't help some noise."

He smiled, shaking his head, "Are you kidding? No, we love it. We watch you turn and the sun hits your wings. Oh no, you don't disturb us. We love to see you."

Yes. Oh, yes.

Creatures Great and Small

When I slid open the hangar door, a sparrow inside fluttered across the vast empty space and landed on a high windowsill. It must have been trapped overnight, I thought, since I had not seen it the previous day when I had rolled Nanna back into the hangar after a few practice takeoffs and landing. The bird flew out, inconvenienced, probably hungry, but healthy and maybe a bit wiser about enclosed airplane nests.

Any other day, that would have been the end of thinking about a creature, but not today. Since rising, I had been haunted by the tale told by another biplane pilot the night before at a fund raising event. I was sitting inside a neighbor's hangar on a metal chair, eating and making conversation with the pilot's wife. During a lull, I looked at a group of neighbor pilots standing outside. The sun was setting, so palo verde and saguaro glowed pale salmon, and the tanned faced of the pilots shone more bronze than usual. A breeze carried sounds of calling quail and cooing dove. Right outside, framed by the hangar opening, there it lay—drop-dead glorious nature.

The speaker was a beefy man, still working to shed the last layers of fat put on as protection against extreme cold for the flight he now recounted. He spoke with a deep, soothing voice in an engaging, personable style. His quest had taken him over large expanses of wilderness. His primary challenge had been the effects of extreme cold on both his airplane engine and his body. Boredom and loneliness had become secondary threats, though, traveling as he did for long hours over thousands of miles of wilderness.

Toward the end of one of the loneliest flight legs, he spotted a herd of caribou. Delighted to see other living creatures, he decided to buzz them. Facing extreme headwinds, his Stearman biplane flew across the ground much slower than usual, so he did not skim over the entire herd quickly, but gradually caught and passed the stampeding animals one by one. As the pilot gained on each frightened and tired animal, it angled off course and turned to face the menace, head bowed, prepared for a clash of antlers that would never come. Finally, only one buck remained ahead of the biplane, thundering on and on, far beyond the rest. The animal never turned to fight as the others had. Finally, unable to run farther, the animal dropped in its tracks. Circling the motionless beast, the pilot cried, sure that the animal had died. "I felt as though I died, too," he said.

In the morning, I thought about his incident and other encounters of biplane and creatures, many about which I have read, some that I have experienced.

My favorites are among the earliest encounters of beast and aerial man. In the milder climate of Kenya, Denys Finch-Hatton flew Karen Blixen in his Moth biplane along the Ngong Mountain across a wooded area to a clearing. As the couple circled and counted twenty-seven buffalo, the animals ceased grazing, bothered by the strange new sounds. One old bull looked up to challenge the roar overhead, and then led a stampede through the bush to a thicket well hidden from observers on the ground, yet visible the air. Another day, Denys and Karen launched for Lake Natron, an azure pool amid a large expanse of barren country, pale and etched like a bleached tortoise shell. As the plane approached, a resting blanket of pink flickered and fanned out, thousands of flamingos. On a third occasion, the flyers chased an eagle that toyed with Moth and, when Denys stopped his engine in mid-air, the bird screeched with surprise.

Creatures great and small got here first. Biplanes and the monoplanes that followed were the newcomers, the ones needing to find their proper place in the ancient kingdom. As aircraft matured, they left the low skies where animals and birds have lived forever. Collisions and near misses became limited to brief path crossings of landing and departing aircraft. But, old biplanes still swim in the lower currents of air and still struggle with citizenship there.

After every flight, I fill a bucket with water and wipe all Nanna's leading edges and wires, so I do not face a marathon wash every few months to remove sharp petrified masses. When I wipe the squished remains of tiny gnats and flies, I am delighted that they are gone and spend no time pondering their existence. Sometimes, my damp cloth comes upon a butterfly wing wrapped around a flying wire, and I feel a twinge of sorrow that my pleasure has cost the life of a beautiful creature that I have admired dancing along Nanna's wing while we rolled through the spring grass. Silly as it is to differentiate between the death of gnat and butterfly, if I were to find a bloody bird feather, my sense of loss would be greater still, although the chances are excellent that I would have noticed a bird strike long before the daily bath.

The bigger the critter, the worse it gets. When I took a mountain flying class, the petite, soft-spoken instructor asked us about contingency plans for one-way airstrips after we had committed ourselves to land. "Gosh, darn, look at those elk on the runway. You don't have room to go around—it's a tight canyon. What are you going to do?" She looked around the classroom, but nobody answered. "Hit 'em," she said. "You've got to do it. If you have to hit something, pick something that moves and can absorb energy. Big trees don't move." In these life and death decisions, trees and humans win and elks lose. Not happy choices, but necessary.

Another time when I left Nanna home in the U. S. to fly another plane in Africa, I felt no qualms about buzzing a runway to discourage lions or baboons from darting out of the surrounding bush to cross our path. I did not feel guilty when a ranger raced ahead of our departing plane, down the dirt runway in a Land Cruiser to scare off one Cape Buffalo, a dozen wart hogs, and a lone giraffe at the far end. Likewise, I was amused, not annoyed, dodging elephant dung while landing on a runway near the

Zambezi River. Nor, do I fret when deer, coyotes, or javelinas loitering along local taxiways and or trotting across runways at my new home airport inconvenience me. Inconvenience is okay, spice in the stew of life.

A reservoir in north central Texas drains south, leaving the northernmost end swampy or just damp in times of drought. During migrations north and south, flocks of water birds congregate there among the exposed tree stumps. This resting place lies along an old route to my favorite grass strip. Years ago, I delighted in coming upon egrets, which at the sound of Nanna's engine cleared a churning wake of white, beating along a few feet above the marsh to land again not far away as we passed and our engine noise faded. I learned over time the preferred altitudes for these egrets and other birds and how many would likely to be flying together, geese and ducks by the dozen, hawks alone or with a couple of hunting buddies. Never have we struck one. Rarely have we come close. The last two years that we crossed that reservoir, I changed our customary route. I did not do so because of any conscious decision. It just happened that one day, I found myself abandoning our straight path and circling west. We followed the tree-lined course of the river that meandered through the dry section of the reservoir. Another day we flew even farther west low above the flat damp, russet lichens that had taken over the silted area. We had begun skirting around the resting flocks. Most of the egrets paid no attention to our passing. Some stretched their beautiful long necks and raised their heads toward us. Occasionally, a pair of great white wings lifted into the air. That had become thrill enough for me. Nanna and I had found our place in the natural order.

We live farther west now, surrounded by mountains instead of the reservoirs of north Texas. Someday, we will fly north, explore a high mountain valley, and see a herd of wild horses. When we drop down to circle for a closer look, perhaps to admire new foals, the herd will hear Nanna's engine, become spooked, and run. When I add power to pull up and away, though, not a one will be dead.

Home by Christmas

"I don't know, Anne," Pam Burgy said over the telephone. "The weather is so iffy right now."

"If I'm up there when a window opens, I can launch. If I'm down here, it could take a couple of days to get there and I might miss it."

"You're probably right."

"Tony offered to pick me up at the airport on his way to your place. I'll see you Friday night."

After I hit the fence at Timber Basin, Howard and I hopped a commercial flight from Spokane and saw our three weeks of carefully knit time and distance from Dallas to Timber Basin unraveled with blistering speed and unrelenting efficiency by an airliner. Then Pam's husband John and Tony Blum set about repairing Nanna. During that summer and fall, I moved to Tucson. By late November, Nanna's repairs were complete, and I was looking for a weather window to retrieve him and bring him to his new home. The flying weather in Arizona was nearly perfect, but the wintry weather forecasts for Idaho were becoming more frequent. Anxious, I had begun pestering my friends every day. Finally, just a few weeks before the holidays, I decided to scoot up north, betting that I would find a way out.

Howard dropped me off at the airport. He had volunteered to come along, but I needed warmth in the back cockpit more than I needed company. For me to stay warm, I had to force the heat from the engine back toward me by zipping a cover over the front cockpit. Poof, no passenger. If he came along, precious heat would escape around him, and I would be like a winter hiker watching smoke rise from the chimney of a distant, snowed-in cabin. Besides, the trip would be miserably cold, probably with some snow and rain showers. I knew that he would not enjoy the flight. I was looking forward to the trip alone with constant problem solving, a good book to read while waiting for weather to clear, and my thoughts.

"I'll be home by Christmas," I said as I left him at the curb and slung my backpack on one shoulder. It contained my flight suit, radio and GPS, foul weather gear, charts, and all the sharp and pointy items disallowed in airplane cabins since the terrorist attacks three months earlier. I wore my more formal change of clothing—blue jeans, cotton turtleneck, a sweater, baseball cap, and my flying shoes, the ones with arrows and notes painted on the toes. I wish I had paid better attention to one of the shoes later that weekend—the one that said "Push Right Rudder."

Low clouds, rain, and snow at Timber Basin kept us indoors until Sunday morning. It was early afternoon, cold, and a metallic winter sun shone upon the white meadows and surrounding evergreen trees. The weather looked like it would hold for the rest of the afternoon. Yesterday, Tony had ploughed the snowed-in grass strip and dragged it with mattress springs, turning it spongy and muddy as the day warmed. Another storm was on its way to pummel the Northwest. If I failed to fly Nanna to an airport with a paved and plowed runway, I might have to wait for the spring thaw to fly out.

We rolled Nanna out of the hangar, onto the muddy track, and down the hill. Tony and I got in and I eased the throttle forward to start our takeoff roll. Nanna labored to start moving across the sodden ground with his wings hanging over the deep snow on both sides. Within just a few seconds, I let Nanna's left main wheel roll into a foot of snow at the runway's edge.

"What happened!" John Burgy's face was pale with terror as I turned my head and watched him run up from the chase plane behind us and stand by my cockpit. "The rudder wasn't moving at all. Did you hit the pole back there?" He stooped down to look at the underside of the left wing.

When he did not shout, and I saw his expression turn from one of terror to one of frustration, I knew the wing was undamaged, but my heart was pounding and I felt like an awful failure.

"I don't know if you were stomping on the rudder there at the end, but I was," Tony said from the front cockpit. "When it didn't clear, I pulled the mixture, sorry."

"Thanks." I said dejectedly. I was the one to be sorry. Would I ever do anything right in this beautiful place?

John and Duane Binnall, our chase plane pilot, hauled Nanna backward out of the snow bank and rolled us back to the starting point for a second attempt. I had felt confident for the first takeoff. The field was satisfactory, I was rested, I had recently practiced takeoffs and landings in another Great Lakes biplane, and Nanna's engine was running fine. After the aborted takeoff, though, I was shaken. I did not know then what I had done wrong. It would be days before I figured out that I had eased the throttle forward and begun rolling on the soggy ground with my feet resting, but not pushing quickly enough, on the rudders. That bad habit extracted no penalty back home on my wide Texas runways. Nor had I noticed or corrected it a week earlier during my refresher lesson at another big concrete runway in Arizona. On most runways, I could start rolling and push in the rudder when Nanna started pulling left, a normal effect of engine and propeller on takeoff. Here the narrowness of the runway, just a swath cut through the snow banks, allowed no such leeway. A little pull left rolled me smartly into the thick snow. What was sloppy technique elsewhere became a near-disastrous error here at Timber Basin. Nor had I ever figured out how the previous June I had managed to hit the fence at the other end of this field, on my last flight in Nanna. The idea that I just missed damaging the wing—again—worried me.

"Let me take it off," Tony said, as though reading my mind. His voice was warm and kind, as always.

"Please do." Bless his heart, I thought. Not only had he given up weekends repairing Nanna's wing after my fence-hitting, stupid pilot trick and hours preparing the runway for our departure yesterday, but he was going to have to fly me out as well. He must have thought I was one plum useless pilot. If he did, he never said so. That was his way.

From the moment the tires began to inch forward, Tony kept Nanna rolling ramrod straight along the track. Better than half the runway fell behind, and still the wheels were slinging up mud. We should be airborne, I thought, but we seemed glued to the ground. We had already passed the telephone pole near where we had agreed we would abort and were approaching the crest of the hill. Tony kept pushing ahead. I felt relieved.

After we had broken ground, sailed over the lake, and vaulted above the forest, Tony said, "I felt the wings taking the weight, so I decided to keep going." Once Nanna's wheels had broken free of the slogging mud, he had shot like a pebble out of a slingshot, the engine generating maximum power in the cold air.

"Good decision. I felt the same."

"You've got the airplane." Tony waggled the stick, which I took.

"I've got the airplane," I confirmed. Finally, yes, I had the airplane.

It had been over five months since Nanna and I had flown together. I felt stiff, like I did if I had not exercised for days, then bent over to stretch and found that my knee had grown farther away from my bowing head. We climbed and circled the field to test the rigging and be sure that the engine was running okay for the flight to Spokane. If anything seemed unsafe, we would land. I did not fancy landing at Timber Basin that day. Things would have been going to hell in a darned big hand basket for me to try. Rather, I would run for the clear, paved, long, and wide runway that waited only a few miles across the lake.

John and Duane in the high wing chase plane took off behind us and headed for Spokane. Satisfied that we were good to go, I cut the imaginary cord with Timber Basin and headed after them.

Clouds matted the sky, but below them the air was clear. The outlines of cars and trucks, ridges of mountains, icy edges of streams looked crisp and clean. Nanna's engine gobbled up the brisk, dense air, so different from the warm, summery breaths of his last flight here. We followed the winter wonderland of a valley between evergreen mountains dashed with snow.

I dialed the radio for the Felts Airport information and called the tower controller who cleared me for the shorter of two parallel runways. Both were many times wider and longer than Timber Basin.

"Now, Anne, if you're not comfortable landing on the short one, just ask for the other one." Although Tony's words sounded like a mother hen's, his voice did not sound strained or nervous. I bet he had his hand close to the controls, though, and his feet on those rudders. Poor Tony, I had really put him through it on that first takeoff.

"I'm fine with this one." I had grown steadily more confident on the flight down. Like riding a bike, you never forget how to fly. I just had to warm up. Turning to final, I became delirious at what I saw ahead. Why lookey there, I could see the long runway beyond Tony's head. Not only that, but here I was still high above it, and I could see the sides of that dang surface rising to meet Nanna's wheels. This place was a monster compared with Timber Basin. We landed without incident. I was one for three. It was a start. At that moment, I knew that everything was going to work out getting home.

We landed at two airports in Spokane that afternoon, first to show off John and Tony's work to a fellow aircraft restorer, and last to a hangar where Nanna spent the night assured of a paved, plowed runway for the start of the trip home.

Then the four of us piled into the chase plane and raced sundown back to Timber Basin. Duane flew a fast pattern and then dove toward the runway to shoo away deer that spent their evenings there. On the second pass, he landed in failing light.

257

The minute we touched down, pounds and pounds of mud and grass clumps pelted the wings and fuselage like machine gun fire. We rolled down the hill to the runway's end, then turned off and taxied up to John's place, slinging mud all the way. We lurched across the ruts until the wheels slid effortlessly onto the concrete outside the hangar. Duane kept taxiing where ordinarily we would stop and pile out. The propeller cut a circle through a makeshift plastic curtain to the otherwise open-air hangar, leaving a hole like a cartoon character plowing through a wall. I guess he figured we had enjoyed enough of slogging through mud for one day. My nose was running from the cold.

The harsh light of the cold hangar fell upon four people, all of us relieved and happy to have saved Nanna from forced hibernation in an Idaho winter. I was itching to head for home the next day. The others must have been relieved that my departure would simplify life at Timber Basin. I suspect the stories of Nanna and his whacky mom get better every year. "By gosh, she tore up a wing on the way in," I can imagine them saying, "and darned if she didn't almost do it again on the way out!"

Tony's family and I drove back to Spokane that night. The next day's snow showers, low visibility, and a pressing need for a new transponder kept Nanna on the ground. The following day, we launched southeast under a low layer of cloud, heading for The Dalles on the Columbia River. From there I planned to head south down the valley east of the Cascades. An alternate route farther east would take us through more desolate, risky country with no promise of better weather. The third possible route through northern California's central valley had turned into an impassable, soppy mess from an incoming weather front.

Soon after scooting away from Spokane, the edge of the cloud blanket appeared, a wintry sun lit a brighter path ahead, and I relaxed. We flew across an assortment of farms, forests, rivers, and towns. The land along our path varied from low valleys to uplifted rifts and small mountains. Great snow-capped ones pierced the horizon. The first leg the trip had begun to feel more like a pure pleasure flight than a mission.

We were seventy miles away from our destination airport with an hour and a half left before sunset, and I was cold to the bone. I noticed that we were traveling only seventy miles per hour across the ground, slow for us. When we were sixty miles out, we were doing sixty. At fifty miles, only fifty. The feeling was like shinnying within inches of the top of a pole and then slipping back down repeatedly. As if that strengthening headwind was not enough, a wall of snow careened toward us and the clear air began to turn milky. We were not going to make it. I pulled Nanna around hard. We began traveling a hundred miles per hour faster back to Hermiston. Nanna stayed outside for the first night in many months. He was brutally cold, but felt not a flake of snow.

Wednesday brought a bright clear morning, but headwinds hammered us again, and by the time we reached a midday thaw stop at Redmond, another gloomy sky loomed ahead. Still, we managed to cross the rest of Oregon that afternoon under sharp low overcast skies that I so enjoy. We had passed small airports along the way and I noticed many had snow on the runways, so I was concerned that to venture beyond Klamath Falls might bring sunset before the next cleared runway. We slipped into Klamath Falls between military jet trainers.

The following morning was damp, windy, and cold, but no snow or rain fell at the airport. We would probably find some farther south, but I decided to head out for a look. If we could not get through, we would turn around and I would spend the day reading. We had already penetrated far enough south that I could count on getting out eventually, so my mood had turned mellow and fatalistic. If we did not get out of Oregon today, we would tomorrow, or the day after. Military operations kept the runways clear at all times here. This was not Timber Basin, where at some point relentless snow would choke off the runway until spring. Christmas was still a couple of weeks away, after all.

I prepared to taxi for takeoff, cockpits secure, belts and harnesses all in place, engine start moments away, and I adjusted my sunglasses. A lens fell out. It dropped between my legs, bounced once like a rim shot, and fell through the hole in the cockpit floor onto the belly fabric.

Through the plate glass windows nearby, pilots who had been glancing at Nanna and me with mild curiosity, watched more intently now, baffled, as I unbuckled and got out. As I lay down on the cold wet ground and scooted under the belly, one moved right up to the window of his warm and comfortable den and watched the show as he drank his coffee. As I felt the chilled dampness work its way to my back, through flight suit, sweaters, and turtleneck, I noticed an item that might have caused another cockpit exit. Somebody had placed chocks on Nanna's right main wheels, and I had not noticed them during my preflight check. I walked around and pulled them out.

Cold and wet, I began talking myself out of launching at all. After all, I thought, I would probably have to turn around anyway. I looked longingly at the comfortable couches a few feet away and the coffee pot just down the hall. How warm everyone inside looked. Why not just go back inside and kick back for the day? No, press on. Get in and get the heater going, and the temptation would pass. It did. I started the engine and sat for a few minutes hunkered down low where the heat was strongest as I listened to the recorded takeoff information and then switched frequencies to become familiar with the voices of controllers on duty.

"...ready to taxi, southbound," I called when the engine temperature dial had rotated into the green operating range.

"Two-tango-echo, say again type aircraft," the tower controller said, sounding warm and relaxed. I imagined him holding a hot cup of coffee and wearing a short-sleeved shirt, one with palm trees on it.

"Two-tango-one-alpha, a Great Lakes biplane," I answered the question, then keyed the mike a second time. "Now, be careful not to confuse us with all the other open-cockpit biplanes launching this morning."

I did not hear him laugh, but the pause was long enough for a good chuckle and his voice betrayed at least a smile as he sent me on my way. "Roger that, taxi to runway two-five…"

Within a few minutes, we were holding at the end of the runway running Nanna's engine up, rearing to go. I looked around at snow everywhere, glittering in the sun. A flight of two fighters roared along on another nearby runway and lifted off together. Sights like these would not last many more hours. Eager as I was to get home, I knew I would soon miss these scenes, unusual for us, accustomed as we were to grassy fields and milder climes. The next time we landed, the snow might be gone forever.

Nanna and I made it fifty miles south, a thousand feet above the highway, to the point where a flight briefer had warned that we might encounter low ceilings. The briefer was right. We could not continue descending along this unfamiliar terrain safely. We diverted east and climbed way up to hurdle south for clear skies. The detour would cost me a hoped-for Mt. Shasta fly-by, but I knew we would be back here one day to explore. While flying above the clouds, we found a rocket tailwind with a healthy assist from a mountain wave above ten thousand feet, which we rode the rest of the day, making it from the Oregon border, Reno for lunch, and down the Owens valley. I reset my target airport repeatedly as wind and altitude stretched our fuel supply. Halleluiah, I had begun to sweat in my foul weather getup. I turned down the heater and unzipped the front of my flight suit.

Since flying off Timber Basin, I had dressed purposefully as usual for the wintry excursion: two pairs of socks, tennis shoes, underwear, cotton tights and turtleneck, two cashmere sweaters, a flight suit, a neck warmer, leather helmet with goggles, a windbreaker, and fur-lined gloves. I also carried a silk knit facemask, which I never donned. I was cold at times, but Nanna's heater kept me reasonably warm. How I did admire the old airmail pilots who flew without a heater in even worse conditions—and on a fixed schedule.

By the time we landed and tied down at the next airport, I was sweltering. I took my time in the cockpit as I often do after a long flight, resting my head on the headrest, slowing marking down meter readings and making notes on my log sheet. Hot as I was, I wanted to linger over the inner warmth that comes from a successful flight. Reaching home soon had become a lead pipe cinch.

Shirt-sleeved pilots tying down their planes shot puzzled glances at me and my foul-weather get-up when I finally did step down from Nanna's wing. The sun was setting below the mountains that ring the Los Angeles Basin. I looked around at the high desert. No snow, for sure.

Friday, the wind blew through the Cajon Pass into Los Angeles at about sixty miles per hour. I had to force Nanna's nose down as we shot through like water from a fire hose. Once through the pass, we aimed for an airport near the base of the mountains. The wind was still strong and kept blowing us sideways away from the mountains. To counteract the wind, I pointed Nanna's nose toward the mountain, so we moved nearly sideways, like a crab. I began to doubt that we would be able to land. Suddenly, five miles out from the airport, howling winds became zephyrs and our landing routine. I met my Stearman friend Ken McCullough and we pulled Nanna into his hangar. The artist who had painted Nanna's original details arrived and repainted bits of worn or damaged decoration while Ken and I tweaked rigging, aiming for the perfection so elusive to biplanes.

With mixed emotions, eager to get home, but hesitant to end my first outing with Nanna in so many months, I pulled up to the departure runway the following morning at sunrise.

"Is that the Lakes that was at John Burgy's place?" asked another departing pilot over the radio. The world is a small place, indeed, for biplanes.

"Affirmative. I left there a few days ago. Heading for Arizona."

"So long."

I was not eager to fly in the weather that had been forecast for that Saturday, severe turbulence with major up and downdrafts across California and into Arizona. To minimize the buffeting, I had decided to make a high spiral climb to get out of the mountain turbulence and live with whatever headwinds we found there. Once aloft, though, the air turned out to be smooth and the winds calm, so I trimmed Nanna for a leisurely climb passing above the Banning Pass and Palm Springs. Forecasts are funny things, sometimes weather turns out worse, sometimes better. When I find conditions better, it is like a little gift, a morsel of chocolate on a smooth white pillow. To get such a gift on the last day of this trip, the day I mark as the end of an era for Nanna and me, our Texas era, made me happy.

As we followed I-10, the highway we had taken to Texas five years earlier, I remembered Amy sleeping in the front cockpit, her head bobbing. I recalled many more flights, short ones on weekends, long ones in the summertime. I thought about the future, how many times I would retrace this route between Tucson and California in the future, what month-long trips might we take. I felt again the joy of the day I first soloed in Nanna, turning into the sunset from base leg to final, "If I never fly this airplane again, I'll be happy for this one perfect moment." Only now I amended it, "If I never fly this airplane again, I'll be forever grateful for our years in Texas."

As we approached Buckeye Airport near Phoenix, my thoughts turned to landing at our new home, fast drawing close, the slender runway at La Cholla. The sheer terror of repeating my dismal history with a narrow runway the last two tries and the knowledge that I would probably land in a stiff crosswind, gave me pause. So, Nanna and I lingered at Buckeye to practice landing in a hellacious wind. We did just fine, right on the centerline, wing into the wind, no drifting, and just a tiny bounce.

"Wind strong enough?" The pilot in a twin-engine plane had been waiting beside the runway for us to land so he could depart. What he was really asking was, what were we doing out on a windy day like this.

"Perfect."

We flew around the pattern twice more, touching down once and flying low along the centerline the second, then turned toward home, more confident. We flew over flat irrigated fields and through the odors rising from feedlots full of cattle and dust. As we passed Picacho Peak and headed for the Tortolita Mountains, the farms disappeared. Desert engulfed us now, the tall saguaro in every direction, arms raised skyward with prickly pear clustered around their bases like bunches of green grapes. Mesquite and palo verde cast long, full shadows across the smaller plants that gave the ground a bumpy texture. We skirted the base of the range. Only a few more minutes and a journey that had begun in Dallas a half year earlier would end.

The short winter afternoon was nearly gone when I first saw the runway at La Cholla. It lay among homes widely scattered and hangars everywhere beside roads that doubled as taxiways. We flew overhead to check the windsock. Its tail pointed southwest, but not rigid and stiff, as expected. The wind had subsided, blowing gently across the runway. We flew alongside and glided down effortlessly until the tires touched.

Chirp.

Nanna and I were home.

One Hundred Ten and Still Flying

Someday I will discover that climbing into Nanna's cockpit takes too great a toll on my body, or I will make a mistake. I will miss seeing traffic that I should have seen, land badly without understanding why, make a dangerous pilotage error, or perhaps do something even worse. Then the little voice within will whisper, "You've had a good run, quit now."

Knowing this, I avoid spending leisure time on anything I will be able to enjoy later as the mind fades or the need arises for cane or wheelchair. I will not soon book the Alaskan cruise to sit and watch fjords and glaciers pass before my deck chair. I will not fly to Paris to buy a baguette and cheese from the corner grocer, stroll along the boulevards, and eat roast chicken with pommes frites at the brasserie in Place Victor Hugo. I will not float along the canals of Europe on a crisp fall day, wrapped in a blanket, warmed by a brilliant sun as I read a book about the canals and glance up occasionally to enjoy a country garden lovingly tended or watch laughing children at play. These things I long to do, but I have put them aside for a later season.

Now, I fly.

Later, in my sunset years, between cruises and canals, I will sit in my study or my garden and fly again with Nanna. Instead of climbing up, strapping in, donning helmets, moving levers, and pushing pedals, I will use a different set of flying tools—logbooks, charts, and photo albums—and exercise a different set of skills— memory and imagination. I know my enjoyment then will be as complete as it was on the original flights, because even today when I kneel and open a chart on the carpet, a familiar point captures my attention and beckons me to following an old route as though I was passing there above the earth again. Vivid details erupt like fireworks from the vast and mysterious warehouse of my mind.

In some ways, these remembered flights improve upon the originals. Less pleasant aspects, like oppressive heat, an ugly junkyard, or the acrid smoke of a paper mill tend to fade, leaving dramatic sights and pleasant sensations. I can fly the same flight many times, like a repeat feature on a music player: a first tracing of a route restores the basic flight; the second is enriched as more details of the flight emerge; the third, people met on the ground along the way come into focus. My game is to fly and re-fly each route until the mental well is dry. Sometimes I have to dig at a bit. If I open a chart and have only a vague memory of my route, I check in my logbook for stops I made. From there I search for a wisp of memory: How warm? What time? What season? Who was in the front cockpit? Who was at the airport? Where did we stay the night before? When scraping the gourd of memory yields no further flesh, I put the flight aside. The following morning another detail, the smell of smoke from a fire or a particular boat docked on a lake, pops out as though buried in the squirt of toothpaste rolling onto my brush.

It may be too soon to know which flights along what charts will become the cream that rises to the top, but some segments play such vivid movies now that it is hard to imagine that others might submerge them. I find myself smiling as a film, long archived, threads itself on the projector of my consciousness. I begin to feel the air swirling around the back of my neck. I am a hundred or a thousand feet above a river or road, in the sunshine or cloudy sky, feeling warm or cold. I am flying again.

To understand these imaginary flights requires a familiarity with the charts that evoke them. Every chart cover shows the same map of the continental United States blocked into rectangles. The area covered by each rectangle is called a sectional chart, or just a sectional. The largest city within a sectional dictates the chart's title. A single northeastern chart, *New York*, covers much of that state and most of eight smaller ones, while the state of Texas shows up on eight different sectionals. The charts are two-sided, north and south. If the chart is titled *Houston* or *Jacksonville*, its colors are lowland hues, palest of greens with blue for water, whether rivers or oceans or canals. *Denver* and *Salt Lake City* show graduated shades of brown used for the higher ground, the darkest brown being the highest elevation. Interstate highways show as two parallel lines, smaller highways as one. Rivers and lakes are solid blue or blue polka dots if they sometimes go dry. Two crossed picks indicate a mine. Most chart notations are obvious from common sense, but a legend exists, and there are books for anyone pining for excruciating detail. The charts alone are interesting; coupled with memory, fascinating.

I may look at that cover map of the whole country and select one chart from a favorite area to open and start a mind journey. I may open the file drawer of alphabetized charts and pick out all the ones that cover the route of a particular trip. I may let my mind select for itself by looking at a chart cover as my gaze passes over the squares until one shouts, "Pick me." Of thirty-seven possible sectional choices, I have folded and refolded thirty-two of them while strapped into a cramped cockpit on summer flights. I have no doubt that I will cover the remaining five before Nanna and I quit flying together.

Whichever method I choose in the winter of my life, I will pull from the bookshelves the logbook and scrapbook covering those weeks so long ago and carry them to my favorite chair, where my wrinkled and age-spotted hands will open the first chart of the trip.

The first chart I pick up is *Dallas – Ft. Worth*. There are nearly a dozen more stacked below it for the Big Sky trip. We had sketched out the trip (planning would be too precise a term) nicknamed early on the "Greats" trip—Great Lakes, Great Plains, Great Mountains. As usual, the trip ultimately renamed itself, this one to Big Sky. As I open the first chart to the south side and unfold the accordion panels of paper into my lap, the blob of bright yellow shows the shape of a metropolitan area as it would look lighted at night from miles above. My finger snaps to the solid blue circle depicting Addison Airport, Nanna's home for five years, always our starting point. As I follow the route along the chart now, I find myself shaping each printed detail into a hook to fish out a memory. I know I did not study the chart that July morning, though. I already knew every reservoir, every road, and every train track all the way to the Oklahoma border.

We took off and turned to the north, picking up I-35. The morning was hot, well over one hundred degrees already, made hotter by cockpits full of backpacks, jackets, and sleeping bags that blocked air from circulating about our sweating legs. (I laugh. We would use the jackets on only one cold evening in Duluth, would never use the sleeping bags, and would mail them all back home in a couple of weeks along with dirty laundry and bits of memorabilia that Howard could not resist collecting along the way.) As we hurtled toward the first reservoir, Kevin, my flying buddy from the local air museum, out giving a paying customer a ride, pulled up on our wing in the big yellow Stearman, followed along for a bit, and then waggled his wings in a farewell salute and peeled off toward home.

Right away, I close *Dallas* and open *Wichita* and *Kansas City* only briefly.

By the time we landed for fuel just one hour later, we were exhausted. The heat had left our arms and legs crusted with salt. How far north before it got cooler? Soon, please soon. I rarely envied riders in cars below, but that day, I would have been happy to be down there on the interstate in air-conditioned comfort instead of in the steaming heat above it.

We only made it to the outskirts of Kansas City before a low-hanging line of rain clouds stop us and every other small plane heading for Oshkosh in our tracks. Nanna was the first to make a break for it the next morning. I wonder if a nervous pilot I remember managed to get out that day.

I fly onto the *Chicago* chart, remembering how eager I was to cross a northern stretch of the Mississippi for the first time. I saw it off to the right of my chart, but not yet from the air. I had in mind to cross near the bridge at Dubuque, where years before I had crossed heading west onto winding and undulating roads through enchanted farmlands in Iowa. Later that afternoon we would land at Oshkosh to attend the big air show. Oh, how I had prepared for that arrival, listening to audio tapes of air traffic controllers from a prior year and studying arrival procedures. Like every pilot, I shuddered at the thought of making a mistake or looking like a novice entering the Mecca of aviation. I was ready.

First, I needed gas. I probably had enough, but delays could happen getting in to Oshkosh— it would become the busiest in the world these next few days. We were heading toward Cedar Rapids. Marion looked like a good place to stop. I saw from the chart that it had a relatively short runway, but I still would not need even half of it.

We flew overhead. The runway may have been plenty long, but it was also very narrow. It was even narrower than one near home flanked by lots of tall trees, the one that scared me off unless the wind was calm. At Marion, I saw no trees or any other obstructions. The wind was light. The place looked downright friendly with its faded windsock, worn looking wood building, and assortment of small planes. As we rounded the bend for the final approach, the runway completely disappeared behind Howard's helmet and Nanna's nose. The black pencil mark of a strip was too short for me to see the far end poking up over the nose, and it was too narrow to show itself beneath us from this height. I did not know yet if we had lined up right. I became uncomfortable descending to no place, but comforted myself with a memory of pilots discussing blind landings like this. "If you see the runway, you're going to miss it." Somehow, the thought did not help.

In the last seconds before touchdown, narrow bands of darkness rose up to flank Nanna. Chirp, we were down and rolling on something hard and smooth, yet I saw little but green grass whizzing by.

"Nice job," Howard said. He did not remind me that just a few miles away the big city airport had great wide runways, his earlier nominee for our fuel stop.

"Thanks. That was an interesting one."

We climbed the steps to the airport office, our legs enjoying the freedom, our muscles welcoming exercise after hours of cockpit atrophy. Among the workers and pilots milling about the counter floated a heightened sense of frivolity, an undercurrent of elation. Being close to Oshkosh, a stream of transient aircraft was beginning to roll into little airports like Marion. Planes were raindrops, flowing into tributaries at the edges of the country and into larger streams and rivers leading to the ocean itself, Oshkosh. The transient pilots who stop here were like kids floating in inner tubes along the waters of aviation to a great beach party at the end.

"Nice Lakes," one of the local pilots remarked as he penciled his name into the rental log on the counter.

"Thanks. He's glad to be down. Quite a runway you've got here."

I heard chuckles. I looked around at conspiratorial faces.

"Oh, nobody much lands on the runway. We use the grass."

Soon, we were back in the air, and I refolded the chart to the north side. The Mississippi River was a wide blue snake a few inches away on the chart, but when I looked up I did not yet see it beyond the rolling farmland. The fields varied so in color and shape that it was hard to believe that farmers, not artists, had been hard at work here. Such variety and contoured patterns must have been the result of the hard lessons from the dust bowl, but I preferred to think that farmers, bored with convention, chose to paint intricate patterns with the tools at hand, plow and seed.

"Old Man River, that old…" I tucked my chin down to lower my voice as I launched into the song from *Porgy and Bess*. It was our custom to sing crossing state lines and when moved to song, inspired by major landmarks. That we often could think of no appropriate lyric rarely stopped us. Needs be, we made up one by changing a few key words in a familiar one.

"Where?" Howard stretched his neck to see ahead. "I don't see it."

"Look left, about ten o'clock. See how it's coming toward us? …that old man river, he just keeps…"

"…rolling along." Howard's head nodded as he joined in.

How wide it looked, even from afar, much wider as we approach Dubuque than when we saw it the year before flying from Vicksburg to Memphis. This northerly stretch ran along a more definite lowland path through the hills, more stable and determined than its frilly, confused southern belle cousin dancing across the flatter lands flirting east and west, even turning back north, leaving ponds and false rivers from abandoned paths.

We crossed to the north of the city, the surrounding hills set apart from one another by lengthening shadows. I looked upriver wondering where it started. We would find the source many days later.

We approached Ripon, the starting point for the standard arrival procedure for the Oshkosh fly-in. I had my charts properly folded, I had memorized my landmarks and frequencies, and I knew what to say to the controllers posted along the route and directing aircraft—nothing. "Listen, but do not talk," the instructions said. The first controller would be standing at Ripon with binoculars and a radio to give us a shorthand name like "blue biplane" instead of the official "Great Lakes biplane November-two-two-tango-echo" and tell us where to fall into the line of airplanes leaving Ripon along the railroad track that ran to the airport. I had listened to a tape recording of a busy time when dozens of planes converged at once on the tower at Whitman Field in Oshkosh. I knew that for the days ahead, Oshkosh would be so crowded that two airplanes would land at once on a single runway, one starting at the end and the other in the middle, while a third would land on a perpendicular runway. I was nervous.

As often happens, I was prepared and braced for the worst, but the tiger turned out to be a pussycat. I had no problems at all from the time the controller mistook me for a "Pitts over Ripon" and sent me off along the railroad track far behind another airplane and with nobody close behind me. The tower controller cleared me to land a full minute before my touchdown. Descending to land, I had the full view of the airport grounds, covered already with planes and tents and people milling about. On the ground, a marshal waved his flags as soon as we pulled off the runway onto the grass, directing us to a row of vintage airplanes parked in a premium spot.

In my scrapbook are page after page of photos of airplanes and people from Oshkosh. Three are favorites: a man laboring with cleaning cloths and potions to remove finger prints from the engine of his prize-winning Bonanza (to this day we call our tie-down neighbor and new friend Larry the "show plane slave"); my dad and I sitting in the shade of Nanna's wing watching a sleek white sailplane painting gentle arcs across the sky as an orchestra sounded over the loudspeakers; my dad sitting in the front cockpit of the show's camouflage-blue Dauntless dive bomber with me in the rear as his tail gunner.

I open *Green Bay*. Surrounded by the light green paper that depicts the lowlands of Wisconsin and Michigan, the blue of Lake Michigan and the ruffled curve of its western coast pulls my gaze southward. There is Lake Winnebago.

Oshkosh and its crowd of aviation enthusiasts and airplanes grew smaller and faded into the summer haze below us. We had barely escaped Whitman Field before it closed for the afternoon air show, so I felt relieved. No further pressures existed. Howard and I had no plan for the remaining day beyond exploring something of the Great Lakes region. We had no commitments, no deadlines, no reservations, and no destination in mind. I had studied the chart and knew that plenty of airports ahead sold fuel. We could satisfy any exploratory whim and stop whenever we felt a need to attend to stomachs, bladders, or stiffening legs. Sometime in the next few days, we would turn west toward the Great Plains, the centerpiece of this trip, but no such decision faced us now.

I was glad to be away from the crowds. No matter how friendly and interesting the people, how impressive the aircraft, after a couple of days, I begin to suffocate. I felt as though I had been mingling with guests in a house throbbing with music, full of color and texture, elegant furniture, floral bouquets, and architectural detail that drew my eye here and there, a feast for the senses. Yet, I longed to retire to an uninhabited room where everything was simple and white except a single red rosebud in clear crystal vase and quiet, except for a guitar playing softly. Ahead we would see wide-open spaces, punctuated in simple ways, perhaps by a lone building or a solitary railroad track running to the horizon. When we landed, we would meet people one at a time in their natural habitats.

As we rounded the lake, Oshkosh lay on the other side, and I was a kid running away from the schoolyard after the last bell on the last day of the year. From the chart I knew that the waters along our way north would grow progressively dominant: this small lake, a larger bay and then the great lake itself. We passed over the city of Green Bay to follow the western coastline of Lake Michigan. Cities had disappeared. Towns were becoming smaller and the time flying between them longer. Fewer and fewer fields had been carved from the forest until all that was not water was one continuous forest stretching far into Canada.

From Escanaba, following the lake perimeter road through the marshy forests that separated us from the more northerly Lake Superior, we turned gradually east, and then southeast until the miles and miles of bridge spanning the Mackinac Straits came into view. I tuned the radio to the frequency of upcoming airports and discovered that neither custom nor treaty had resolved the pronunciation of Mackinac Island.

"Mack-i-naw traffic..." called one pilot.

"Mack-i-nack traffic..." called another.

Finding out why became reason enough to stop there for the night. Besides, sunset was approaching.

"Want to stop at Mackinac County?" Howard asked.

"How about Mackinac Island instead?" I began the negotiation we frequently had toward the end of a flying day. The two airports were a few miles apart. The county airport was larger and close to a town. The island looked relatively unpopulated. Howard and I had different criteria for such selections. He would always opt for a larger, busier airport likely to have more amenities and certainty. I preferred small and funky hotbeds of the unknown.

"No fuel there and it's getting late."

"We could refuel in the morning. I think this is the island with a famous old hotel from the turn of the century."

"What if we land and can't find anything? Then it'll be getting dark and we'll be stuck. We won't have anyplace to eat. Kind of risky."

"Nah. Let's take a chance."

"Okay." He said it with that resigned tone I had come to expect when we communicated along the boundaries of our individual risk envelopes. Always the good sport, he agreed to go along with my preference.

I felt the warmth on the back of my head diminish as the sun plummeted toward the horizon and we passed over the county airport. I watched Howard's head turn with longing toward the nearby city, like an ancient mariner watching Barcelona disappear as he sailed forth with his whacky captain toward the edge of a flat earth. We breezed across the few miles of water to an island that was a small hill, the only land rising above the surrounding disc of water and forest. The island appeared to be populated with trees alone. A few houses began to show through the forest, but nothing appeared large enough to be a hotel. We saw no roads, no cars. Soon, we could see the swath cut across the hilltop, the airport.

"I don't know about this. Are you sure you want to land here?" Howard's head was swiveling back and forth looking for signs of civilization as though we were about to crash land and needed to find the most promising direction for the hike out.

"Don't worry. It's an adventure. You'll see. Check out three o'clock." On the downwind leg I caught a reassuring glimpse of buildings on the south side of the island. Oh, how I hoped we were not in for a bad experience after such a glorious day. Howard would never say, "I told you so," nor would he pout or complain when things did not turn out well, but he would sit quietly with a distant look, imagining that parallel universe where, following the safer choice, he was hiking no long distances, eating better, and sleeping in greater comfort.

"Uh-huh. Okay." The sound was almost a groan as we turned onto the base leg.

Landing became a glide into a forest. The treetops rose up to meet us. Suddenly all the water, our day's constant companion, disappeared. We were in a glade with one building and a few other small aircraft. Their owners had abandoned them. We finished our evening airplane chores and headed for the small, clean, but empty terminal. Howard walked with his backpack slung over his shoulder, water bottle and camera dangling around his neck, bags of charts and sleeping bag swinging along his side—an aerial accidental tourist. I breathed easier when we found the door unlocked and I saw vending machines and couches. It would be possible to survive here overnight. I felt even better when I spotted a phone with what looked like a slim phone book dangling from a chain. Before we had a chance to look up any numbers or make a call or become anxious because we couldn't find a hotel, salvation arrived. It came with the clop, clop, clopping of a fringed surrey drawn by two chestnut draft horses starting up the circular driveway. The driver, a fresh-faced teenager, stopped at the front door and dropped off her fare.

"Need a taxi?" She asked. Backpacks flew onto the seat and we climbed aboard. Her blonde ponytail swung like a third horsetail as hooves clop-clop-clopped back downhill along the one-way road that wound beneath a canopy of ancient trees. The trunks were thick and dark, the underbrush lush and green. The air in this enchanted forest was moist and dense and a breeze rustled the leaves overhead.

Our driver was Dolla, a veterinary student working a summer job. We were barely out of the airport before she radioed and made some hotel reservations and suggested a couple of restaurants. All the while, we asked questions about her and the island. As we have concluded so often by chatting with young people at work in the countryside, civilization appeared safe in the hands of the next generation. Soon, we turned onto the main street of town, a clean bright road lined with gingerbread facades and window boxes bright with geraniums. The road served horses, bicycles, and pedestrians. There were only four power vehicles on the island and those only for emergencies.

"Here we are," said Dolla. The surrey stopped in front of a white wood porch of a charming Victorian hotel. Howard appeared as relaxed now as he had looked anxious when we first landed.

"Great." I turned and said to Howard.

To myself I said, *whew*.

I will fly on the *Lake Huron* chart only briefly. I rest my finger near the edge, below the locks on the Canadian border.

To get to the locks, we took the highway carved through deep green timber. I looked back at Lake Michigan across the long and tall bridge that joined the Upper to the Lower Peninsula across the straits. The morning was cloudy and the air damp. I began to notice how uninhabited these forested northern lands were from here on up through Canada. Texas was vast, but I found a town or house or cow or at least an oil well from time to time. Some trips in Texas carried me over the piney woods, but the trees there looked shorter and less deadly than these hardened northern cousins. Flying over forests was not something I liked very much. The safety of flat landing fields as far as the eye can see had spoiled me. We followed the lone road north from Mackinac. I wondered if the forest hid small cabins. It was summer, so no smoke from chimneys gave them away.

There, ahead lay gray-blue water, closing in from both sides, lakes converging. Between them, details of the locks at Sault St. Marie emerged. Thin channels of calm water ran between narrow islands of grass edged with concrete. Two of the locks had been drained and looked like concrete tubs. A lone iron ore vessel had just ridden the watery elevator to Lake Superior, while a gaggle of tiny sailboats and pleasure cruisers huddled together in another for the reverse trip to Lake Huron.

As we circled to take photos, we flew outside the country briefly. Nanna was a real globetrotter, last winter Mexico along the Rio Grande, now Canada.

I pick *Green Bay* off the floor where I had dropped it earlier. This time I turn it to the north side. Too bad the mapmakers could not just have fit that little jog up to the locks on this chart.

I open it full wide.

We would fly all the way along the southern shore of Lake Superior to Duluth that day, ending our Great Lakes portion of the trip. We did not know that when we departed the locks, though—only that we would head west. At some point, the light would fade or we would tire. Then we would land. That was all we knew at the start.

The temperature was mild, the sky smattered with clouds as we followed roads that hugged the shoreline for a while, cut across a neck of land, and returned to the shore. Even when the lake dropped out of sight, water was everywhere: large lakes, small ponds, millions of puddles. Short lines clumped together covered the chart, telling us to expect marshy land. Yes, we saw it.

By the time we passed Chequamegan Bay the benign clouds above had begun to change. I looked off to my right at the lake.

I had always thought Superior the most sinister of the sister lakes. I looked at the water that consumed most of the chart and saw the monster beak pointing west above an open maw. Something else, missing from most maps, was the beady eye made by Isle Royale. The beast was watching us, too. If that were not frightening enough, the government had painted large blue boxes inside the monster's snout and outside along the Canadian border to proclaim the areas dangerous and "PROHIBITED." This was the sort of place the military dropped bombs, hid things, or protected very important people and buildings. All was not graveness and danger, though. Nearby lay a chunk of space at the tip of the monster's nose surrounded by softer looking magenta lines of a Military Operations Area, "Snoopy East" and another beside it "Snoopy West." Here we were allowed to fly near Snoopy and the Red Baron's home, but must beware of busy military pilots likely to be flying fast airplanes and not looking for us.

We were flying along the rills that fell into the lake east of Duluth when the air cooled and began thickening. Out on the lake, fog appeared, a watery broth turned to white gravy, rolling closer and closer. No longer were we flying level, but dropping lower and lower to stay below clouds changing from romantic and misty wisps to solid gray masses promising rain.

Somewhere ahead, Duluth Sky Harbor Airport sat on a narrow isthmus. Not a moment too soon, as the closing clouds erased from the waters the last pools of sunlight, the runway came into view. We dipped farther down to stay in the clear air, flew a low traffic pattern, and landed. All around us seaplanes rested directly on the tarmac, their floats looking like ungainly feet of ducks out of water.

"Quick, get the cover," Howard shouted as we clamored out of the cockpits.

I unlatched and flipped open the lunchbox, grabbed the black tarp, and tossed it the over the cockpits. By the time we snapped it down, the rain was falling hard. We were drenched and a bit chilled by the time we reached a nearby building.

As usual, Howard tended to ground transportation and lodging arrangements. Soon, we were rattling over a clanking bridge, off to town. That night we wore our jackets, the only time we did so on the trip, and the only time we did not resent the precious space they consumed in our backpacks.

We stayed on the *Green Bay* chart for much of the following morning, a couple of hours of it waiting at the airport for a morning fog to burn off. We knew that the rest of Duluth was clear and sunny, but the city proper did not sit as we did out in the steaming lake.

When the fog looked bright enough, we hopped into Nanna. As the last wisps cleared, we took off to the west. Looking left, I saw bright sky, shoreline, and the large port full of commercial vessels, many of them long, heavy ore ships. We were just another pleasure craft lifting into the sky. To the right, I saw the monster's beak across a lingering prehistoric fog. We were an ancient bird escaping. Farewell, monster lake.

"Blasting in effect today 2000Z Hibbing VOR R009/15 miles." This had been the warning from the morning briefing. In plain English, it meant that an active mine some fifteen miles northeast of a white transmitter that looked like Paul Bunyan's bowling pin, government-designated as "Hibbing," would this afternoon spew into the sky dirt and rock (up to two thousand feet I had been told by a local). If we flew near there during the blasting period and managed not to be hit, we could count on hearing great booming shocks.

It was still early for all that fuss. The danger warning added to the magnetism of the little mine symbols on the chart. We headed for them to see for ourselves. We followed another road through more forested lands into a wonderland of lakes, each formed by a giant cookie cutter pressing through thick terra cotta dough. The darkness of the blue water suggested that the straight-cut edges plunged deep. These must have been abandoned open-pit mines that nature had transformed.

Farther ahead, we saw puffs of dirt rising from a large hole, an active mine. What we thought might be an early blast turned out to be the wake of a speeding pickup truck rushing down dry and dusty corkscrew roads along the sides. The mine bustled with activity of trucks and equipment that appeared large even from high above. Conveyor belts, processing plants, railways, and roadways marked the producing mines. One day, nature would transform this one, too, from a played-out mine into a sheer-cliff lake. The aesthetics would improve when nature returned as caretaker.

As I open the *Twin Cities* chart, I question again whether it depicts a land full of lakes or a shallow inland sea stuffed with islands. Through my magnifying glass, I see water labeled "Lake This" or "That Lake," so someone has decided the former. Minnesota is one wet state.

We headed across the watery forest from the mines northwest

of Duluth. At many points along this westerly route, we could have turned and flown straight to the North Pole without flying over a single town or building or even a person. What a grand empty place lay along my right shoulder. I saw nothing but water, forest, and sky.

If we had flown north, we would have intersected the route taken long ago by another Anne as she headed for the Orient with Charles. Although the Lindberghs had taken every precaution and wrung much of the risk from the operation, still I wondered what she must have felt as she reeled in her radio antenna and turned her goggled eyes from her rear cockpit to look at the last outpost of civilization as it fell behind. Even knowing that many others have made such flights, I could not shake the unease of contemplating hurling myself into such wilderness. I had caused myself the same feeling of distress when flying along the Atlantic Coast. I can turn east and cross the ocean, I would think. If I had enough fuel, I would land somewhere in Europe or Africa. Or, would I?

There was no ocean here to consider, and I was becoming more comfortable above the forest. We were no safer than before, nor were we more at risk. We had simply endured more time without incident. As a safety measure we still flew along highways, because what little population existed would pass along them should engine trouble occur. East of Bemidji, we passed along a square pond on an island within a lake, a nesting of water I have seen nowhere else.

The next item on our aerial scavenger hunt was a statue of Paul Bunyan. We knew that at least two existed in Minnesota, one along a highway somewhere and the other in Bemidji. The chart identified nothing obvious along the highway, but Bemidji lay as a perky yellow spot right along a lakeshore, a snap to find. Surely, something as large as Paul would pop right out at us. We darted across the lake, circled the town, but found nothing.

"I give up, where could it be?" I asked.

"I don't have a clue," Howard said.

"Maybe we could see it better if we were looking up at it." I turned north along the shoreline and descended nearly to the treetops. When the town thinned to nothing, we circled back. I was confident in this approach to the search, as I saw towers sticking up. Surely, a skyscraper statue, the world's largest man, would show himself, as well. Nothing appeared along the first half of the town. As we arrived beside town center once more, a bright spot of blue down low in an open plaza caught my eye.

"Babe, there's Babe," I said banking right over buildings near the shore. There beside a large blue ox with wide white horns stood a wooden Paul with his red shirt and broad shoulders. He looked relatively small and insignificant in comparison to Babe, and not even as tall as a flagpole.

"No wonder. What a wimp," Howard said, raising the camera to click another trophy find.

"They look so much bigger in pictures." I felt like a kid going back to visit an old neighborhood and seeing the house in which I once lived, always surprised at how small it looks.

When we tired of watching tourists watching us, we bolted on toward another of the day's targets, a small liquid one. We found a long, narrow road heading our way south and followed it. Ahead I saw the lopsided pear-shaped water we sought, Itasca. We slowed down to trace the perimeter, dipping a wing so Howard could photograph the trickle of a stream flowing away from the pond. To myself I hummed, "Old Man River, that old man river…" Today, we would not follow these few gallons of water on their circuitous journey, joining other gallons along the way through a chain of towns and cities, the last, New Orleans. As we departed, I bid farewell for this trip to the Mississippi, looking forward seeing its sibling, the Missouri soon.

We were in buffalo country. At some motel or airport counter along the way, we had seen a brochure touting the world's largest buffalo. The next morning we found the brown and gray, concrete-like statue south of Jamestown, North Dakota. From the air it looked enough like a buffalo, but not huge. Besting such a "world's largest" claim would have been easy for some enterprising town with surplus funds.

"Pretty wimpy if you ask me," I said.

"I agree."

"No big deal. We'll see plenty of real buffalo." Oddly, we never did, although I am sure we would have had we known where to look or been more vigilant.

About an hour later, Nanna's engine was purring along nicely. We were flying a few hundred feet above a highway that rose and fell below. I saw that Howard was reorganizing his charts and other cockpit paraphernalia. I knew this because his head was bending forward, and he had just bumped the throttle with his left elbow. I nudged it back into position. I was enjoying the solitude found in few places besides a tandem, open-cockpit biplane. I was alone with my own thoughts in my own space, yet I was only a couple of feet from another human being. We could communicate at will, but choose not to for long periods, each drinking in the wonder of what we saw, snapping the images for later recall. I let my eyes wander over the large eighteen-wheelers on the highway as we gradually passed each one about as fast as I would expect. The wind must have been nearly calm.

The deep green forests were behind us now. The land was no longer so flat. Brownish green hills rose in our path and fell away, rose and fell. We had no items on our scavenger list for today. Whatever showed up to amuse or interest us would be fine. Out of the corner of my eye, something on an upcoming hill startled me. It was black and white, and it was very large. I looked around for a building or sign that might present a clue. There was none.

"Howard, Look!"

His head popped up, too late to see. I circled back for another look.

"A cow?"

"Surely the 'World's Largest Cow.' I don't know, maybe 'World's Largest Jersey'?"

"Bigger than the buffalo, anyway."

There must have been a good story about how that large, painted statue came to sit alone on a remote stretch of North Dakota highway. I have always wondered why.

Opening the *Billings* chart, I remember how our trip shouted to us that it would accept none of the names contemplated thus far. It could no longer be "Great Lakes & Plains" or just "The Greats." "I am Big Sky," it announced to us over and over as we watched clouds and colors and storms sweep above the plains. If some god of the heavens ever descended and pronounced that I must choose only one charts-worth of territory to fly, *Billings* would make the short list. It was the most surprising land to me, up there in the middle of no-place full of hardly anybody. If the mapmakers had chosen to trim the chart off along the western edge, the city of Billings would have fallen off and the remaining chart would have been renamed *Bismarck, Dickenson, Minot*, or *Williston*, after another prominent city. I would have to move it in my alphabetical chart files next to peer cities like *Atlanta, Denver, Miami*, or *Washington*. The contrast in the scale of the cities was as extreme as the contrast in the scale of the land. Big Sky country grew small cities in wide-open spaces.

The chart painted places I knew so little about, places I had never been. To have seen it for the first time in skies of sparkling sun and then thundering, booming storms and from an open cockpit was a highlight of my life.

Here was a chart low and green on the east rising through higher cream and yellow elevations to the start of the browns of the western mountains. Across the palest yellow plains cut the blues of the broadest rivers ruffled with the river valleys, the

Missouri and the lakes formed by the Garrison and Fort Peck dams. As grand as the chart was, it did little justice to the land itself.

We crossed the Missouri River where Lewis and Clark wintered at Fort Mandan, now unrecognizable as modern-day Bismarck. That shimmering, bright day would carry us back with the Corps of Discovery along stretches of the Yellowstone and Missouri unchanged in the centuries that separated our journeys. They had departed from this point with unreliable maps looking for a passage to the Pacific. The geography held nothing but surprises for them, for us there would be none. We sought only adventure and had accurate maps of every inch of the land we would transit. Every mountain, river, pass, road, and airport was a lead pipe cinch for us to find—we thought.

We struck out north from Dickenson across the surface of North Dakota, tables of green and gold fields with a jagged edge that soon fell away hundreds of feet into a bowl of badlands. I had been expecting badlands that I remembered from childhood, South Dakota's austere canyons of pale bleakness, with spiky, parched rocks, bunched together and with cars streaming through along a single dusty road. When I saw instead the subtle blends of green and striations of red, gray, and brown on rocky hills, I was surprised. These badlands should be renamed somewhat-naughty-lands, I decided. They covered so much square mileage that I despaired that anyone should not behold them as we did sliding above, swallowing them in great gulps, yet able to lower our gaze to sip a detail of a ledge here, a ravine there.

At the other side of this bowl of hills, the jagged edge of another table appeared, and, like sherbet between courses of a meal, we savored the greens and golds of cultivated lands once more. At a crossroad sat a reminder that people lived on this vast and empty plateau, a lone white church with a tall steeple like the ones that poke through treetops in a New England town square. Here, though, there were no trees for it to pierce. Still, it looked

287

as purposeful and resolute. I turned my head to look for homes of the congregation and stores where the people shopped, but saw none.

Far ahead, the pale wall of Lake Sakakawea's farthest shore emerged on the horizon. As we drew closer, the shores parted for a shock of color, water of robin egg blue. The dammed river grew startlingly wide as we approached its high banks. Soon the road we were following ended, then barren brown earth fell behind, and we were flying above calm, bright water, a mirror to the few clouds sweeping across a sky as blue as the water. Eager for another taste of the badlands before dusk, we left the river, knowing we would soon return. Slowly, we made our way south to the Little Missouri River valley. The early evening sun deepened the greens and browns, heightened the striped contrasts. The badlands became new to us again in the waning day. We banked toward the Yellowstone River. There, I looked upriver at the gleaming water that flowed along the main channel and the glittering water that trickled over rocks and around islands, all of it so unspoiled as it made its way toward us from the mountains. How easy it was to see the ghost explorers nearing the end of their ordeal, in a pirogue gliding down to camp near the confluence of the Missouri.

That evening, we slept in a motel with musty, dark halls hung everywhere with large portraits of beauty queens where windows should have been.

When I flew along rivers, I often scooted Nanna off to one side so that we got the full view of the river and a good bit of its valley. This sometimes put us over a road, as it did the following morning leaving Williston. An added bonus, the road ran along a railroad track. The air was crystalline, smooth, and cool. When the road and river carried us back to the Yellowstone fork, we turned down its channel once more.

That river drew me like few others on our summer journey. Had I been making decisions for Lewis, I would have argued to take the Yellowstone route over the Missouri. Along its shores now grew a variety of crops that I could not name, but some looked dark green and matted like beans. I recognized the corn. Looking down through the stalks was like looking into the deep pile of velvet. Alongside them all, the river ran clear and silver blue.

Howard and I had decided to continue along the Missouri into the Rocky Mountains, so we did not travel far along the Yellowstone, but soon turned back. The Missouri twisted and turned through a broad, fertile valley. Along the valley floor, farms and homes looked different from the larger grain operations on the higher, broad plains to both sides. The scale of the riverbed farms was smaller and the variety of crops greater. Their greens ran like an accent thread through the checked fabric of gold and brown. The road we followed ran straighter than the river's curves, so we watched our river run away and return repeatedly as we moved west. The occasional false river, an unattached loop, showed where some change had caused the river course to shift. Sometimes, we would follow a loop of water away from our road and then back, but found the river's game of hide and seek a delightful and lazy one to watch from the road. There it went. Here it came again. It never arrived or departed in quite the same way, each bend a random marker of a summer idyll.

In the distance, a train rumbled toward us. I nudged Nanna down toward the track to watch the details of the yellow locomotive emerge. Once past the cabin, we turned and gave chase. This was the only time on the trip that we chased a train. It is not Howard's favorite gambol. But that train on that morning simply had to be chased.

Malta Airport was to be our fuel stop. Such places were becoming more and more rare the farther we penetrated the hinterlands. Approaching the town, I pinpointed where the airport was on my chart and fixed my search to the left. I saw the runway in the distance and, drawing close, saw five huge, yellow "X" marks spaced along the runway shouting up at us "don't land here."

"I have the field, but look at those X's," I said.

"I don't see any," Howard answered.

Is the man blind, I was thinking. I looked forward and saw that he was peering down to the right. I glanced that way and saw nothing but fields and roads and said, "No, look over here to the left. See the chart? It's left of the road."

"No, it's on the right."

After a few more of these wordy but worthless exchanges, each growing more adamant, frustrated, and loud, I saw what he had sighted. A brand new, black runway with bright white lines and numbers lay a half mile farther down the road. It was two miles from my deserted one, the only one on the chart.

We landed. I folded my chart back to the front cover to check the expiration date. It was current.

"This must be a new airport," I said to the fellow who appeared with a ladder to help pump our gas.

"Been open a few months," he replied, snapping open the ladder.

"It's very nice. Any reason it's not in the right place on the chart yet?"

"I keep trying. When we closed the old airport, we filed a Notam," he said, wincing and shaking his head as he spoke of the Notice to Airmen, a tidbit of late-breaking information from the government, "but it expired."

Howard was climbing the ladder and taking the fuel nozzle I handed up to him. He looked at me first, and then raised his eyes toward the heavens.

"I was about to land at the old airport. I probably didn't have enough gas to keep going. Lucky that Howard spotted you here."

I thought to myself that it was fitting we modern explorers taste the unexpected in this part of the country as those before us had. Who moved the airport? The question paled in comparison to our forbearers' query, "Who moved the ocean?"

This was a Lewis and Clark moment.

With regret, I fold *Billings* and put it aside. I open *Great Falls*, a brown, brown chart of rising terrain.

That afternoon, we continued on, staying north of the Missouri River in Montana, as we had done most of the afternoon. The fields below were strips of land alternately planted and lying fallow like lengths of striped fabric unrolled from the bolt, draped on nature's inmate fields. "Look, prison farms," I said over the intercom. We cut back toward the river from Big Sandy, a small airstrip west of the Bearpaw Mountains, a distinct stark bunch rising a few thousand feet above us. The afternoon was pleasantly warm, the sun shining in a sharp blue sky. Clouds, sparse here, looked thicker and darker to the south.

Charts showed no highway running to Lewistown, where we were heading to stop for the night. Howard was flying, following a maze of narrow roads that led southeast, practicing his pilotage along the roads and drainages. That left me free to empty my mind of flying matters and to let all that my country offered wash over me. A ranch passed below. I wondered which refugee from civilization, a pioneer descendant, movie star, or militia member, lived there. I made up their stories. We continued along our road as it dropped off the slope of the mountains, and looking down the valley toward the junction of the Judith River and the Missouri, I saw the road touch the bank—and stop. Strange. Another road began on the far shore no more than a few car lengths away. That a bridge was missing puzzled me until we draw closer and, tied at the north side, I saw the ferry, a remnant from centuries past used to transport wagons and horses from one dirt path to another. Now, presumably, it shuttled cars.

Across the river, we climbed onto a wide expanse of dry grass with few distinctive features, making its several roads ambiguous, so Howard enlisted me back into navigation service. My lollygagging was over. I studied the chart and matched the road

I saw below with the bends and sharp turns of the black lines on the chart leading to Christina.

The air cooled and grew damper, clouds of various shapes thickened, pierced by shafts of light, painting that extravagant, show-off sky that appeared nowhere but the northern states. We were now in shadows, and the temperature was dropping. The wind picked up, buffeting Nanna's wings. The ion smell of an approaching storm surrounded us.

A lone railroad track, a biplane's godsend, led us steadfastly to a wet runway at Lewistown. Between showers, the young woman who greeted us with a grin as big as the sky itself snapped a photo of Nanna. It probably still hangs on her bulletin board among those of all the unusual visitors to that remote outpost of aviation.

The following morning, Judith Gap intrigued me. Beloved Judith already had her namesake river, and it appeared she had deserved a gap, as well. Her pass fell like a saddle between the first ridges of the Rockies and the Snowy Mountains set apart to the east. After days of flying over plains and the few smaller isolated hills and mountains we had skirted yesterday, I felt we were getting to the main event of the trip as mountains go. Approaching these highlands from the plains reminded me of standing chest-deep on a smooth ocean floor, pushing gently off the sandy bottom to float over many shallow swells, then watching a monster wave roll toward me and preparing myself to push off more forcefully when it arrived. Yes, we would need to do some climbing.

The morning had broken clear and mild. Still, the weather forecast kept us from penetrating farther into the mountains. The likelihood of high winds and thunderstorms in the unfamiliar, craggy, and hemmed-in terrain was frightening enough to keep us safely along the rim, with a clear shot east to escape any surprises rumbling over the mountaintops. It was disappointing to come so close to the mountains' door and miss strolling in, but we would return someday for that. Today, fate handed us a different adventure.

If we had made the run up the Great Falls on down to Yellowstone and Jackson Hole, we would have missed a part of the river that had struck such a chord days ago, the Yellowstone. Here it tumbled out of the mountains at Big Timber. We turned to chase it eastward. Even from hundreds of feet, the water looked clear and fresh as it flowed, sometimes smooth and calm, sometimes generating rapids, through a verdant and winding river valley dotted with farms and clean little towns. I am a sucker for shimmering water on sunny days and this was as good as that combination ever got. Large, forested islands split the river into two courses in places. The land along the river rose into a narrow slope laced with tributaries before erupting skyward into dark green-forested foothills. We stayed with the river until it turned back toward Billings, and we banked away to follow the road south to Cody where we landed for the night.

"What are the chances we are going to use all this stuff?" I stood beside our pile of worldly belongings just emptied onto the tarmac from lunchbox and cockpits.

"Slim," Howard said at once.

"None. Shall we ditch the sleeping bags and jackets, maybe these dirty clothes, too?" I pushed the candidate items into a separate pile with my foot to dramatize the sizeable improvement in our comfort such a decision would make. The air had been growing warmer by the day as we drifted south. Texas was still topping a hundred degrees. The elimination of these items might improve air circulation around our cockpits enough to cool our legs.

"Yes, let's do."

We rented a car, drove into town, and found an establishment capable of shipping our items home. The dirty clothes would ripen fully by the time we smelled them again the following week.

We had hoped to fly into Yellowstone the next day, but storm forecasts blocked us once more. Instead, we drove in and nearly missed the deadline for leaving the park before the exit closed for the night. The forecast that kept us from flying turned out to be wrong. Had we flown, though, we would have missed the bright, full moon rising before us, filling the windshield as we wound along the dark, sometimes terrifying roads back from the park.

Great, I get to open *Billings* again.

Some images of flights are so vivid that I have captured and stored them in my mind like master film prints in a Hollywood vault. I can close my eyes and see them projected. Following the Bighorn Canyon between Cody and Little Big Horn is part of that personal film library.

The Bighorn River flowed through sheer cliffs far below a bleak, rocky plateau. Along that high, forbidding surface ran a winding road. Approaching from the west, far enough away to take in the whole of the plateau and river canyon, it looked as though a giant had pulled a hard-crusted bran muffin apart into two halves. One uneven, crumbly edge would fit to the other should they ever again be pushed back together. The Bighorn River turned into a reservoir because of a dam thirty miles downstream. Green water grew darker and bluer as we inched toward the dam and plains beyond. Wakes of powerboats disturbed every turn of the river, yet the surface returned to a mirror of calm immediately as they passed, fair warning that to disappear here was to disappear forever.

Beyond the canyon and dam, the Bighorn River flowed north and led us back out onto plains stretching beyond the horizon. We followed it nearly as far as the junction with the Little Bighorn, then cut across the fork formed by the two rivers along the road that led to Crow Agency. There beside a modern interstate highway and a few park buildings, but otherwise isolated, lay the battlefield where General Custer and Crazy Horse struggled. That patch looked much like all the other undulating land for miles around, all grasses and no trees, insignificant compared with the canyon we had recently departed. We headed south.

Goodbye again to *Billings* and back onto *Cheyenne.* I will soon run out of charts for this trip.

The Black Hills was an area we wanted to explore. We approached from the west, having stopped for fuel at Buffalo, Wyoming. From there we picked up the interstate and began noticing motorcycles heading east. Some were alone, others traveling together in pairs or packs of three, four, five, and more. Something was up. I looked at the chart.

"Where is that Harley event held every year?" I asked Howard the question as I unfolded my chart for clues.

"I don't know."

"Do you know when they hold it? Isn't it around now?"

"I don't know."

"Look at all those bikes." I said and watch Howard's head turn and look down.

"Yeah. Look's like something."

"Sturgis! That's it!" Over along the top edge of the chart I had spotted the little town with the name that sounded so familiar. Beside the town sat a solid magenta circle with little protrusions, the symbol for a non-tower airport with a paved runway and fuel. "And they have an airport—and gas."

"Let's go."

No doubt, Sturgis, South Dakota, during the great motorcycle migration was an amazing place on the ground, as we would later discover, but from the air it was mind boggling. The roads into town were full of arriving Harleys, Indians, and probably every other make of bike as well. From our cockpits, they all looked pretty much alike, lots of shiny black and chrome with tanned and leathered riders. As soon as we reached the outskirts of Sturgis, every hillside was dotted with camp sites, every street flowed like molasses with vehicles. Along every byway stood the gleaming, glittering mechanical steeds. We flew low enough to see plenty of detail, and then turned away from town toward the airport.

We flew between two hills. In the opposite direction came an ag plane towing a banner. Upon landing, we learned, not surprisingly, that we would never find a room for the night, but were welcome to camp at the airport.

Howard and I looked at each other and shook our heads.

"Timing is everything," I said. We had carted our sleeping bags around for weeks and had just mailed them home. It was growing late, so we decided to fly on the short distance to Rapid City. As we prepared to fly out, another tow plane trailing a hook swooped down and then pulled up sharply to snag its banner. It peeled off the ground and floated away before us like leather fringe from a hog-rider's jacket, "EASTRIDERS...ALL NIGHT PARTY EXIT 30." Yep, the revelers were moving into high gear now. We followed the banner to town and right down the main street like a kid tagging onto the end of a parade.

Within minutes, we reached Rapid City. It throbbed with bikers as well. We parked Nanna on the airport ramp beside a business jet belonging to a talk show host, also an avid biker, who had flown in for a celebrity-wrestling match, one of the main events of the gathering. I liked the way Nanna, chunky and perky, looked next to his sleek white cousin.

At our hotel, we saw elevators fill up with stockbrokers and schoolteachers, perhaps even a deacon or two. All wore combinations of black leather, fringe, sweatbands, and lots of skin, much of it tattooed or pierced. A slender blonde with a braid down her back and a headband got in with a male companion, both decked out in leather for the streets.

"Where did you all come in from?" I asked her.

"Florida."

"Wow, that's a ride."

"Oh no, we don't ride. We have our motorcycles trucked in. Most people do. It would take too much vacation time to get here. We're on our way to drop ours off now."

"His and her motorcycles, hmmm." I had always remembered the babe riding in back, reclined against a tall backrest, knees high, locks flying, but times have changed, even in Sturgis.

"The only way to go."

The restaurant and parking lot bulged with bikes and riders. From every direction came the rhummm-rhummm-rhummmming of engines. Each motorcycle sparkled, whether parked or rolling along with its rider slung nonchalantly in the saddle. To my untrained eye, every single one looked perfect: no oil streaks, no dust, no scratches, and no cracked leather. We had stumbled into an adult fantasyland full of shiny toys. Our elevator acquaintances pulled out of the garage as a flight of two, turned onto the main drag, engines revving.

"Cool, real cool," I said to Howard as we watched them depart.

"Is cool still a word?"

"Cool? Boss? Bitchin? Pick one you like."

At the airport, our celebrity jet neighbor had departed. For us, a day of Black Hills, granite monuments, badlands, and otherwise aimless flying lay ahead. It was an uncommonly tourist-like morning. At Mount Rushmore, I felt that I was one of hundreds looking at the same thing, a strange feeling after so many days of not sharing our sights. The parking lot was full of cars and buses. I could see dark spots in the plaza, people looking up, no doubt. We looked down but were not allowed to fly close enough to see it well, so we moved on.

The monument in progress at Crazy Horse was a big improvement, so massive, so proud by comparison. That day, what protected him from closer inspection were small and unthreatening-looking clouds, ones that could as easily move away or blossom rapidly into thunderheads. Local pilots had warned of the frightening speed of storms developing in the Black Hills, so we flew conservatively that day. From my perspective high above, neither of the human works, grand achievements though they were, struck me as competitive with nature's Big Horn Canyon, the endless plains, or the Yellowstone River.

Even the badlands here in South Dakota seemed smaller scale, not nearly as important as North Dakota's. A bright sun washed the dusty bleached spires and subtle geologic banding, a starkly beautiful patch of earth. We flew along the boundaries then struck east to Phillip for a quick fuel stop and return to the skies for another leisurely afternoon.

We had started the day without expecting to see any particular landmarks. We had been out for weeks and flown nearly fifty hours, a long time to hold right rudder to compensate for Nanna's right-wing-heavy rigging problem. In general, we were heading home. The point had arrived as it does in every trip, where eagerness for the new and novel experiences had begun to wane, and the yearning for the familiarity of home had begun.

"What would you think about stopping in El Dorado to introduce ourselves?" I referred to the small town in Kansas, east of Wichita, where the Patty family ran the primary parts and maintenance business for Great Lakes biplanes like Nanna.

"Okay." Howard's voice sounded neither enthusiastic nor reluctant. It came across the intercom in the solid, even tone that so reflected the kind of person he was. He had been flying, but had just turned control back to me because the soles of his shoes had overheated from contact with the metal rudders that picked up heat from the firewall.

"We can be there by early this afternoon."

I knew that we could. While Howard was flying, I had punched the El Dorado Airport into the GPS to get a general heading. That was the easy part. Then I struggled to open, fold, turn, and refold three charts to estimate where a series of straight-line segments would fall if it were humanly possible in a two-foot wide cockpit to draw a straight line across a route that was seven chart-feet long. That task completed, I picked potential fuel stops along the way. Much of the country we would cross would be new to us, first in South Dakota, then Nebraska. The chart showed prairies falling onto wetlands. Not until we crossed the border into Kansas would the terrain become familiar. We had flown through Kansas on the first legs of the trip and stayed on the ground there for a day when weather had pinned us down.

With a half days worth of travel sketched out, we flew on a few hundred feet above the vast bright prairies speckled with shadows from the clouds drifting overhead. I wondered what the people living in such a remote area were like as Nanna's wing passed alongside a ranch house. A fence surrounded the home and its few shade trees, but no lawn or garden broke the natural turf. Beyond spread more open rangeland mottled gray, brown, and green. No golden wheat fields lay end to end here like those we had seen in the North Dakota plains. This was open rangeland. Had not a narrow track run from the house to a two-lane road that continued for many miles before connecting with a highway, the place would have looked completely isolated. Here was the place loners had settled to eke out their livings during the westward migration of centuries past. Here, no doubt, the loners remained.

On we flew, coming upon one more of these remote outposts until we flew off the chart. Goodbye, *Cheyenne*.

I open the next chart, *Omaha*. I see all the blue speckles and think, ah, yes, water everywhere.

We had left behind none of the remoteness, but the landscape had changed. Evidence of moisture began to appear—greener expanses, ducks, and geese. With every mile, more ponds showed in the rolling terrain, nirvana for waterfowl.

We had decided to make a direct run to Patty Field in southern

Kansas. With no particular landmarks along our path and with many of the trip days that we had allotted for weather delays unused, the morning's journey took on an even more peaceful, unhurried quality than usual. We had time enough to strike out in a bold new direction, if we so desired. We did not. We had covered so much ground already, had so many fine days enjoying the best our country had to offer, that we were ready to return to our everyday worlds. We had two summer trips under our belts now, so many memories. Over the winter, we would hibernate and digest. Come spring, a new itch would start.

The *Wichita* chart comes next.

As Nebraska fell behind and Kansas rolled in, Howard and I swapped piloting duties. On my time off, I still followed along the chart, practicing pilotage skills, a more difficult task in homogenous land without mountain peaks and other readily distinguishing features. I compared the bend in a road to one on the chart and looked for confirming radio towers and river crossings.

On the road below, I began to see automobiles passing large trucks instead of the more common sight of days past, the lone pickup speeding along. As the roads became busier, towns grew larger, and cities began appearing on the horizon. There was Wichita. Look at all those airports on the chart, one named Cessna Airport—this was airplane country, the birthplace of many aircraft, including Nanna.

We picked our way around the edge of the big city to the small town of El Dorado, then east a few more miles to Patty Field. From the air, the only hints that the field was an airstrip were the bright orange windsock, a couple of painted tires at each end, and two buildings that looked like hangars. No airplanes sat along the runway. We circled the field several times to gauge the wind and the condition of the field. Nobody had answered my radio calls for landing advisories. We had no permission to land at this private strip, but reasoned that if a Great Lakes biplane is not welcomed by his makers, then the world has gone crazy, and someone would just have to shoot me.

The grassy field was wide, but short. The breeze blew softly out of the south, so I flew Nanna parallel to the field toward the nearby water tower, and then banked gently, slowed to a minimum speed as we dropped down over homes to be sure we did not roll too far upon touch down, and descended to the grass. We had not landed on grass even once before on this trip, it suddenly occurred to me. The turf was solid, but not in the harsh manner of concrete or asphalt that scrapes tires like sandpaper. The earth seemed to give a little when we landed, and the soft ground caressed the tires. Whummmmppphhh. The grass slowed the rolling wheels right away.

"I don't see anybody around," said Howard. A dark passage to the largest white hangar opened and a large young man in a sleeveless blue shirt and faded baseball cap appeared, then went back in and closed the door.

"Wow, he didn't even wave." I began to have reservations about this surprise stop. Within a minute, the man reappeared, walking along the side of the hangar. He pointed to a good place to shut down and waited.

"Hi. We just stopped to say hello," I said as I stood in the cockpit, tightened up my bib overall straps, and climbed out. "I'm Anne Hopkins. This is Howard Richmond."

"Hello," Howard said, following me onto the wing, then stepping down onto the grass beside me. We walked toward the man. The Kansas air was moist and hot.

"Brent Patty." He extended his hand, squinting into the sun. We had spoken on the phone before, and he knew about my airplane from Nanna's hangar accident two years earlier. Nanna's wing had dropped onto a hoist arm when a cable broke, crunching the leading edge. Brent had supplied some of the parts for the repair. We spent a few moments reliving that awful few months.

"I've still got my rigging problem. Right wing is heavy."

"We can fix that." He said it quietly in a matter-of-fact way.

"When can I bring him back up from Dallas?" I had given up hope for improvement, but I could tell I was working with a man who did not make idle boasts.

"Anytime in the next month would work."

I turned to Howard, and we began working out a time for him to help with a ferry operation involving Mr. Mooney, his airplane.

"It won't take long," Brent said. "Are you busy this afternoon?"

My jaw must have dropped. For the three years that I had owned Nanna, I had engaged several rigging experts and countless amateurs for the job. None had ever opined that this was a straightforward afternoon job. Such black art always took a day or more, and it had never resulted in noticeable improvement. When the last person suggested tearing the fabric off the rudder because it was too tight and warping was the problem, I threw in the towel. Face it, I was destined to live and fly permanently pushing the right rudder and picking up the right wing by tilting the stick to the left. Old planes were just plain difficult. I looked at Howard in disbelief.

"Go for it," he said, "We're in no hurry."

"Pull on around front. Have you eaten?" Brent started walking back the way he came.

"No," I said climbing back onto the wing. Howard began walking around the hangar with Brent. I checked my watch. It was almost one o'clock.

"Take the pickup on into town if you'd like," Brent handed Howard a set of keys and began pointing as he related driving directions. Howard rumbled out of the gravel driveway like a kid with a new toy.

I started the engine and pulled Nanna around to the front of the open hangar. Inside the large door opening was a jumble of airplane and parts, tools, rags, and animals. A biplane that Brent had been working on sat on the oil-stained and dusty cement floor with its cowling removed. The single open room, if emptied, would have held several fully assembled airplanes. Filled as it was, only one could fit.

I plopped down on the grass to observe. Few activities are more rewarding than watching a craftsman make magic with a few tools and a lot of knowledge. Brent had disappeared into a small room off to one side of the hangar and emerged with a level, a gripping tool something like tweezers, and a large, shiny metal object with knobs, long arms, and a tension gauge—something that might have been left over from the Inquisition. He lifted Nanna's tail and rested it on a barrel, then began moving about and climbing up on the wings to check with the level.

"Falls off in a stall?" Brent squinted into the sun and looked my way with a single open eye.

"Yep, to the right," I said. What should happen during stall practice was for Nanna to drop his nose like a diver rolling forward off a board. Instead, when his wings stalled he lurched like a drunk falling sideways off a stool. This was a dangerous habit if the pilot did not know to expect and compensate for it.

"We'll fix that."

Back he turned toward Nanna. He began twisting flying wires loose, measuring the angle of the wing, and attaching his magic torture tool to the flying wires to measure their tension. The stall problem would never go away altogether, but the rigging and handling characteristics did improve dramatically. Most times we returned to Patty Field, Brent would work on it a little bit more. I could tell that being unable to solve the problem completely vexed him. After the final try, we guessed that when a previous owner had flipped over on the back that the frame had been bent enough that the problem would never completely go away.

The old two-tone brown truck turned back into the driveway. Howard joined me and we ate our sandwiches. While Brent worked, we sat, watched, and visited with his children that wandered in and out, father Cliff as he puttered with an ancient airplane he was building from scratch, and the family animals. Over the years we visited at Patty Field, the menagerie might contain a single cat or dog, or a litter of one of the other. I think that first day we had cats.

For the rest of the day, Brent loosened and tightened wires, I flew a test flight and reported any changes, Brent fine-tuned, I flew, and so on until by late afternoon I was beaming at the results. Adding a trim tab would take out any remaining yaw, something we decided to hold off on until we returned for the annual inspection the following winter. I felt like a person who had been told that my leg was permanently lame, had given up hope, and then happened upon the magician with a cure and walked away without crutches and barely a limp. Hallelujah, brother.

Besides making great progress with the rigging, we had traveled back into the olden days of biplanes. Nanna and I lifted off a field smelling of summer grass, rising over the white tire boundary and Kansas fields green and gold with crops. We turned back over the narrow lane lined with age-old trees that led to the county road, climbed over white wooden houses with pickup trucks parked out front, passed beside the town's water tower and on to the sparkling reservoir nearby. When we finished one set of tests, we headed back for a slip down final to touch down and roll with wheels bouncing gently across tufts of grass and weed.

"Thanks for dropping everything to do this today, Brent. What do I owe you?" I asked as we pushed back from the hangar, ready to head for Oklahoma and then home.

"Nothing. We'll work on it some more next winter."

I open the *Dallas* chart again. I had opened it just hours earlier at the start of my memory trip when the rest of the sectionals lay in a neat pile. Now they are in disarray, many still partially open on the floor around my chair to the spots where I had flown years ago and had drawn my finger across just minutes earlier. Scrapbooks, too, lie open around me. My logbooks rest in my lap.

I remember how I felt that day leaving Patty Field.

We might have floated along for days longer making more memories and savoring the fresh ones: laughing about the Sturgis "EASYRIDERS" banner, the misplaced airport at Malta, remembering fondly new friends like Brent Patty and his family, or a thousand other details of nearly sixty hours in the air and all the other hours in between. A little internal bell told us it was time to go home. That was the beauty of these trips, we listened to our own harmonious timepiece, not someone else's clanging alarm.

We stopped for fuel, planning to touch down at our home field at Addison Airport in Dallas by sunset. I checked the weather. The line of storms that formed off and on all spring and summer along the Red River between Oklahoma and Texas were on again late that afternoon, and in a big booming way. Stillwater, our fuel stop, became our overnight stop instead. A tall young man with a receding hairline, glasses, and a relentlessly friendly and enthusiastic manner took us in hand, found us accommodations and transportation, and agreed to meet us early the next day so we could beat the heat—it had been over one hundred degrees for weeks—into Dallas.

When we arrived the following morning, there he was standing by Nanna's wings, freshly rinsed by overnight showers and gleaming in pale light filtering through a thin overcast layer of clouds. The young man reminded me of a kid who had found a stray puppy and did not want the owners to show up and take it away.

"I'm taking flying lessons," he said as we completed fueling.

"Soloed yet?" I watched his expression to judge his passion for flying.

"Oh, sure. But I've never flown in anything like this." He looked longingly at Nanna. My heart melted.

I looked at Howard and he said, "Okay. We've got time."

"Climb in, then," I said.

The youth lit up a few more watts. He was all elbows and knees climbing in and his long feet nearly dislodged the windscreen as they passed into the cockpit. For a moment, I thought he was not going to fit, but at last, he did. I breathed a sigh of relief. To snatch away the promised flight would have been unthinkable.

"Slouch or lean forward if the wind hits you too hard," I said, as we taxied out. We took off south toward the tall buildings downtown.

"You can take the airplane now," I said. I felt the stick shake and released my grip. "You've got the airplane."

"Got it. My mom lives on the other side of town."

"Let's head that way then."

We swept around the far side of the city and found the modest house. We circled a couple of times then flew away for the few minutes it took to return to open countryside. He flew Nanna with increasing confidence as he learned by trial and error the proper amount of rudder to use as he banked into his turns.

When we landed and pulled to a stop, I could see his head in the front cockpit nodding and shaking. "Great. That was great. Thanks a lot. Oh, thank you. Great. That was just great." What a wonderful start to a morning, leaving behind a happy memory in another soul.

Howard and I got set to leave. We headed out to the runway for departure. The short leg home took us around a few more showers. Not that Nanna needed another wash, but when we found a rain cloud with a curtain of water thin enough to see through, I could not resist taking a dip. We flew toward the darkening spot. I smelled ion, saw the first few specks of mist on the windscreen, and then the larger splatters of the cloud's central drubbing. I saw the water dribbling into the front cockpit along the edged of the windscreen and Howard swiping at the waterfall to keep it off his legs. I watched the stream hit the leading edge of the wings, flow back in rivulets, and fall away on the wind. Suddenly it was all over. We were again in the clear.

Nanna would arrive home cleaner than he left, as would our spirits. Ahead lay the skyline of Dallas. The last of the prairie sod passed beneath our wheels. We were pushing it behind, as though kicking open our roll-top desk again. The clutter of modern life was still there, lying in wait to bury us. Somehow, though, it all looked foolish and unimportant. Without any conscious thought, my mind had sorted through priorities, and the big unimportant slugs had sunk to the bottom where they belonged. Years later, I would probably not even remember what they were.

"Two-tango-echo, cleared to land," a female voice called to us from Addison Tower. Stephanie was on duty. "Welcome back. We missed you."

The sun is setting. Hardly enough light comes through the window to read the chart titles strewn on the floor around my chair. I am stiff from sitting. As I finish folding each one and putting them back in order, I look at the cover on top. I reach to switch on the table lamp beside me. As I do, I bump the magnifying glass I have been using to read the small print. My eye catches the words "Great Falls" on the chart cover. Ah yes, up at the top of Idaho lies Timber Basin. I remember. I start to open the chart again, then pause. It is getting late, too late to take off again now. Perhaps tomorrow.

No, tomorrow is my birthday. Hah! Think of it. I'm a hundred and ten and still flying.

Glossary

Chart. A map designed for aviation. For historical reasons, pilots rarely use the word map, although a chart is a map.

GPS. Global Positioning System, a device that uses satellites in earth orbit to pinpoint locations on or above the earth surface. These devices, now commonplace, came into everyday use in general aviation aircraft in the decade of the 1990's.

Hobbs. The meter that measures how long the engine has been running, roughly equal to elapsed time. See also *Tach.*

Join. A maneuver in formation flying used to bring together airplanes. The lead airplane flies an arc. The wingman flies a smaller arc inside the leader. Eventually, the wingman will catch up due to the shorter distance traveled.

Knots. Nautical miles per hour, a word derived from knots on a rope used by sailors to determine speed of a ship. Airplane and wind speeds are frequently stated in knots.

Rudder. The moveable vertical piece of an airplane's tail that makes the nose move left or right, similar to the rudder of a boat. The rudder is controlled by the pilot's feet on left and right rudder pedals.

Stick. A control used to dip a wing down or lift it up and for pitching the nose down or up. In a biplane it is attached on the floor between the pilot's legs.

Tach or Tachometer. An instrument that counts hours of engine use, recording more hours at high power than at lower power. The tach will record fewer hours than the *Hobbs.*

Taildragger. An airplane with larger main wheels forward and a smaller wheel aft (sometimes a tailskid). This arrangement makes the plane's nose stick up and guarantees the pilot poor forward visibility while sitting on the ground, but much greater clearance for the propeller than an airplane with *tricycle gear*, which has a nose wheel instead of a tail wheel and sits more level. In the air, these differences do not matter.

Touch and Go. Takeoff, fly a rectangular pattern, descend again back to the runway, land briefly (touch), and take off again (go). Once, with a large jet coming in to land behind me, a tower controller trying to keep ample spacing between our aircraft, said, "Cleared for touch and go. Give me a little touch and a lot of go."

Transponder. A device that emits signals so that remote receivers can know an airplane's location and altitude.

VOR. Very high frequency Omnidirectional Range. A transmitter that looks like a large, white bowling pin on the ground. Aircraft tune in a VOR frequency to help determine their positions or provide a navigation target. GPS is moving quickly to reduce pilots' reliance on VORs.

Printed in the United States
15717LVS00006BA/3